A Policy Reader in
Universal Design for Learning

A Policy Reader
in Universal Design
for Learning

Edited by

DAVID T. GORDON, JENNA W. GRAVEL,
and LAURA A. SCHIFTER

HARVARD EDUCATION PRESS
Cambridge, Massachusetts

Library of Congress Control Number 2009927818

Paperback ISBN 978-1-934742-38-9
Library Edition ISBN 978-1-934742-39-6

Published by Harvard Education Press,
an imprint of the Harvard Education Publishing Group

Harvard Education Press
8 Story Street
Cambridge, MA 02138

Cover Design: Perry Lubin

The typefaces used in this book are Sabon for text and Myriad for display.

Contents

Related Supports

Assessment

Designing Learning for All Learners

MARTHA L. MINOW

How can public policy help us envision and implement a new kind of curriculum—one that expands learning opportunities for everyone rather than requiring students to negotiate the constraints of traditional schooling? That is a central question posed in this collection of insightful essays, and the authors make an effective case that universal design for learning (UDL) provides a compelling answer to that question.

In fact, universal design for learning is one of the few big and truly transformative ideas to emerge in education over the past two decades. I first heard of UDL in the 1990s when I was approached by David Rose and Anne Meyer of the Center for Applied Special Technology (CAST) about becoming a partner in the National Center on Accessing the General Curriculum, an initiative funded by the U.S. Department of Education to explore ways to improve education for students with disabilities. When David and Anne described the UDL principles and showed examples of UDL in practice, I recognized that this vision paralleled my own emerging ideas about what inclusive education should be.

In my work, I have explored ways to ensure that rights and opportunities reach those who have been marginalized by the majority or by tradition. Children who seem different from their peers—different because of race, disability, refugee or immigrant status, religion, sexual orientation, gender, language spoken at home, economic class—have too often been denied equal opportunities to learn. Even enlightened school systems and policy makers often respond to students who differ from the real— or imagined—norm with uneasy and contradictory policies. At times, schools assert identical treatment for all as the notion of equality; at other times, schools seek to accommodate differences but do so in ways that can be stigmatizing, exclusionary, or oppressive in their low expectations of students' potential. The very same school system may enact inclusion in the general education curriculum for individuals with disabilities alongside programs of separate instruction for students whose home language is not English. And affixing a label—such as disabled, or English language learner—may be the only way to provide individualized help in school, at the cost of stigmatizing a student and at the risk of failing to recognize how individual needs fit on a spectrum rather than falling within clear categories. The U.S. Supreme Court's 1954 declaration in *Brown v. Board of Education* that racially segregated public education is inherently unconstitutional started rather than resolved the task of ensuring equal educational opportunity for all students. A constant stumbling block has been how to recognize individual differences without producing exclusion or stigma—and how to ensure equal treatment without neglecting individual need. This dilemma of difference arises because of the constant reiteration of a norm against which individual student differences are compared; ignoring a student's difference may extend equal treatment without accommodation, but identifying a student's difference risks producing exclusion, stereotype, or shame.

Here is where universal design for learning is transformative. Its set of principles exposes and proposes remedies for several fundamental biases in a traditional curriculum that imagines a "normal" student and hence marginalizes anyone who does not comfortably fit that norm. Those biases proceed on the assumptions that (1) print is the best medium for acquiring information; (2) writing is the best means for expressing what one knows; (3) the ability to learn and engage in rich content depends solely on mastering these particular media; (4) "book smarts" are what matter most to learning; and (5) those who find print inaccessible or difficult deserve a less challenging, less rich, and less stimulating curriculum. Driving these assumptions is another more harmful one: that some individuals simply will never learn as much or as well, and that is their problem, not a problem for the standard educational system.

CAST's extraordinary work with individual students has demonstrated that students who were thought to be "unteachable" because of severe disabilities can in fact learn when provided with appropriate materials and instruction in a safe environment. Not only *can* they learn, but they demonstrate hunger for knowledge, intellectual creativity, and capacity for expressing insight that lie at the core of education at its best. As David Rose and Anne Meyer have stated elsewhere, UDL was born of the realization that there is nothing "wrong" with a particular individual who has not been learning; rather, the curriculum has been inadequate to meet that individual's needs. The curriculum, not the individual, needs fixing.

This was an "aha" moment for me as well. I had long understood how a building with stairs at the entrance excludes a person who uses a wheelchair while a ramp opens access to that individual—and can ease access for a parent pushing a stroller and a person walking a bicycle as well. I had not understood, though, that for some people, a physical book is like the stairs to a building: a cause of unnecessary exclusion. I suddenly realized that securing the rights of individual students with disabilities to sit alongside other students in the general education classroom does not solve the access problem if the curriculum itself imposes barriers to learning. Universal design for learning calls for constructing the methods for communicating the curriculum with all possible students in mind in the same way that universal design in architecture directs up-front planning of the physical building for all possible uses.

Hence UDL invites creative uses of media and methods to ensure access for students with physical, attention, and cognitive differences. And we should not be surprised to find that the results hold potential benefit for students who do not have disabilities. Students who are learning English and students who are distracted by problems at home can find curricular materials engaging and accessible because of supplements like glossaries and other interactive features. UDL also focuses on the potential issues of motivation and engagement in learning and acknowledges that not every student comes or stays ready and eager to learn every day and every minute.

Here the universality of this approach becomes salient: materials designed with interactive and visual dimensions help address the undeniable generational shift in how people learn and what they want to learn. New generations of "digital natives" are born into a world of digital, portable communications devices; many use a mouse before a pen and live in a world of electronic images and sound more than print. These features of the new world dramatically change how young people acquire and use information, how they organize themselves socially, how they communicate and collaborate, and even how their brains work. Many in this generation need to touch what they are learning, to navigate through material in an order and plan of their own making, to share and collaborate, and to combine humor and irreverence with even the most serious learning. Digital natives don't read instructional manuals first; instead they try something, and if it doesn't work, try again, and if that doesn't work, they keep trying. They are democratic in their approach to information; they want to explore it, share it, and assess its content even before knowing its pedigree or place in the canon. And they like multiple modes of presentation: images and sounds are as critical as words. Here UDL's focus on engagement holds promise for educating every member of the new and successive generations; its capacity to work through multiple modes of presentation and to enable students to navigate, create, and collaborate can cultivate the passion for learning that is the most essential goal of education.

I agree with the editors of this volume that UDL deserves the attention of all who have a hand in shaping public policy (see the introduction). The law on the books calls for access to the general curriculum for students regardless of ability or disability, but realizing that vision requires more than simply telling people what the law requires. UDL offers the means to implement the vision of equal educational opportunity. The past decade has brought significant gains toward this vision. For example, the development of a National Instructional Materials Accessibility Standard (NIMAS) ensures that students with print disabilities get the classroom materials they need in appropriate formats and at the same time as their peers. The U.S. Congress in 2008 embraced UDL in the Higher Education Opportunity Act and directed postsecondary institutions and teaching education programs to follow UDL principles. These are positive steps but just a beginning.

Much more needs to be done to close the gap between the ideal of equal educational opportunity and the practice, especially in K–12 education. This book gives anyone who cares about equal educational opportunity sufficient knowledge of UDL principles and their origins to join efforts to address the most intransigent challenges facing public education today. By imagining all the different ways that people learn, those who apply universal design for learning can make a difference for all individuals.

Martha L. Minow
Dean of the Faculty
and Jeremiah Smith, Jr.
Professor of Law,
Harvard Law School,
September 2009

Introduction

DAVID T. GORDON, JENNA W. GRAVEL,
AND LAURA A. SCHIFTER

Over the past decade, as the standards-based reform movements of the 1980s and 1990s have flowered, the federal government has increased emphasis on the need to educate all learners to high standards. As a result of the No Child Left Behind Act of 2001 (NCLB), all states have standards in English and math, and schools are held accountable for ensuring that their students—both in the aggregate and by subgroup (including students with disabilities and English language learners)—achieve those standards. In addition, the Individuals with Disabilities Education Act (IDEA) includes a commitment to provide equal opportunities for students with disabilities to learn in the general education curriculum.

These commitments have dramatically raised expectations for most stakeholders in education, including teachers, students, administrators, researchers, publishers, parent advocates, and policy makers. However, the burden of accountability has fallen on those with the least control of the curriculum and its implementation: the students. In other words, the educational system continues to locate the source of failure in students or, on occasion, their teachers, when in fact the curriculum itself— education's goals, methods, materials, and assessments—is incapable of serving the increasingly diverse populations found in our classrooms.

In recent years, universal design for learning (UDL) has emerged as a set of principles to meet the challenge of expanding educational opportunities for *all* learners. UDL proposes to relieve students of the burden of adapting to an inflexible, "disabled" curriculum and instead to provide teachers and students greater flexibility and opportunity where it matters most—in the classroom, at the point of learning.

The UDL framework is relatively new—the term was coined by researchers at the Center for Applied Special Technology (CAST) in the mid-1990s. However, UDL principles reflect a century or more of insights from education research and practice along with new findings from neuroscience regarding how individuals learn. Taken together, UDL principles offer a research-based lens through which to critique and improve the design and implementation of the curriculum.

Given UDL's roots in research and practice, much of what has been written on UDL deals with creating and deploying instructional goals, methods, materials, and assessment. This includes two previous books published by Harvard Education Press: *The Universally Designed Classroom: Accessible Curriculum and Digital Technologies* (Rose, Meyer, and Hitchcock, 2005) and *A Practical Reader in Universal Design for Learning* (Rose & Meyer, 2006). *A Policy Reader* is intended as a companion volume to the prior books and, with the *Practical Reader* and a forthcoming *Research Reader*, will form a handy trilogy for reference and reflection.

The field is still nascent, and much work remains to be done in addressing key issues in education policy via UDL at all levels—federal, state, and local. To date the most significant work in policy has occurred at the national level. For more than a decade, the U.S. Department of Education has invested in UDL research and practice as part of a larger effort to expand access to the general education curriculum. Other federal agencies, such as the National Science Foundation, have made significant investments in applying UDL to the development of curriculum and assessment. In fact, in 2008, Congress included the statutory definition of UDL in the Higher Education Opportunity Act (HEOA). Within HEOA, Congress made provisions for incorporating UDL into teacher preparation and professional development programs as well as state report cards on teacher quality.

In 2006, the National UDL Task Force, led by the National Down Syndrome Society, was established with representatives from more than twenty organizations representing teachers, principals, state directors of education and special education, special education, civil rights, and disability rights advocates, parents, and others. The task force has worked together for UDL implementation and to incorporate UDL into policy. It achieved success with the HEOA and has now turned to the pending IDEA and NCLB reauthorizations.

Finally, at the state level, several states—including California, Michigan, New York, Indiana, Louisiana, and Kentucky, to name a few— support efforts to apply UDL to teacher preparation and in-service development, instructional materials, and assessment. These efforts are often launched and driven by educators, administrators, and advocates who sense the need for a bold new approach to deliver on the promise of equal opportunity in education. They are, however, subject to shifts in policy and funding priorities.

Also notable is the inclusion in recent federal special education law of a National Instructional Materials Accessibility Standard (NIMAS). NIMAS will soon make print instructional materials, including textbooks, more readily available in digital formats—preparing the way for the widespread use of technology-rich, customizable learning environments. While not specifically a UDL initiative, NIMAS sets the stage for applying UDL to instructional materials development, since flexible digital formats can more easily be loaded with learning supports than can printed materials.

The field is clearly growing, and this volume contains some early documents and related articles that help the reader understand the UDL perspective on a few core issues related to education policy.

In the first section (Overview), we include some pieces that place UDL in the context of the larger education field. David Rose and Jenna Gravel, who along with their colleagues at CAST have defined the principles and guidelines of UDL, draw playful and important parallels between an everyday technology—Global Positioning System—and the work that education is trying to accomplish. We need to be clear about our goals and flexible in the means of achieving them, they write. Two other overview pieces, by David Gordon and Tom Hehir, place UDL in the larger context of education reform (Gordon) and disability rights (Hehir).

Section two (National Considerations) provides helpful points of reference in understanding how UDL might inform discussions about accountability (Rose) and access to the curriculum as provided for by

NCLB and IDEA (Karger). We have also included some recent documents from Project Forum, a program of the National Association of State Directors of Special Education, in cooperation with the U.S. Office of Special Education Programs. These two documents show potential avenues for growth and major challenges facing the field of UDL, especially around penetrating state and local practice.

In the third section (Related Supports), we have included two pieces that aim to sort out or clarify some major issues for policy: (1) How does UDL relate to assistive technology (and how, in turn, does NIMAS connect the two) and (2) how does it relate to response to intervention (RTI)? Especially important is the discussion in chapter 10 on NIMAS. As the authors write: "The true promise of NIMAS is that it provides a flexible but sturdy foundation for curricula that embody UDL and capitalize on ATs to make that learning accessible to everyone. Realization of the promise of NIMAS will be apparent as a cultural shift for students with disabilities: the shift from a focus on *access* to a focus on *learning*."

Finally, section four (Assessment) explores one of the most urgent issues facing policy stakeholders. How do we measure student learning, teacher effectiveness, and the efficacy of our education systems in general? Standardized assessments come under special scrutiny as the authors question how they might be improved to accomplish what they intend to accomplish. In this respect, the discussion of UDL and assessment aims to arrive where the NIMAS discussion does: with a focus on learning and how to open opportunities for learning to more and more people.

In total, this book is a conversation starter—a first glance at the policy writings of a new field. As UDL's place in the national discussion about educational improvement continues to grow, many more questions will need to be addressed, including the cost of implementation and the supports, resources, and further research that will be needed to scale up UDL.

REFERENCES

Rose D. H., Hitchcock, C., & Meyer, A. (2005). *The universally designed classroom: Accessible curriculum and digital technologies.* Cambridge, MA: Harvard Education Press.

Rose, D. H., & Meyer, A. (Eds.). (2006). *A practical reader in universal design for learning.* Cambridge, MA: Harvard Education Press.

CHAPTER ONE

Getting from Here to There

UDL, Global Positioning Systems, and Lessons for Improving Education

DAVID H. ROSE AND JENNA W. GRAVEL

Establishing good educational policies and practices depends first and foremost on being clear about what we want to achieve. What is the goal of education in the twenty-first century? In writing the universal design for learning (UDL) guidelines with our colleagues at the Center for Applied Special Technology (CAST), we have argued that the goal of education is not simply the mastery of knowledge but the mastery of learning. Education should help turn novice learners into individuals who are *expert* at learning—individuals who know how to learn, who have already learned a great deal, and who want to learn even more. At commencement all graduates should be well prepared in their own individual ways for a lifetime of learning as content-area experts (if they choose), masters of trades and crafts, artists, scientists, or whatever else life has in store.

UDL is an approach that addresses and redresses the primary barrier to making expert learners of all students: inflexible, one-size-fits-all curricula that raise unintentional barriers to learning. Learners with disabilities are most vulnerable to such barriers, but many students without disabilities also find that curricula are poorly designed to meet their learning needs. Traditional curricula—and, for that matter, the policies that support them—are too prescriptive in how students reach the end goal of mastering learning. They provide few routes to success, requiring individuals in all their diversity to follow the same narrow roads.

Of course, diversity is the norm, not the exception, wherever individuals are gathered, including schools. When curricula are designed to meet the needs of the broad middle—at the exclusion of those with different abilities, learning styles, backgrounds, and even preferences—they fail to provide all individuals with fair and equal opportunities to learn. Curricula should make clear the goals of learning and then provide guided support for reaching those goals.

In this chapter, to illustrate the principles of UDL, we describe an instrument that many of us use every day: the Global Positioning System (GPS) that many of us now have in our cars. (Hertz Neverlost, TomTom, and Magellan RoadMate are examples of commercial instruments.) The GPS is a good analogy because it embeds many of the same features that are needed in education. In fact, the GPS may serve as a better example of UDL than most traditional educational curricula.

ONE GOAL, MANY ROUTES

The GPS guides travelers to their final destinations by asking three important questions:

- What is your present location?
- What is your destination or goal?
- What is the best route for reaching that goal?

To assist individuals in finding their present location, the GPS offers multiple options. Users can click a button that reveals their exact location, type in a starting point, or speak their present location into the instrument. The GPS builds in these alternatives to ensure that it will obtain an accurate starting point for every user. We highlight this feature of the GPS because in schools, we often do not know the "present locations" of our students. We might have twenty-five students in a classroom, and each student has unique background knowledge as well as varying strengths and weaknesses; these twenty-five all start in very different places. When we think about the GPS in relation to UDL, it is clear that the GPS builds in features to account for this diversity among individuals.

Once the starting point has been determined, the GPS then addresses the question, "What is your destination or goal?" Again, the GPS assists individuals in setting their objectives by offering alternatives. For example, you can choose to enter your destination by yourself, or you can search from previous destinations. If you do not know the exact location, you can even choose to select from the Yellow Pages. The GPS very rarely restricts users to only one option; it embeds a wide array of choices to support travelers in selecting their objectives. In terms of UDL, the GPS understands the importance of setting goals and providing the necessary supports to reach them.

Finally, the GPS supports travelers in selecting a route. The GPS does not assume that there is only one way to get travelers to their destinations; it recognizes the need to offer alternatives so that users can choose the route that best suits their needs. For example, you can select your route based on the shortest time, the most use of freeways, or the least use of freeways. In fact, some systems even allow you to choose the most scenic route. When we think about the GPS in terms of UDL, it is asking, "What *kind* of route do you want?" or "What kind of route is *best for you*?" This ability to customize according to individual preferences is a key element of UDL.

The GPS is a perfect analogy with which to illustrate UDL because these three questions—determining a present location, setting a destination or goal, and selecting individualized routes—are crucial when we think about student learning. Students are highly diverse, and this means that they are going to need to take different paths to achieve the same goals.

The GPS is faced with two different challenges: getting *you* to your destination on time and getting *everyone* to their destinations on time. This second challenge is a very different challenge from the first. It is not just about providing multiple routes to take one individual from the airport to the Children's Museum, for example; it is also about being responsive to the many different travelers who want to go to the Children's Museum. Each traveler will start in a different place and will have varied needs and preferences that the GPS must accommodate. Both of these challenges are interesting from a design standpoint as well as from a technology standpoint.

The GPS is able to address these vastly different challenges by embracing technology. In fact, the GPS utilizes technology well in the ways that we want education to use technology well. To get travelers to their destinations, online technology is much more effective than a traditional printed paper map. The GPS also draws upon the power of technology to differentiate. The GPS recognizes that there are many paths, and this awareness allows different people from different places to all get to the same objective. The GPS takes full advantage of the power and flexibility of technology in its design, and we hope that schools will be able to harness this power in the design of their curricula as well. Of course, it is worth noting here that even in low-tech environments, curricula can and should be responsive to individual needs. Technology can make this easier to accomplish in some settings but is itself never a substitute for a well-designed curriculum or thoughtful, responsive instruction.

UNIVERSAL DESIGN FOR LEARNING

UDL helps meet the challenge of diversity by suggesting flexible instructional materials, techniques, and strategies that empower educators to meet these varied needs. A universally designed curriculum is designed from the outset to meet the needs of the greatest number of users, reducing the need for costly, time-consuming, and after-the-fact changes (Rose & Meyer, 2002). Three primary principles guide UDL:

> *Principle I: Provide multiple means of representation (the "what" of learning).* Students differ in the ways that they perceive and comprehend information that is presented to them. For example, those with sensory disabilities (e.g., blindness or deafness), learning disabilities (e.g., dyslexia), language or cultural differences, and so forth may require different representations of information in order to access and understand the same content. Moreover, no one type of representation is optimal for a particular kind of content. For example, printed text may be a better medium for teaching and learning history than science and mathematics. In reality, there is no one means of representation that will be optimal for all students or for all types of learning; providing options in representation is essential.

Principle II: Provide multiple means of action and expression (the "how" of learning). Students differ in the ways that they can navigate a learning environment and express what they know. For example, individuals with significant motor disabilities (e.g., cerebral palsy), those who struggle with strategic and organizational abilities (e.g, executive function disorders, ADHD), and those who have language barriers approach learning tasks very differently and will demonstrate their mastery very differently. Some may be able to express themselves well in writing but not oral speech, and vice versa. In reality, there is no one means of expression that will be optimal for all students; providing options for expression is essential.

Principle III: Provide multiple means of engagement (the "why" of learning). Students differ markedly in the ways in which they can be engaged or motivated to learn. Some students are highly engaged by spontaneity and novelty while other are disengaged, even frightened, by those aspects, preferring predictable routine and structure. In reality, there is no one means of engagement that will be optimal for all students; providing multiple options for engagement is essential (Rose & Meyer, 2002; CAST, 2008).

CAST drafted the *UDL Guidelines* (2008) to address the call from teachers, administrators, curriculum developers, and policy makers for guidelines to help make applications of UDL principles and practices more concrete. Each principle has three associated guidelines, and each guideline offers several specific options or "checkpoints" (see figure 1-1). These guidelines and their associated checkpoints articulate evidence-based options that should be considered to ensure that students with a full range of abilities and disabilities can access and progress in the general curriculum.

AN ANALOGY FOR EDUCATION: HOW THE GPS ADDRESSES UDL PRINCIPLES

Sadly for education, the commonly available GPS exemplifies the principles and guidelines of universal design for learning better than most

FIGURE 1-1   Universal Design for Learning Guidelines

I. Provide Multiple Means of Representation	II. Provide Multiple Means of Action and Expression	III. Provide Multiple Means of Engagement
1. Provide options for perception • Options that customize the display of information • Options that provide alternatives for auditory information • Options that provide alternatives for visual information	**4. Provide options for physical action** • Options in the mode of physical response • Options in the means of navigation • Options for accessing tools and assistive technologies	**7. Provide options for recruiting interest** • Options that increase individual choice and autonomy • Options that enhance relevance, value, and authenticity • Options that reduce threats and distractions
2. Provide options for language and symbols • Options that define vocabulary and symbols • Options that clarify syntax and structure • Options for decoding text or mathematical notation • Options that promote cross-linguistic understanding • Options that illustrate key concepts non-linguistically	**5. Provide options for expressive skills and fluency** • Options in the media for communication • Options in the tools for composition and problem solving • Options in the scaffolds for practice and performance	**8. Provide options for sustaining effort and persistence** • Options that heighten salience of goals and objectives • Options that vary levels of challenge and support • Options that foster collaboration and communication • Options that increase mastery-oriented feedback
3. Provide options for comprehension • Options that provide or activate background knowledge • Options that highlight critical features, big ideas, and relationships • Options that guide information processing • Options that support memory and transfer	**6. Provide options for executive functions** • Options that guide effective goal-setting • Options that support planning and strategy development • Options that facilitate managing information and resources • Options that enhance capacity for monitoring progress	**9. Provide options for self-regulation** • Options that guide personal goal-setting and expectations • Options that scaffold coping skills and strategies • Options that develop self-assessment and reflection

educational curricula. The following section explores the features of the GPS through the lens of the UDL guidelines.

Principle I: Multiple Means of Representation

Guideline 1: Provide options for perception

In order to ensure that information is equally accessible to all learners, the UDL guidelines point out that it is critical to provide several options in the way that the information can be perceived. If we present information that is accessible through only one sensory modality—a spoken lecture, for example—students who are deaf or hard of hearing or students who simply have trouble processing auditory information will not find the information accessible. If our information is presented only through printed text, students who are blind or have low vision will be unable to access the content. Providing options (e.g., captions for the lecture, voicing for the visual text) are essential for equitable learning and teaching.

The GPS, much more than most lectures or textbooks, automatically provides the perceptual options recommended in the UDL guidelines. First and foremost, it presents all of its key information by visual and auditory means. Visually, it uses maps to display your location and text to provide directions, locations, and landmarks. But it also presents the same information aurally by "talking you through" each step of your journey and reading any text aloud. If you have a visual impairment, with the GPS you can navigate purely through spoken words and sounds. If you are hard of hearing, you can navigate entirely by visual information. Finally, the GPS builds in options to customize the display of information. In most GPS units, you can make the screen brighter, adjust contrast, increase or decrease the size of images, increase or decrease the volume, and so forth. The GPS recognizes the diversity of perception among travelers and provides multiple representations of information.

Guideline 2: Provide options for language and symbols

The UDL guidelines also prompt us to consider providing options for the language and symbols in which information is represented. Students in our classes have different strengths and weaknesses with language; if we present information primarily through text, students who have difficulty decoding, students with dyslexia, or students who are English language learners will not have equitable access.

The GPS, in contrast to textbooks, provides many options for the languages and symbols it uses. For information presented in text, the GPS provides the option to hear it read aloud automatically; for information presented orally, the GPS provides visual options; for information presented in English, the GPS allows users to select the language with which they are most comfortable. Finally, there are even alternatives for language itself. The GPS has a "beep system" that obviates the need for language at all. The various beeps associated with "turn right," "turn left," and "stay straight" allow travelers to reach their destination entirely on the basis of sounds.

Guideline 3: Provide options for comprehension

The UDL guidelines also prompt us to consider providing options for comprehension, recognizing that students differ widely in their preparedness to assimilate new information into usable knowledge. They stress the importance of providing information that has "cognitive" options: alternative representations that highlight critical features or provide prompts and models to guide effective information processing, for example.

Typical GPS units provide multiple cognitive options to enhance comprehension. To draw attention to useful information, for example, many GPS units have a built-in product demonstration that highlights the important features of the device for novice users. More importantly, there are many cognitive options in how the GPS displays information. For many users, the optimal representation is a coordinate spatial map view where they can get a "big picture" view of their progress and direction. For others, the optimal representation is a "landmark" view: a list that shows them the turns and signposts that lie ahead. For still others, the optimal representation is an even smaller chunk of information: just the next turn to be watching for. The GPS provides each of these options with a simple press of a switch.

Principle II: Multiple Means of Action and Expression

Guideline 4: Provide options for physical action

The UDL guidelines also encourage us to provide options for physical action so that students' motor skills do not act as a barrier to expression. For example, if you asked your students to express what they know about the causes of the American Revolution through a written essay, those students with motor disabilities would not be able to give you an accurate picture of what they know because the motor demands of the task would interfere with fluent expression. Consequently, the guidelines encourage us to provide multiple options for student action.

The GPS has alternatives for physical actions built right into its design. To enter your destination, you have the option of speaking the name of the destination into the device instead of typing it. This feature benefits travelers who have motor disabilities as well as those whose hands are occupied by the steering wheel. The GPS also features embedded word prediction: you type in the first few letters of a destination, and it will predict your word. In three simple clicks, you can enter your destination.

Guideline 5: Provide options for expressive skills and fluency

The UDL guidelines also suggest providing options for the skills that underlie expression and communication. These options are necessary because students differ widely in the fluency with which they can use various media and tools to express themselves. For unskilled novices it is important to provide scaffolds that can be gradually released as those learners develop fluency and independence.

The GPS is certainly not an instrument or medium for communication, but it does provide important scaffolds for the novice. For one, most GPS units provide an option to "simulate" the trip ahead, modeling the sequence of turns and choices that the driver will ultimately follow. When you actually proceed along the route, the GPS scaffolds you by breaking your trip into small, manageable steps instead of overwhelming you with the whole sequence at once. Last, like a good mentor, it prompts you "just in time" to make the right choices.

Guideline 6: Provide options for executive functions

The UDL guidelines also stress the importance of providing support for what are called the "executive functions": setting goals, making plans and strategies, and monitoring progress.

The GPS provides many options for these executive functions. At the outset, as we noted earlier, it prompts you with options for setting your goal and then provides options in choosing the type of plan you would prefer for reaching that goal. Additionally, one of the most powerful features of the GPS is the immediate feedback it offers to travelers so that they can more easily monitor their progress. What is especially interesting, and instructive, is the kind of feedback that is provided. Instead of harshly saying, "Wrong, go back!" the GPS instead simply says, "Calculating new route." This is a great example of UDL in its explicit recognition of two things: that you have already made progress and that from where you are now a better route can be found. In terms of UDL, we want to monitor students' progress (and help students to develop the skills to monitor *their own* progress) so that even after making mistakes, they can find the best route toward achieving their learning goals.

Principle III: Multiple Means of Engagement

Guideline 7: Provide options for recruiting interest

Because students differ significantly in what attracts their attention, and learning requires attention, the UDL guidelines recommend options for "recruiting interest." One of the simplest options, one supported by a great deal of research, is the offering of choices. Students are much more highly engaged when they are able to make relevant choices themselves.

Not surprisingly, the GPS engages the driver's interest in large part because it offers choices in almost every aspect of its design. By far the most important choice is that of destination. With a GPS, the choices in where to go are nearly infinite; they can range from specific addresses, to business locations, to public facilities, and so on. But there are many other choices. As noted above, users have choices in how information should be displayed, what language is used, how selections are made, and so forth. By embedding options, the GPS gives users a sense of control and autonomy over their driving experience. This sense of control and autonomy is essential for students as well.

Guideline 8: Provide options for sustaining effort and persistence

The UDL guidelines also prompt educators to provide options for sustaining effort and persistence. Many kinds of learning, particularly project-based or inquiry learning, require sustained attention and effort. However, students differ considerably in their ability to independently sustain the attention that many lessons require. The UDL guidelines suggest options that can help, such as options to keep the goal salient and "in mind."

The GPS would seem to place a lower demand on this guideline because the designer can assume a highly motivated user from the outset (the user has chosen to purchase and use the GPS). But the GPS does include important design features that are very relevant. In particular, most units provide a consistent multiple representation of the goal (often at the very top or bottom of the screen) that constantly reminds you not only where you are going but how much time and distance remain, what time you will arrive at your present pace, and so forth. These design features all serve to keep the goal very salient, an important UDL checkpoint.

Guideline 9: Provide options for self-regulation

The UDL guidelines also stress the importance of developing students' intrinsic abilities to regulate their own emotions and motivations. The ability to self-regulate—to strategically modulate one's emotional reactions or states in order to cope or engage with the environment more effectively—is a critical aspect of human development. Some students are able to develop self-regulatory skills on their own, either by trial and error or by observing successful adults. Yet many other students have significant difficulty developing these skills.

This guideline is probably the least applied in the design of the GPS. Quite simply, the designers are not attempting to build independence or self-regulation—both of those goals lie well beyond the scope of getting from the airport to the convention hall. And in that lack of scope lies the critical difference between what a GPS does and what an educational system does, as we shall conclude in the next section.

IS THE GPS REALLY A GOOD MODEL FOR EDUCATION?

As we have illustrated, the current GPS effectively embodies most of the UDL principles and guidelines. But it is important to recognize the limitations of the GPS as a model for educational design. To put it starkly, the GPS is an excellent model of universal design, but not of universal design *for learning*. The difference lies primarily in the goals: the GPS is designed to optimize performance; educational curricula *should* be designed to optimize learning. That is a big difference.

The different goals of the GPS are most apparent when a traveler visits a particular city, say Boston, several times. On the first visit they would primarily experience the advantages of the GPS: it would help them save time in reaching their destination. But on the next visit the limitations would be more apparent: they would likely find that they remember very little about Boston, about its distinctive topography or landmarks, about how to navigate the peculiar landscape and roads of Boston, how to find and orient themselves to the city's various neighborhoods, and so forth. Most disturbingly, the traveler would find that they are almost as dependent on the device on their subsequent visits as on their first. They find that they have learned one thing for sure: how to depend on the GPS.

The expectations for education are higher. Its goals are not merely to improve immediate performance but to build future capacity—the capacity to be effective in almost any setting because the learner is more knowledgeable, more skillful and strategic, more engaged and motivated. The goal of education is to increase *independence*, not dependence.

It is evocative, and therefore instructive, to imagine the redesign of the GPS with learning rather than performance as its goal. Several differences immediately come to mind. At the outset, the GPS would offer a broader range of options, some that instruct in the most efficient routes for reaching a destination and others that build understanding of a city's topography, landmarks, history and culture, tourist attractions, or architecture.

In truth, a really "educational" GPS would deliver information that best matches the context in which you are traveling with your own stated interests and/or prior experience. By asking a few carefully constructed questions (which you would answer by voice, not typing, of course), it could adapt the level of its teaching to your present level of knowledge.

That is but one example. With carefully engineered options, the GPS could also mentor you more deeply by prompting you to stop and investigate various aspects of the city and check your learning with queries that would guide further exploration. It could also be used to develop skills and strategies rather than simply knowledge: skills for navigating in new cities generally, techniques for driving more cost-effectively, strategies for estimating distances and speeds more accurately, experiments in the physics of motion and acceleration.

CONCLUSION

When we think about the GPS in terms of the three principles of UDL, we can see there is an incredible amount of flexibility built into this device that reduces barriers and increases options for all users. This chapter has illustrated the many effective UDL features built into the GPS, and we wish that the curricula in our classrooms were just as effective. To improve our classrooms, we should focus on those same questions addressed by the GPS: Where is each student? What are each child's goals and objectives? What is a good route for this child? The GPS is much better at addressing these questions than our traditional curricula because so many of the UDL guidelines are integrated into its design. The GPS shows us that we can do so much more for education; we must work to make our curricula as responsive to individual differences as this little piece of technology.

When you finally reach your destination, the GPS narrator announces: "You've arrived." You may not have taken exactly the route you expected, and you might have wondered whether the method was in fact madness. But in the end you reach the destination you set out to find with just the right amount of support. Wouldn't it be great if our curricula could promise and deliver the same?

REFERENCES

CAST. (2008). *Universal design for learning guidelines version 1.0.* Wakefield, MA: Author. Retrieved online May 20, 2009, from http://www.cast.org/publications/UDL-guidelines/version1.html.

Rose, D. H., & Meyer, A. (2002). *Teaching every student in the digital age: Universal design for learning.* Alexandria, VA: Association for Supervision and Curriculum Development.

CHAPTER TWO

School Reform: Are We Just Getting Started?

DAVID T. GORDON

The little blue bound booklet, all thirty pages of it, grabbed the public's attention in 1983. *A Nation at Risk: The Imperative for Educational Reform* read the dramatic title. Inside, the report, issued by the U.S. secretary of education's National Commission on Excellence in Education, warned of a "rising tide of mediocrity" that threatened to swamp U.S. schools: "If an unfriendly foreign power had attempted to impose on America the mediocre educational performance that exists today, we might well have viewed it as an act of war." Providing an education with high academic standards for all learners must become an urgent national priority: "Our recommendations are based on the beliefs that everyone can learn, that everyone is born with an urge to learn which can be nurtured, that a solid high school education is within the reach of virtually all, and that lifelong learning will equip people with the skills required for new careers and for citizenship" (National Commission on Excellence in Education, 1983).

The idea that academic achievement for all students should be the primary goal of educational policy and practice was something new (Graham, 2003). In the early twentieth century, schools had aimed to provide elementary workforce skills and an understanding of American civic values, which would foster democratic practices in a society continually replenished by newly arrived immigrants. College preparation was reserved, by and large, for elites. By the end of World War II, the

U.S. Office of Education was emphasizing the need to prepare 20 percent of students for college and 20 percent for skilled occupations. The remaining 60 percent would receive "life adjustment education" focused primarily on practical subjects such as home economics, social guidance, and vocational training, subjects with immediate utility (Ravitch, 2000, pp. 328–329).

The conventional wisdom that most students didn't need a robust academic education carried over into the fifties, when large high schools with highly differentiated curricula, numerous social and athletic opportunities, and few rigorous academic requirements became the norm (Ravitch, pp. 362–365). After the Soviet Union sent *Sputnik* into orbit in 1957, public pressure grew for stronger math, science, and foreign language preparation for students on the college-prep track. The tide of a stronger academic emphasis appeared to raise all boats: high school graduation rates rose more than 10 percent in the early 1960s, to nearly 77 percent (higher than today's), and educational attainment increased across racial and socioeconomic categories during that same period (Snyder, 1993).

By the seventies, following heady days when bold federal initiatives to combat discrimination based on race, gender, socioeconomic status, and disability promised to increase opportunities for all, expectations had changed. Yet along with these expectations came the sober realization that soaring rhetoric and pots of public funds alone would not improve schools. A number of blue-ribbon panels diagnosed what was ailing schools and, in some cases, prescribed solutions. Reports issued by the College Entrance Examination Board, the Twentieth Century Fund, the National Science Board, the Southern Regional Education Board, and others were "thoughtfully written, insightfully analytical," writes historian Patricia Albjerg Graham, "and each sank like a stone from public view" (Graham, 2003, p. ix).

Providing physical access to schools for minorities and individuals with disabilities was in and of itself a significant social achievement. Now the emphasis shifted to ensuring academic success as well. And how could educational opportunities be guaranteed for all? The authors of *A Nation at Risk* favored more of everything—more content, more standards and expectations, more time in the school day, more support (and expectations) for teachers, more money, more accountability tied to standardized test scores. So began the era of school reform.

STOP-AND-GO REFORMS

While a number of state and local reform efforts were already under way when A *Nation at Risk* was issued, such efforts grew exponentially in the months and years following the report. In the state of Arkansas alone, 122 education bills were passed in a twelve-month period during 1983–1984. Forty-four states raised graduation requirements, especially in math and science, while dozens of states raised standards for teachers and mandated more classroom instructional time (Schwartz, 2003). A new generation of governors, especially in the South—governors such as Bill Clinton of Arkansas, Richard Riley of South Carolina, and Lamar Alexander of Tennessee—made school reform a priority. The flurry of activity was impressive, though lacking any national coordination.

The initial state-level reforms faced resistance from educators and their unions, who resented the top-down approach to reform. As a result, the National Governors Association (NGA) proposed a bottom-up approach, giving schools more autonomy in exchange for more accountability. "To sum it up," said NGA chairman Lamar Alexander in 1986, "the governors are ready for some old-fashioned horse-trading. We'll regulate less, if schools and school districts will produce better results" (quoted in Schwartz, 2003, p. 133). Principals and teachers would take responsibility for improvements in curriculum and instruction—and be called to account for the results. Policy makers would support efforts to build a stronger teaching corps by funding career development and in-service training. In reality, school finances, personnel, and to a large extent curricula remained in the hands of lumbering district bureaucracies and the unions with which they dealt. Autonomy was a phantom. (In just a few years, a more dramatic proposal would be made: to give "charters" to groups of educators, parents, businesspeople, and others to found and operate public schools, innovating in whatever ways got results.)

In 1989, President George H. W. Bush and the nation's governors, led by Arkansas's Bill Clinton, met in Charlottesville, Virginia, where they agreed to establish national K–12 education standards and assessments. In doing so, they adopted six national goals to achieve by the year 2000, including that all students would master "challenging subject matter in the core academic subjects"; that U.S. students would be "first in the world in science and mathematics achievement"; that universal literacy among American adults would be achieved; and that the high school graduation rate would rise to 90 percent. It was not enough for states to develop models of excellence and innovation: they had to take such models to scale in order to extend to all students rich opportunities to learn (Sadovnik, Cookson, & Semel, 2000).

In many ways, Charlottesville launched what we now call "standards-based" reform (Elmore, 2003). Though several states, such as California and Maryland, had recently begun designing comprehensive state strategies with aligned curriculum frameworks and assessments, Charlottesville rallied national stakeholders with different interests and ideologies in a common cause. Business leaders joined the cause, as did the American Federation of Teachers, whose president, Al Shanker, became one of the decade's most prominent spokespersons for strong standards and assessments. This broad and bipartisan commitment to standards-based reform survived even as governorships, the White House, and the U.S. Congress changed party hands.

The nineties were a time of great experimentation and were not without controversy. Charter schools proliferated, providing "hothouses" where innovations could be developed and tested outside the usual constraints of district management and collective bargaining. The number of charters grew from two in 1991 to more than 4,300 by 2007 (U.S. Department of Education, 2008). Voucher programs, like charter schools, aimed to give more authority to parents by enabling them to use public funds to send their children to private or public schools. Privatization of school management and services was tried, ostensibly to provide more fiscal accountability and to free up educators, especially school principals, to focus on instructional leadership rather than buses, buildings, and budgets (Knowles, 2003). In 1991, the chief executives of several major corporations established the New American Schools Development Corporation to find and fund school reform models that would "break the mold" and help take such models to scale, offering professional services, consultation, and capital investment (Bodilly, et al, 1996). Home schooling soared, with more than one million students learning at home in 2003, double the number educated at home in 1990 (National Center for Education Statistics, 2006).

Since research suggested a strong correlation between school success and school readiness, states also placed a new emphasis on early childhood education during these years. They added prekindergarten programs, raised teacher licensing requirements, and established school readiness standards. By 2001, forty-six states and the District of Columbia funded some kind of preschool program, though only a few (including Georgia, New York, and Oklahoma) made strides toward offering universal preschool (Griffin & Lundy-Ponce, 2002).

In 1994, with his national health care reform faltering, President Bill Clinton turned to education. His Goals 2000: Educate America Act aimed to provide a more coherent, or "systemic," approach to education policy at the federal, state, and local levels. In a year of epic defeats—ending with the Republicans controlling the House of Representatives for the first time in forty-eight years—Clinton managed to build a high level of bipartisan support for his education initiatives. Washington offered funding to states to develop content standards and appropriate assessments for reading and mathematics at three grade levels; it also required states to hold schools receiving Title I funding accountable for student performance (Sadovnik et al., 2000). Later, Clinton would also initiate efforts to support teacher professional development and make new technologies more accessible at the classroom level. The federal government was still reluctant to exert too much control over education across the fifty states, but it was getting bolder.

Though Washington funded various educational organizations to draft standards in areas such as history, English language arts, and science, efforts to establish national standards never got traction. Without a system for balanced reviews of the frameworks by impartial expert panels, the standards got mired in ideology and politics. History standards that portrayed Western accomplishments in relentlessly negative terms drew fire across the political spectrum. Whole language and phonics advocates carried their decades-long battle into the standards arena. Discussions of math standards followed suit, pitting proponents of a "new math" focused on problem solving against those who favored more traditional arithmetic instruction.

Where state standards became highly politicized, as in California, educators at the school-building level were left to make sense of shifting messages and mandates. Whole language and new math were "in," then they were "out," or at least were forced to become curricular bedfellows with phonics and basic arithmetic (Gordon, 2003). This wobbliness at the policy level often left teachers and administrators confused as to what was expected at the classroom level and what would satisfy the demand for better performance on standardized tests.

During the 2000 election season, with the next Elementary and Secondary Education Act (ESEA) reauthorization approaching, momentum grew for new federal leadership in education reform. Vice President Al Gore, the favorite to win that year's presidential election, proposed a $115 billion plan that would have included national content standards, merit pay for teachers, reduced class sizes, support for universal pre-kindergarten, and more rigorous teacher requirements and in-service evaluations (Gore, 2000). George W. Bush, having made school reform his showpiece as Texas governor, proposed "a fresh start for the federal role in education" (Bush, 1999) in which Washington would hold states accountable for educational improvement, support "scientifically-based" education research, invest federal dollars in charter schools and character education, and fund an early childhood reading program. History tilted Bush's way.

In No Child Left Behind (NCLB)—as ESEA was renamed at its 2001 reauthorization—the president sponsored and signed a bill that, in one swoop, aimed to impose standards and accountability on all U.S. schools. Students would learn to high standards, as measured by standardized tests. Teachers would have to be "highly qualified" and demonstrate their skill. Schools would have to demonstrate annual progress toward the goal of leading all students to basic proficiency in mathematics and reading/language arts. Policy makers would have to do a better job of monitoring and, presumably, funding schools to ensure success. Furthermore, every school, district, and state would have to demonstrate not just overall progress but progress by traditionally disadvantaged students in a number of different categories. Test results would be sorted by racial/ethnic identity, disability, limited English proficiency, and socio-economic status. With Bush leading from the right and his unlikely ally, Senator Edward M. Kennedy, leading the left, NCLB won strong bipartisan support.

For all its broad support and big declarative statements about how finally to achieve academic success for all, questions about how to assess progress under NCLB were raised almost immediately. To critics, the new law relied dangerously on a simplistic definition of academic success—test scores. Harvard scholar Richard F. Elmore noted that in the early years of the accountability movement, "reformers had an expansive view of performance that included, in addition to tests, portfolios of students' work, teachers' evaluations of their students, student-initiated projects, and formal exhibitions of student work" (Elmore, 2004, p. 203). Standardized tests are appealing to policy makers because they are cheaper to administer, easier to grade, and deliver simple results, added Elmore, but are they the accurate measures of student performance that good decision making, both at the policy and the instructional level, requires?

For most Americans, patience and longsuffering are hardly regarded as essential political virtues—perhaps because we reserve the right to change our minds every two, four, or six years in elections that invariably promise "change" for the better. The planning and execution required to adopt and then drop new practices and programs can masquerade as progress—activity being mistaken for effective action. Yet, as historian Maris Vinovskis writes, education is a field where the "process of identifying promising educational practices, rigorously testing their effectiveness in model programs, and then trying them out in different settings often can take fifteen to twenty years" (Vinovskis, 2003, p. 116).

LOOKING AHEAD

For all that we have *not* accomplished and have *not* learned, we have in fact learned many lessons during the past thirty years, some by trial and error, some by attentive research and study. A few general lessons—by no means comprehensive—can serve as guideposts for tomorrow's work.

Academic excellence begins early

Scientific knowledge of children's learning, behavior, and development has changed dramatically in the last quarter century (Commission on Behavioral and Social Sciences and Education, 2000). For decades, researchers have gathered strong evidence that effective early childhood education has lasting benefits in preparing children not only for later school success but also for success in life. Research suggests that children who participate in high-quality pre-K–3 programs are more likely to perform better in math and reading throughout their school careers and are more likely to graduate from high school than their peers who do not attend such programs (Wiltz, 2006; Peisner-Feinberg, Burchinal, et al., 1999). Early childhood education programs—especially those with a planned curriculum aligned across the years from prekindergarten through third grade—are especially important for children of low socioeconomic status and for English language learners, since they are far less likely to have the kinds of rich language, literacy, and learning experiences at home that will prepare them well for school ("From Literacy to Learning: An Interview with Catherine Snow," 2005).

In one landmark study, the Perry Preschool Project, researchers examined the long-term effects of high-quality early childhood education on low-income three- and four-year-olds. Beginning in 1962, the study followed participants into their forties. Those who participated in preschool did better in school and at work, had higher earnings, and committed fewer crimes on average than those who did not take part in preschool programs. Overall, the study estimated a return to society of more than a $17 for every $1 of public funds invested in the program (Schweinhart, 2005).

Another longitudinal study followed some 1,500 students from low-income, largely African American families who participated in the Chicago public schools' Child-Parent Center (CPC) program. With federal Title I funding, the CPC provides educational and family support services for children in grades pre-K through 3. A fifteen-year study culminating in 2001 found that attendees completed more years of education than peers of comparable socioeconomic status who did not participate in preschool, were less likely to be placed in special education or get held back in school, demonstrated higher scores on cognitive literacy and school achievement measures, and graduated from high school at a much higher rate ("Preschool Yields High Returns, But Not All States Are Investing," 2003).

Small schools seem to work better

A growing body of evidence suggests that small schools are better places to learn, on balance, than large schools. Research shows that students who attend small schools (generally, high schools of seven hundred students or fewer; K–8 schools of three hundred or fewer) perform better in core subjects such as reading and math, complete more years of higher education, have better attendance records, and report better relationships with teachers and other students (Cotton, 1996; Wasley, Fine, et al., 2000). Kathleen Cotton's meta-analysis (1996) found that small schools tend to be safer, reporting fewer incidents of violence and vandalism. They appear to encourage more parental participation and teacher-parent communication. And they tend to mitigate some of the effects of low socioeconomic status, providing disadvantaged students with opportunities to work more closely with adults who know them by name. Nine of ten studies reviewed by Cotton found strong correlations between small schools to lower dropout rates.

Small schools can not only help reduce the anonymity of students, but can have a similar effect on teachers as well, providing better conditions for collaboration with colleagues. As rising enrollment rates pressure states and districts to keep schools large, increasing numbers have experimented with creating "schools within schools" to replicate some of the favorable conditions of small schools while making do with existing facilities and structures. Of course, other conditions—teacher preparation and support, instructional time and standards, and so forth—will also help determine the success or failure of any school to provide effective education for its students. But both research and anecdotal evidence strongly suggest that smaller schools support better teaching and learning (Lawrence, Bingler, et al., 2002).

The small-schools movement lost some of its shine after a $2 billion initiative by the Bill and Melinda Gates Foundation to fund 2,600 small high schools failed to show significant improvement in student test scores after a few years. In fact, students in the Gates schools were outperformed on certain measures, including mathematics, by students in larger schools nearby. However, attendance rates were higher at the Gates schools, suggesting greater student engagement and interest in schooling. The Gates experiment does not refute the larger body of evidence in support of small schools as much as it raises questions about curriculum and instruction, as well as teacher preparation and development, in the Gates schools themselves (Ravitch, 2008). The Gates experience shows that organizing small schools is not enough. Due attention needs to be paid to what happens inside those schools. But given a strong curriculum and high-quality teaching, the opportunity to humanize and personalize the educational experience for young people through a small-school environment offers a clear advantage over a more impersonal one.

The diversity of student populations is much greater than we ever realized

The diversity of student populations is increasing—and with it the need for renewed commitment to teach all learners to high standards. The underlying premise and promise of the past three decades of reform is that all learners, regardless of race, socioeconomic status, ability, or background, deserve the best education we can provide. Since 1980, the populations of U.S. classrooms have changed dramatically. According to a 2005 U.S. Population Survey, 12 percent of U.S. residents are foreign-born, nearly three times the level of thirty years ago. More than 20 percent of all U.S. school-age children were born to immigrants—and more than a quarter of all low-income schoolchildren (Capps, Fix, et al., 2005). Most of these are Latino and, like African American students, have struggled to close the gap between their academic achievement and that of their white peers ("Latino Achievement: How to Close the Gap," 2003).

Coinciding with this increase in immigration has been a new emphasis, especially in federal legislation such as NCLB and the Individuals with Disabilities Education Act (IDEA), on the right of students with special needs to receive a high-quality education based on the same standards and accountability measures as the general population (Hitchcock, Meyer, et al., 2005).

At the same time, advances in neuroscience and education research have revealed that diversity is much more than something we can see. Recent advances in the cognitive sciences have given us a whole new understanding of the subtle but significant differences in the way each person learns. As education researchers David H. Rose and Anne Meyer have written: "When two students perform the same academic task, the patterns of activity in their brains are as unique as their as fingerprints" (Rose & Meyer, 2002, p. 18). This recognition needs to be taken into account, especially as we standardize both the curriculum and the way student learning is measured.

Curricula need to be flexible and responsive to individuals

A promising way of addressing student diversity is through universal design for learning (UDL). While all students deserve the same opportunities to learn, they do not all learn in the same way, nor do they demonstrate their knowledge and mastery of skills uniformly. What science now confirms, good teachers have known all along. Yet this insight has not always translated into effective curriculum because the curriculum has been traditionally viewed as a fixed entity to which individuals must adapt. That is, the means of achieving common academic goals have been rigid and prescribed, excluding those who might otherwise attain academic expertise through diverse means. Knowing what we now do about the great diversity of individual learners requires us to embrace a different strategy for pursuing a common endpoint: we need to remain open to multiple means of getting there. The UDL principles, which reflect insights from brain research into how vastly different individual learners are, call for

- Presenting information and content in different ways (the "what" of learning)
- Providing options in learning strategies and expression (the "how" of learning)
- Stimulating interest and motivation for learning (the "why" of learning) (Rose & Meyer, 2002)
- When applied carefully in the design of curriculum, these principles have the potential to expand learning opportunities for all by lowering barriers to learning.

Technology well deployed can increase learning opportunities
New technologies present us with extraordinary opportunities to individualize instruction in ways that help all students learn to their fullest ability. Typical classrooms are filled with barriers for learners with special needs and gifts. For example, the overwhelming reliance on printed materials—textbooks, for example—limits opportunities for students to whom printed text is inaccessible. These might include students with physical disabilities such as blindness, but they also include those with learning disabilities. Furthermore, inflexible curricular materials hamper students who do not have disabilities but who may learn more effectively in other ways—by listening, through arts, or with highly graphical displays.

The advent of universally designed learning technologies—especially portable and powerful multimedia—offers new opportunities in content presentation and also student assessment, providing new tools to gauge what students are learning *during the instructional process* so that instruction can be adjusted. In doing so, these technologies make the learning experience more about content and less about format—opening multiple pathways to the same destination of a high-quality, standards-based education (Rose & Meyer, 2005).

The inclusion in IDEA 2004 of a National Instructional Materials Accessibility Standard (NIMAS) makes printed instructional materials, including textbooks, more readily available in digital formats—preparing the way for the widespread use of technology-rich, customizable learning environments (NIMAS Development & Technical Assistance Centers, 2008). Of course, previous waves of technology have failed to change the classroom in the ways their advocates promised. But what is different this time is the ubiquity of technology tools in the everyday lives of children. They live in a nearly wireless "mediasphere" where video iPods, cell phones, instant messaging, and blogging are reshaping fundamental definitions of what it means to be literate. New technologies can no longer be supplemental to core academic endeavors; they must become intrinsic to learning goals and processes if schooling is to remain relevant in a swiftly evolving culture (Dalton, Rose, & Christodoulou, 2005; Rose & Meyer, 2002, 2005).

*   *   *   *

In some ways, the reform of our educational system is just beginning. That would be some solace if we didn't recognize that the impact of every failure in education—as opposed to, say, in manufacturing—is incalculable. Thirty years represents three generations of schoolchildren whose education will impact the rest of their lives. In marking the twentieth anniversary of *A Nation at Risk* a few years ago, education historian Patricia Albjerg Graham wrote of a discussion she had had in 1981 with a superintendent about the challenges facing his district's schools. "You don't understand," the administrator had said. "We run social welfare institutions, not academic ones" (Graham, 2003, p. viii). The idea that public schools, and not just elite private academies, should offer all students a challenging curriculum, high learning standards, expert instruction, performance-based accountability, and the lifelong opportunities that such an education affords—this idea had not yet taken root. Within a few years, it had. Yet most observers would agree that, clearly, this ideal has not flowered in enough—or even in *most*—classrooms. Seeing that it does is our primary assignment for the next several decades.

REFERENCES

Bodilly, S., Purnell, S., Ramsey, K., & Keith, S.J. (1996). Lessons from New American Schools Demonstration Corporation's demonstration phase. Santa Monica, CA: Rand Corporation.

Bush, G.W. (1999, October 5). The future of educational reform. Speech given at the Manhattan Institute for Policy Research, New York, NY. Retrieved June 29, 2009 from http://www.manhattan-institute.org/html/bush_speech.htm

Capps, R., Fix, M., Murray, J., Ost, J., Passel, J., & Herwantoro, S. (2005). *The new demography of America's schools: Immigration and the No Child Left Behind Act.* Washington, DC: Urban Institute. Retrieved May 20, 2009, from http://www.urban.org/UploadedPDF/311230_new_demography.pdf.

Center for Education Reform. Retrieved online May 20, 2009, from http://www.edreform.com/_upload/ncsw-numbers.pdf.

Commission on Behavioral and Social Sciences and Education. (2000). *Eager to learn: Educating our preschoolers.* Washington, DC: National Academy Press.

Cotton, K. (1996). *School size, school climate, and student performance.* Close-Up No. 20. Portland, OR: Northwest Regional Educational Laboratory.

Dalton, B., Rose, D., & Christodoulou, J. (2005). *Technology's role in advancing literacy and achievement for diverse adolescent learners.* Report prepared for the Carnegie Corporation of New York. Wakefield, MA: CAST.

Elmore, R. F. (2003). Change and improvement in educational reform. In D. T. Gordon (Ed.), *A nation reformed? American education 20 years after A Nation at Risk* (pp. 23–38). Cambridge, MA: Harvard Education Press.

Elmore, R. F. (2004). *School reform from the inside out: Policy, practice, and performance.* Cambridge, MA: Harvard Education Press.

From literacy to learning: An interview with Catherine Snow (2005). *Harvard Education Letter 21* (4), 7–8.

Gordon, D. T. (2003). The limits of ideology: Curriculum and the culture wars. In D. T. Gordon (Ed.), *A nation reformed? American education 20 years after A Nation at Risk* (pp. 99–114). Cambridge, MA: Harvard Education Press.

Graham, P. A. (2003). Foreword. In D. T. Gordon (Ed.) *A nation reformed? American education 20 years after A Nation at Risk* (pp. vii–xi). Cambridge, MA: Harvard Education Press.

Gore, A. (2000). *Al Gore on the issues: Education.* Brochure. Al Gore for President 2000. Retrieved June 29, 2009 from http://www.4president.us/issues/gore2000/gore2000education.htm.

Griffin, D., & Lundy-Ponce, G. (2002). *At the starting line: Early childhood education programs in the 50 states.* Washington, DC: American Federation of Teachers. Retrieved May 19, 2009, from http://www.aft.org/pubs-reports/downloads/teachers/EarlyChildhoodreport.pdf.

Hitchcock, C., Meyer, A., et al. (2005). Equal access, participation, and progress in the general education curriculum. In D. H. Rose, A. Meyer, and C. Hitchcock (Eds.), *The universally designed classroom: Accessible curriculum and digital technologies* (pp. 37–68). Cambridge, MA: Harvard Education Press.

Knowles, T. (2003). The academic imperative: New challenges and expectations facing school leaders. In D. T. Gordon (Ed.), *A nation reformed? American education 20 years after A Nation at Risk* (pp. 39–52). Cambridge, MA: Harvard Education Press.

Latino achievement: How to close the gap. (2003). *Harvard Education Letter, 19*(6), 5.

Lawrence, B. K., Bingler, S., et al. (2002). *Dollars & sense: The cost effectiveness of small schools.* Cincinnati, OH: KnowledgeWorks Foundation.

National Center for Education Statistics. (2006). *Homeschooling in the United States: 2003.* Washington, DC: NCES. Retrieved May 20, 2009, from http://nces.ed.gov/pubs2006/homeschool/.

National Commission on Excellence in Education. (1983). *A nation at risk: The imperative for educational reform.* Washington, DC: U.S. Department of Education. Retrieved May 19, 2009, from http://www.ed.gov/pubs/NatAtRisk/index.html.

NIMAS Development & Technical Assistance Centers (2008). *Progress on implementation of the National Instructional Materials Accessibility Standard (NIMAS).* Policy Brief. Wakefield, MA: Author. Retrieved June 29, 2009 from http://nimas.cast.org/about/resources/policy_brief-2008-04.

Peisner-Feinberg, S., Burchinal, M. R., Clifford, R. M., Culkin, M. L., Howes, C., Kagan, S. L., Yazejian, N., Byler, B., Rustici, J., & Zelazo, J. (1999). *The children of* the cost, quality and outcomes study go to school: Executive summary. Chapel Hill: University of North Carolina at Chapel Hill, Frank Porter Graham Child Development Center.

Preschool yields high returns, but not all states are investing (2003). *Harvard Education Letter, 19*(5), 6.

Ravitch, D. (2000). *Left back: A century of battles over school reform.* New York: Simon & Schuster.

Ravitch, D. (2008, November 19). Bill Gates and his silver bullet. *Forbes.com.* Retrieved online July 12, 2009 from http://www.forbes.com/2008/11/18/gates-foundation-schools-oped-cx_dr_1119ravitch.html.

Rose, D. H., & Meyer, A. (2002). *Teaching every student in the digital age: Universal design for learning.* Alexandria, VA: Association for Supervision and Curriculum Development.

Rose, D. H., & Meyer, A. (2005). The future is in the margins: The role of technology and disability in educational reform. In D. H. Rose, A. Meyer, & C. Hitchcock (Eds.), *The universally designed classroom: Accessible curriculum and digital technologies* (pp. 13–36). Cambridge, MA: Harvard Education Press.

Sadovnik, A. R., Cookson, Jr., P. W., & Semel, S. F. (2000). *Exploring education* (2nd ed.). Boston: Allyn & Bacon.

Schwartz, R. (2003). The emerging state leadership role in education reform: Notes of a participant-observer. In D. T. Gordon (Ed.), *A nation reformed? American education 20 years after* A Nation at Risk (pp. 131–152). Cambridge, MA: Harvard Education Press.

Schweinhart, L. J. (2005). *The HighScope Perry Preschool Study Through Age 40: Summary, conclusions, and frequently asked questions.* Monograph. (Ypsilanti, MI: HighScope Press).

Snyder, T. E. (1993). *120 years of American education: A statistical portrait.* Washington, DC: National Center on Educational Statistics.

U.S. Department of Education (2008). *A commitment to quality: National charter school policy forum report.* Washington, D.C.: Author. Retrieved June 29, 2009 from http://www.ed.gov/admins/comm/choice/csforum/report.html.

Vinovskis, M. A. (2003). Missed opportunities: Why the federal response to "A Nation at Risk" was inadequate. In D. T. Gordon (Ed.), *A nation reformed? American education 20 years after* A Nation at Risk (pp. 115–130). Cambridge, MA: Harvard Education Press.

Wasley, P. A., Fine, M., et al. (2000). Small schools, great strides: A study of the new small schools in Chicago. New York: Bank Street College of Education.

Wiltz, S. M. (2006). Research points to the long-term benefits of preschool. *Harvard Education Letter, 22*(1). Retrieved May 19, 2009, from http://edletter.org/current/prekresearch.shtml.

CHAPTER THREE

Policy Foundations of Universal Design for Learning

THOMAS HEHIR

> I can still recall the smell, pungent mix of ammonia and human waste. I can still recall the rows of metal beds, the children and adults who were forced to lie in them, day and night. I can still recall the racket in the ward, the bedridden residents' crying, moaning, yelling, and pleading. The year was 1971, and I was an undergraduate taking my first course in special education . . .
>
> Our professor assured us that these children and adults were capable of far more than was apparent during our visit, and that we would visit other sites where we would see that these students could learn and have full lives. These other sites included special schools and classes in which more fortunate students were learning to read, write, and laugh. However, though some children were getting a chance at a better life, children with significant disabilities were not guaranteed a right to an education. They could be denied entrance to school.
>
> —Thomas Hehir, *New Directions in Special Education*
> (2005, p. 1)

Since the 1970s, policy, practice, and litigation have pushed educators to think of better ways to educate students with disabilities in school. The dynamic of the major federal special education law, the Individuals with Disabilities Education Act (IDEA), is different from other education laws in that, from the beginning, advocates have sought to fundamentally change schools and other systems that serve children and youth rather than keep them static. And, given the strength of the parent and disability lobbies, Congress has frequently responded by strengthening the law and expanding its provisions. As a result, when there are innovations in practice, they tend to become incorporated into policy, and policy pushes educators toward new innovations. Further, parents have significant leverage to promote change through exercising their due process rights under IDEA. Though relatively few parents go to hearings, the few who do can have a major impact on the education system due to the high-stakes nature of these disputes (Hehir, 1990).

The experience of including students with significant cognitive disabilities is an example of this. Innovative educators, pushed by parents and supported through IDEA discretionary programs, began experimenting with ways to include children with significant disabilities in general education classrooms. As these children became successful, IDEA was amended in 1997 to provide greater impetus to this movement, requiring individualized education plans (IEPs) to include a greater focus on access to the general education curriculum and placement-neutral funding formulas. Further, parents successfully used the due process system to leverage change. What was once an experimental innovation is now widespread. Though we need to continue to promote the development of better inclusive options, children with significant disabilities are being included in every state and most school districts.

This same dynamic has led to greater access for children with disabilities and is currently building a foundation for educators to embrace universal design for learning (UDL). The development of UDL, a new and innovative concept in the 1990s supported through IDEA discretionary programs, is now incorporated in IDEA 2004 with its requirements for National Instructional Materials Accessibility Standard (NIMAS) and the movement toward response to intervention (RTI). A detailed discussion of these changes follows.

THE HISTORICAL PERSPECTIVE

Section 504 and IDEA—The 1970s

The legal foundation on which both inclusion and UDL have been based predates these concepts. The passage of Section 504 of the Rehabilitation Act in 1973 and IDEA (P.L. 94-142) in 1975 laid the foundation for UDL by emphasizing the need to educate students with disabilities in the "least restrictive environment" (LRE). In other words, the law now mandated that, "as much as appropriate," students with disabilities should be educated in general education classes with the appropriate aids and supports. Removal from the mainstream should occur only when inclusion cannot work. "As much as appropriate" is relatively vague, making it a dynamic standard rather than a static one, and ultimately it has been defined by the courts. In the 1970s, most practitioners considered integration for students with disabilities appropriate for those who could make it on their own with relatively little support. The definition of "as much as appropriate" expanded over time as practitioners developed more effective ways to educate students with disabilities in mainstream environments, and the courts have recognized these innovations.

Legal Foundation in the 1980s and 1990s

In the 1980s, parents—particularly parents of children with mental retardation—started challenging the segregation of their children, relying heavily on the concept of LRE and the due process provisions of IDEA. Even though segregation was widespread, parents argued that segregation was inconsistent with the intentions of LRE. In the field, innovative educators demonstrated that students with disabilities could be integrated into the mainstream, and this gave the courts the evidence they needed to rule in favor of the parents' case for inclusion.

In 1981, *Campbell v. Talladega* led the charge by questioning the efficacy of segregation and questioning low expectations. The court's ruling requiring that students with disabilities have contact with nondisabled peers established the precedent toward inclusive education. *Roncher v. Walter* in 1983 introduced the "portability standard," which acknowledged that if services could be offered in a nonsegregated setting, then a segregated placement was inappropriate. In 1989, *Daniel RR v. State*

Board of Education established the two-pronged test to determine whether an inclusive setting is the appropriate placement: With the use of aids and services, can the child be educated in the regular education classroom? And if the child must be removed from the general education classroom, is the child participating with nondisabled peers to the maximum extent appropriate? Finally, in *Sacramento City School District v. Holland* (1994), the Ninth Circuit Court of Appeals upheld a district judge's ruling that inclusion in a regular class is the least restrictive environment—and the U.S. Supreme Court refused to hear the case, allowing that ruling to stand.

These rulings built a strong legal foundation against removal unless school districts had tried to support students in general education classrooms prior to removal. These decisions, the mechanisms of LRE, and due process would ultimately push inclusion in a very powerful way to change practice in American schools and set a foundation for UDL.

Technology and Integration—The Early 1990s

By the early 1990s, the integration of students with more complex needs became more commonplace in American schools, and two major developments—advances in technology and the concept of universal design—helped support this integration. The concept of universal design, especially in architecture and in technology development, had begun to penetrate the culture. Disability policy, including the Assistive Technology Act, ensured that new technologies were being developed to be accessible for people with disabilities. Televisions included closed captioning capabilities, public buildings had curb cuts and automatic doors, and so forth.

In light of these advancements, conversations began about how to apply universal design to education. Understanding the developments in technology, we had to start thinking about curriculum and classroom organization in the same way. Organizations such as CAST (Center for Applied Special Technology) began to use technology as a way to support students in inclusive environments through programs like Wiggle-Works (1993), an early literacy program that blended multimedia and computer supports with classic, age-appropriate texts.

It should be noted here that IDEA's discretionary programs played a major role in spurring this innovation. For instance, Madeleine Will, former assistant secretary of education for special education and rehabilitation, promoted inclusion through systems change and regular education initiative grants. During the Clinton years, UDL innovation led by CAST received significant support from the IDEA technology program and the Tech Act under the leadership of assistant secretary of education for special education and rehabilitation Judy Heumann. The dynamic interaction between innovation and regulatory change is established in this following discussion of the 1997 reauthorization of IDEA.

IDEA 1997

In the early 1990s, the Americans with Disabilities Act put tremendous emphasis on people with disabilities gaining access to everything in life; as a result, when IDEA came up for reauthorization in the mid-1990s, the concept of access was central to the discussions. Further, research funded under IDEA was calling into question the widespread practices of segregating individuals with disabilities and basing their specialized curriculum on low expectations. With the 1997 amendments to IDEA, the law now redefined special education as meeting the unique needs that arise out of a child's disability in a way that enables the child to access the general education curriculum. In other words, if a child needs to read braille to access the curriculum, the school district is responsible for teaching braille to that student. In addition to this overall emphasis on access, specific provisions of IDEA 1997 reinforced the potential for UDL to address the challenges imposed by the law.

The regulations of IDEA 1997 included a provision stipulating that the need for a modified curriculum does not justify removing students from the classroom. As a result, general and special education teachers have to consider how to modify the curriculum in the general education setting. Emphasizing access, accommodations, and modifications in the regular classrooms opened the possibilities for the UDL framework to support teachers in meeting these requirements.

An affirmative technology consideration that supports UDL implementation was included in the 1997 law. The regulations require the IEP team to "consider whether the child needs assistive technology devices and services" [§300.346(a)(2)(v)]. As it related to accessing the curriculum and meeting the unique needs that arise out of their disability, IDEA required school districts to consider the technology needs of children with disabilities. With that as an explicit requirement, school districts had to consider technologies such as communication devices and screen readers. Even though UDL extends beyond technology, with the concept of access in the law, people began to shift their way of thinking about educating children with disabilities, making discussions about UDL possible.

Finally, IDEA 1997 emphasized the inclusion of students with disabilities in state accountability systems. This requirement was established before practitioners knew the most effective way to include students in large-scale assessments. Practitioners and policy makers have been trying to negotiate this challenge through accommodations or modifications to assessments, but these negotiations continue to raise concerns over assessment validity. Considering the UDL framework in addressing the question of how we can best include students with disabilities in assessment systems may help to reframe the question—how can we design assessments to anticipate the needs of and be accessible for students with disabilities?

NCLB and IDEA 2004

The education of students with disabilities has continued to shift further toward inclusion and access with No Child Left Behind (NCLB) and IDEA 2004. In NCLB, students with disabilities are included as a subgroup for which schools are held accountable. This inclusion modifies our understandings beyond merely providing access to the general education curriculum to ensuring progress in that curriculum. Schools now need to consider the performance of students with disabilities and make sure their curriculum provides opportunities for those students to succeed.

IDEA 2004 continues to move policy in a UDL direction through the NIMAS and RTI provisions. NIMAS provided the first explicit legal mention of universal design by requiring publishers and school districts to have digitized versions of texts. The statute requires that the state education agency:

(1) As part of any print instructional materials adoption process, procurement contract, or other practice or instrument used for purchase of print instructional materials, must enter into a written contract with the publisher of the print instructional materials to

    (i) Require the publisher to prepare and, on or before delivery of the print instructional materials, provide to NIMAC electronic files containing the contents of the print instructional materials using the NIMAS; or

    (ii) Purchase instructional materials from the publisher that are produced in, or may be rendered in, specialized formats.

[§ 300.172(c)(1)]

The RTI provisions encourage schools to rethink identification of children with certain disabilities with the understanding that all students may struggle in some way with the curriculum and should be provided interventions.

Looking back, the intersection between the LRE principles in special education law with the powerful leverage of due process and the increased knowledge about how to incorporate kids with more complex needs in integrated environments has had a synergistic impact. In other words, policy and practice are impacting each other. As we continue to see the power of universal design for learning in practice and support UDL in policy, we can build on the successful foundation and improve educational opportunities for students with disabilities. We should expect that parents will advocate for UDL in due process hearings and that future reauthorizations will reflect a greater emphasis on UDL.

POLICIES THAT SUPPORT UDL

Some policies currently in place, including RTI and positive behavior interventions and supports (PBIS), help support the concepts of universal design for learning and exemplify the possibilities for the UDL framework in our classrooms.

RTI seeks to identify students who need additional learning support, scaffolds appropriate interventions, and monitors student progress. For instance, RTI calls for designing reading programs that assume every kindergarten, first, second, and third grade will have struggling readers who need a differentiated approach to their reading. Teachers work to design reading programs with the assumption that students come to the task of reading with very different capabilities, while still maintaining the expectation that all students will learn to read.

Designing school behavior programs or discipline programs in a universal way, such as PBIS, is another example of universal design for learning. PBIS requires school discipline programs to assume that students' ability to handle behavior expectations will vary and to support students in developing the behaviors needed to be successful in school and in life.

To implement UDL successfully, we need to support and train teachers to understand the fundamental UDL concepts and support them in the classroom. The inclusion of UDL in the Higher Education Opportunity Act will build the capacity of pre-service programs to teach the principles of UDL, but we also need to invest in in-service training. Once teachers are in the classroom, they can see the applicability of UDL and are receptive toward changing their practices. The model of anticipating diversity in the design of curricula and policies is a form of UDL and can greatly enhance the performance of schools both in the United States and all over the world. Schools, districts, and states can do this now—we know how to meet the needs of diverse learners, and resources are available.

POLICY CONSIDERATIONS

Acknowledging the powerful impact policy has had in the education of students with disabilities reinforces the need for policy makers to consider supporting the implementation of UDL. Even though there is a policy foundation for UDL implementation, there are notable cracks in the foundation, especially with regard to assessment policies. There is a big disconnect between how we evaluate children in a high-stakes environment and what we know is the best way for students to demonstrate what they know. UDL encourages students to learn in the way that is most efficient and effective for them. If we teach students to be efficient and effective learners, we need to evaluate them in the same way.

Assessments are standardized for all students because we deem that to be valid, but assessments lose validity if they assess characteristics of a disability rather than the intended material. For instance, some technologies that enhance instruction and help students to be efficient learners are not allowed in testing regimes. In English language arts testing, only a few states permit the use of a screen reader. A dyslexic student who is print disabled is not allowed to effectively demonstrate learning when taking the test. Even though we are trying to assess reading comprehension, the student flunks because of slow reading fluency, which we already know is that student's deficit.

States should examine their assessment policies as they relate to accommodations and universal design for learning to avoid these unintended consequences. In an era of NCLB, educators raise concerns about how assessment drives instruction, but if states retool their assessments to encourage effective learning, teachers will be able to support effective learning.

THE PROMISE OF UDL

Policy, particularly federal policy, has an enormous influence on the education of students with disabilities and has been a major factor in improving the educational status of these students (Hehir, 2005). In particular, policy has evolved over the years to focus not just on expanding access to educational spaces but to improving educational outcomes of students with disabilities.

This shift in emphasis—from access to learning environments to access to *learning itself*—is a key tenet of UDL (Rose & Meyer, 2002). In a sense, it is the bridge between special education and general education: a concern that all learners get a high-quality education. One of the challenges we face in American education is to reach students who have not traditionally done well in the education system, including students with disabilities, English language learners, and children from low socioeconomic backgrounds. Currently, our learning environments and curricula are too restrictive to support effective and efficient learning for all students. UDL creates a framework to reduce the barriers in education, anticipate the diversity in our everyday classrooms, and embed support into our curricula. The implementation of a UDL framework will open doors in education to all students, especially those not effectively served by our current system.

Change takes place slowly in education, and an important precondition is that teachers be receptive to the idea of change. More students with disabilities are being educated in the general education classroom now than fifteen years ago. Along with this change has come an attitudinal shift. Today, most general education teachers who have students with disabilities in their classrooms think that the students belong there (Wagner, Newman, & Cameto, 2004). This attitude shift is the important precondition. Teachers recognize the appropriateness of diversity in their classroom, and UDL can help give them the tools to effectively accommodate that diversity.

When I do workshops on UDL, teachers love it because I give them tools to do something that is difficult to do—teach all kids effectively. It is one thing to say it is right to integrate students with disabilities into typical classrooms; it is quite another to figure out how to do it well and in a way that allows students to access the curriculum. It is not easy. It is something that requires knowledge, tools, and support. And it requires policies that support UDL implementation.

REFERENCES

Hehir, T. (1990). *The impact of due process on the programmatic decisions of special education directors.* Doctoral thesis, Harvard Graduate School of Education, Cambridge, MA.

Hehir, T. (2005). *New directions in special education: Eliminating ableism in policy and practice.* Cambridge, MA: Harvard Education Press.

Individuals with Disabilities Education Act Amendments of 1997, 20 U.S.C. §§ 1400 *et seq.* (amended 2004); 34 C.F.R. §§ 300.1 *et seq.* (2003).

Individuals with Disabilities Education Improvement Act of 2004, P.L. No. 108-446, 118 Stat. 2647 (amending 20 U.S.C. §§ 1400 *et seq.*).

Rose, D. H., & Meyer, A. (2002). *Teaching every student in the digital age: Universal Design for Learning.* Alexandria, VA: Association for Supervision and Curriculum Development.

Wagner, M., Newman, L., & Cameto, R. (2004). *Changes over time in the secondary school experiences of students with disabilities: A report of findings from the National Longitudinal Transition Study (NLTS) and the National Longitudinal Transition Study-2 (NLTS2).* Menlo Park, CA: SRI International. Retrieved May 27, 2009, from www.nlts2.org/reports/2004_04/nlts2_report_2004_04_complete.pdf.

WiggleWorks (Computer software). (1993). New York: Scholastic, Inc.

CHAPTER FOUR

There Is a Way to "Leave No Child Behind"

Remarks to the NCLB Commission

DAVID H. ROSE

EDITORS' NOTE

In 2006, with the reauthorization of the No Child Left Behind Act looming, a blue-ribbon Commission on No Child Left Behind was established at the Aspen Institute to identify the law's successes and failures and recommend improvements. During that year, the commission—cochaired by a pair of former governors, Tommy Thompson (R-WI) and Roy Barnes (D-GA)—conducted a number of public forums and expert roundtables as part of its review. On August 2, 2006, David Rose, a leading proponent of universal design for learning, took part in a roundtable on the impact of NCLB on students with disabilities.

Rose argued that the promise of NCLB was profound—a guarantee that all children would have equal opportunities to a high-quality education. "A universally designed approach is the most practical way to deliver on the great promise of NCLB, not only for students with disabilities but for all *students—without exception and without retreat," said Rose.*

In its final report, issued in February 2007, "Beyond NCLB: Fulfilling the Promise to Our Nation's Children," the commission cited Rose's testimony and the growing interest in UDL. It also recommended the adoption of universally designed assessments—both large-scale and formative—to make learning environments "more inclusive."

Thank you for asking me to participate in this roundtable today. My name is David Rose. I am chief scientist at CAST—the Center for Applied Special Technology—and a lecturer at the Harvard Graduate School of Education. My colleagues and I founded CAST in 1984 with the goal of expanding educational opportunities for all students, but especially those with disabilities, by joining research-based, best practices in education with powerful new multimedia technologies. The resulting framework, which we call universal design for learning, underlies our research and development, all of which is focused on creating more effective learning environments for all students. Our work is sponsored by the U.S. Department of Education, the National Science Foundation, the National Institutes of Health, and many national and local foundations. The term *universal design* originated in the field of architecture two decades ago, and represented a radical change in the way that buildings were designed. In the old days, buildings had been designed without considering the needs of individuals with disabilities. This method of design resulted in costly after-the-fact adaptations, repairs, and modifications as barriers became obvious, restrictive, and eventually illegal. With the arrival of universal design, architects learned to build in alternative means of access right from the start, so that buildings were more usable and accessible for people with disabilities. In reality, these features—like curb cuts, ramps, and automatic doors—now benefit a much wider population, from cyclists to parents with strollers.

Likewise, úniversal design for learning applies the same concept to education. By designing learning environments from the outset to meet the challenge of individual differences, including the challenges of students with disabilities, we make better learning environments for everyone. As an example, consider the most common learning technology in classrooms—the textbook. In its regular print version, a textbook raises many barriers for students who have disabilities or other differences. Students who are blind, dyslexic, or English language learners, for example, find many barriers to learning in such textbooks. Through universal design for learning, we design digital textbooks that are much more flexible and supportive for students with disabilities—they can easily be transformed into refreshable braille for students who are blind, can speak themselves aloud for students with dyslexia, can provide vocabulary support for English language learners, and can provide cognitive supports for students with intellectual disabilities. These new kinds of universally designed books are now being published by commercial publishers like Scholastic and Pearson, and form the basis for public policy changes like NIMAS (National Instructional Materials Accessibility Standard; see "How to implement increased flexibility for students with disabilities" later in this chapter). With that introduction, I would like to turn my attention to NCLB (No Child Left Behind) and its future for students with disabilities.

NCLB AND STUDENTS WITH DISABILITIES

The principles upon which NCLB is based are enormously promising for students with disabilities. The intent of my remarks is to suggest means of implementation that will more fully realize their benefits. I will take several of the central principles on which NCLB is based as the organizational structure of my remarks, considering in each case what is important for students with disabilities, and then considering changes in implementation that will more fully realize their power. Overall, I will conclude that a universally designed approach is the most practical way to deliver on the great promise of NCLB, not only for students with disabilities but for all students—without exception and without retreat.

Principle 1: Increased Accountability

Why increased accountability is important for students with disabilities
There is no group of students for whom increased accountability is more critical than students with disabilities. In fact, the lack of mainstream accountability for these students, starkly visible in their separation from mainstream educational expectations, programs, teachers, and assessments, has been one of the greatest impediments to their progress. Not

being measured has often meant that they have not been counted. For those reasons, we strongly support the accountability provisions of NCLB, including the focus on measuring adequate yearly progress and especially the provisions that call for attention and accountability for the "disaggregated" groups, including students with disabilities.

How to implement increased accountability for students with disabilities

Accountability requires one thing above all: accurate measurement of results. Without accurate measurement, accountability systems are not only ineffective, they are unethical. Unfortunately, the measurement systems in common use—including most standardized tests—have typically not been designed to measure results accurately for students with disabilities; they have not been designed, developed, validated or standardized for that use. Many of them are demonstrably inaccurate or patently inappropriate. As a result, teachers or aides typically modify or adapt those assessments as well as they can. Most of these local adaptations are not systematic, are not based on research, and often abrogate the standards and methods upon which the assessment was originally based.

To form an adequate foundation for increased accountability, the first step is to use assessment systems that are designed from the outset to be accessible to students with disabilities and to accurately measure their progress. Improved measurement will require two things: (1) a more varied set of measures—not just multiple choice test items—in order to adequately sample the full range of knowledge and skills that students need to master; and (2) measures that have been designed, from the outset, to be accurate across a wide range of students, including those with disabilities. Such measurement systems will be universally designed, and better for *all* students.

Principle 2: Increased Flexibility and Choice

Why increased flexibility is important for students with disabilities

Parents and teachers of students with disabilities, especially students with significant disabilities, often have fewer choices than typically achieving students. There are advocates for increasing available choice through alternatives in the place where education occurs. But most alternative settings—private and parochial schools, and even charter schools or innovative programs in the public system—simply lack the capacity or the inclination to educate children with significant disabilities. Those choices are often hollow ones—choices only of more places that are ill suited or motivated to meet the challenge of students with disabilities.

A more fundamental type of flexibility is needed to give meaningful choices. To meet the challenge of diversity, teachers and parents need pedagogical options and alternatives. Instead they find themselves with only rigid and narrow curricula, teaching tools that are "one size fits all." Faced with high standards, students find that all too often there is only one path to reach those standards, a single path that has not been designed with them in mind, and a path that has many inadvertent obstacles and barriers along the way. In this case, the learning environment itself, not the student, is disabled: it cannot successfully provide students with the equal access to learning that they by law and by right deserve.

How to implement increased flexibility for students with disabilities
The flexibility that is most important to students with disabilities (and their parents and teachers) is in the core curriculum, in actual teaching and learning. To succeed, students with disabilities need flexibility in the way that essential content is presented, flexibility in the means of interacting with material and expressing what they know, and flexibility in the means by which they are motivated and engaged. These kinds of flexibility are essential options that can reduce barriers and provide alternative paths to the same high standards as other students, and they are the options that will have the most profound effects on the education of students with disabilities.

An important first step in ensuring this flexibility has recently been signed into federal law—the National Instructional Materials Accessibility Standard. This standard requires that publishers of print materials, such as textbooks, must provide flexible alternatives—digital versions—for students with "print disabilities." These alternatives provide paths to the same high standards for students who cannot see or successfully decode traditional textbooks. Such alternatives are essential for students with disabilities to reach the same high standards as their peers.

A rigid, one-size-fits-all learning environment is a disabled learning environment. Lacking the flexibility and choice that is a central principle of NCLB, one-size-fits-all curricula limit educational opportunities for most students, and erect barriers that disable many. Increased flexibility is at the heart of all good education and must be at the core of the curriculum. Providing such flexibility is the fundamental premise of universal design for learning.

Principle 3: Increased Use of Evidence-Based Practices

Why increased use of evidence-based practices is important for students with disabilities

Most general education curricula lack a foundation of research-based practices that apply to students with disabilities. These students, already identified as atypical learners, are usually subjected to the same general methods and materials as "regular" students despite evidence that such practices are unlikely to achieve results, and even in the face of obvious mismatches—for example, a dyslexic student being taught history or science with a textbook far above his reading fluency level or a blind student who cannot get a digital or braille version of her physics book. When accommodations for students with disabilities are included in general curricula, they usually are nonsystematic or address peripheral issues—for example, nonsystematic "tips" in the teacher's editions to use alternative activities or groupings—rather than research-based practices that are inherent to the curriculum itself. The result of such practices is an increase in the number of students who are misidentified as unable to learn in many basic and content areas. In reality, there has been too little research on "what works" for students with disabilities within the general curriculum rather than within isolated programs or activities.

How to implement evidence-based practices for students with disabilities

A wealth of research-based practices have proven their effectiveness for students with disabilities. Unfortunately, these practices have been researched and then implemented primarily, if at all, in special education and supplemental programs, not in the mainstream educational curriculum. As a result, students with disabilities must often fail in the mainstream in order to get access to evidence-based practices that would have prevented their failure in the first place. The important next step in implementing evidence-based practices is to build these practices directly into the general education curriculum. The practice of universal design for learning does just that, ensuring that evidence-based practices are available in the goals, materials, methods, and assessments of the general curriculum.

RECOMMENDATIONS

The most important barrier to successful implementation of NCLB lies in the curriculum itself. In most classrooms, the curriculum is disabled. It is disabled because its main components—the goals, materials, methods, and assessments—are too rigid and inflexible to meet the challenge of diversity. Most of the present ways to remediate the curriculum's disabilities—teacher-made workarounds and modifications, unnecessary assistive technologies, alternative placements—are expensive and often ineffective for learning. What is needed are curricula—universally designed curricula—that remove those barriers, that provide more flexibility for teachers and students, and that fulfill the promise of NCLB.

Increase the implementation of accountability for students with disabilities. Encourage the adoption of scientifically validated, universally designed assessment systems (more than just accessible multiple-choice tests) that can accurately measure progress for all students, including those with disabilities. Ensure that measurement systems are not only accurate for students with disabilities, but that they are timely, frequent, and embedded enough in the curriculum to measure progress and inform instruction adequately for all students.

Increase flexibility and choice for teachers, parents, and students. Encourage the adoption of scientifically validated, universally designed curricula in all subjects—curricula that are flexible and adaptive enough to provide high expectations for every student and multiple paths to sustain those high expectations. Creating such curricula and learning materials, and properly training teachers in the principles and practices of universal design for learning, will ensure that parents, teachers, and students have meaningful choices.

Increase the use of evidence-based practices. Encourage the development and research validation of universally designed curricula—curricula that embed research-based practices and flexibility for students with disabilities directly into core curricular methods and materials.

CHAPTER FIVE

Opening the Curriculum to All

The Shared Aspirations of IDEA and NCLB

JOANNE KARGER

EDITORS' NOTE

Joanne Karger wrote this paper just after the 2004 reauthorization of IDEA to explore the intersection of IDEA and NCLB as it relates to students with disabilities accessing the general education curriculum. She provides a historical progression of federal education policy and explains how this progression has culminated in the expectation that students with disabilities have access to and make progress in the general education curriculum and that schools are held accountable for that progress.

Though this article does not specifically reference UDL, it exemplifies the ways in which IDEA and NCLB share a common goal to literally leave no child behind—the same aspiration of Universal Design for Learning. In that sense, the article articulates the question that UDL proposes to answer: how can we educate all learners in effective ways and to high standards?

Karger raises several questions that practitioners face and policy makers attempt to answer in meeting the expectations of these laws, including how to provide accommodations in the general education curriculum and how to effectively include students with disabilities in assessments. Elsewhere in this book, David Rose (in his remarks before the Aspen commission, chapter 4) and Tom Hehir (in chapter 3) locate UDL at the nexus of these debates. Consideration of the UDL principles can provide solutions as policy makers attempt to reconcile these challenges in the upcoming reauthorizations of NCLB and IDEA.

In 1975, Congress passed the Education for All Handicapped Children Act (EAHCA), giving children with disabilities the right to a "free appropriate public education" (FAPE)[1] in the "least restrictive environment" (LRE).[2] Prior to this time, the educational needs of one million children with disabilities were not being fully met [IDEA 1997, 20 U.S.C. § 1400(c)(2)]. A primary purpose of the 1975 law was to ensure that all students with disabilities had access to special education and related services designed to meet their unique needs. The 1975 statute was reauthorized several times; in 1990, it was renamed the Individuals with Disabilities Education Act (IDEA).

By the early 1990s, many improvements had been made in the education of children with disabilities. Early intervention and early childhood special education services were introduced in 1986, and requirements for transition planning were initiated in 1990. Moreover, the number of children with significant disabilities living in residential institutions had decreased dramatically (U.S. Department of Education, 1995). In addition, more students with disabilities were graduating from high school and obtaining postschool employment (U.S. Department of Education, 1995; Wagner, Blackorby, Cameto, Hebbeler, & Newman, 1993). In spite of these positive changes, however, students with disabilities still faced many obstacles. For example, research showed that students with disabilities tended to fail classes and drop out of school at higher rates than students without disabilities (U.S. Department of Education, 1995). In addition, efforts to include students with disabilities in the regular education classroom—commonly referred to as "mainstreaming" and later "inclusion"—often focused on special education as a place, without sufficient attention to necessary supports and services (Hocutt, 1996). Congress summed up the situation as follows: "Despite the progress, the promise of the law has not been fulfilled" (H.R. Rep. No. 105-95, 1997).

The 1997 reauthorization of IDEA attempted to address many of these problems, introducing important changes in the provision of educational services for students with disabilities. One of the most significant changes was the new requirement that students with disabilities have access to the general curriculum—that is, the same curriculum as that provided to students without disabilities [34 C.F.R. § 300.347(a)(1)(i)]. Expanding upon the earlier concepts of FAPE and LRE, the goal was to raise expectations for the educational performance of students with disabilities and to improve their educational results (U.S. Department of Education, 1995). Four years later, in 2001, Congress passed the No Child Left Behind Act (NCLB), the purpose of which was to promote equal opportunity for all children to receive a high-quality education and attain proficiency, at a minimum, on challenging state achievement standards and state assessments (20 U.S.C. § 6301). NCLB includes several requirements that have implications for the participation of students with disabilities in the general curriculum.

On December 3, 2004, President George W. Bush signed into law the Individuals with Disabilities Education Improvement Act of 2004 (IDEA 2004). IDEA '04 maintains the emphasis of IDEA '97 on the promotion of access to the general curriculum, while at the same time introducing a number of changes, including various points of alignment with NCLB. IDEA '04 also alters some of the language used in IDEA '97. For example, throughout IDEA '04, Congress replaced the words "general curriculum" used in IDEA '97 with the phrase "general education curriculum," emphasizing the educational component of the general curriculum. This paper uses the latter phrase found in IDEA '04, unless directly quoting IDEA '97 or NCLB.

This paper analyzes the concept of access to the general education curriculum as mandated by IDEA and further impacted by NCLB. Through a discussion of the interrelationship between IDEA and NCLB, this paper addresses the following questions: (1) What are the legal provisions in IDEA and NCLB associated with access to the general education curriculum for students with disabilities; (2) how do these provisions intersect with one another; and (3) how do these provisions translate into educational obligations for states and school districts? By clarifying the interrelationship between IDEA and NCLB and highlighting the legal and educational obligations incumbent upon states and local school districts, this paper will lead to a more comprehensive understanding of the meaning of access to the general education curriculum.

INDIVIDUALS WITH DISABILITIES EDUCATION ACT

Access to the General Education Curriculum

Congress first introduced the concept of access to the general education curriculum in IDEA '97 by stating, "Over 20 years of research and experience has demonstrated that the education of students with disabilities can be made more effective by having high expectations for such children and *ensuring their access in the general curriculum* to the maximum extent possible" [20 U.S.C. § 1400(c)(5)(A); *emphasis added*]. Similarly, the implementing regulations of the U.S. Department of Education (DOE) for IDEA '97 [3] defined special education as "specially designed instruction" whose purpose is "to address the unique needs of the child that result from the child's disability; and *to ensure access of the child to the general curriculum*, so that he or she can meet the educational standards within the jurisdiction of the public agency that apply to all children" [IDEA 1997, 34 C.F.R. § 300.26(b)(3); *emphasis added*].

The nonspecific term "general curriculum" was not defined anywhere in IDEA '97 or its implementing regulations but was later described in the regulations as "the same curriculum as for nondisabled children" [*id.* § 300.347(a)(1)(i)]. The statute and regulations essentially left the details of the general curriculum to be filled in by states and local school districts.

IDEA '04 both preserves and extends the preceding language of IDEA '97 regarding research and access to the general curriculum, stating, "Almost 30 years of research and experience has demonstrated that the education of students with disabilities can be made more effective by having high expectations for such children and ensuring their *access to the general education curriculum in the regular classroom*, to the maximum extent possible" [20 U.S.C. § 1400(c)(5)(A) (2004); *emphasis added*]. As noted in the introduction, IDEA '04 replaced the words "general curriculum" with "general education curriculum." Moreover, by adding the words "in the regular classroom," IDEA '04 calls attention to the important relationship between access to the general education curriculum and placement in the regular classroom, highlighting the strong preference of IDEA for education in the LRE.[4]

Beyond these general introductory statements concerning access to the general education curriculum, in other places in the respective reauthorizations, both IDEA '97 and IDEA '04 specifically require that students with disabilities be involved in and progress in the general education curriculum. Thus, the overall right to have access to the general education curriculum can, in fact, be viewed as consisting of three interrelated stages: access, involvement, and progress (Hitchcock, Meyer, Rose, & Jackson, 2002).

The first stage, "access," refers to the accessibility of the curriculum to the student. "Involvement," the second stage, can be thought of as the ongoing process of meaningful participation by the student in the general education curriculum and, as such, is an interim phase that links access to progress. "Progress" in the general education curriculum, the third stage, refers not only to a final outcome, but also to an evaluative measure that can feed back into the earlier stages of access and involvement. The three stages of access, involvement, and progress can therefore be thought of as forming an ongoing cycle (see figure 5-1). These stages are not entirely discrete because in certain instances, a provision can arguably fall under more than one rubric. This framework, however, which is utilized throughout this paper, is useful in elucidating the various components of access to the general education curriculum and in analyzing the educational issues involved.

The concept of access to the general education curriculum specified in IDEA '97 and IDEA '04 and described above represents a significant advance in the education of students with disabilities, far exceeding the earlier notion of physical access to the school building and access to special education and related services intended by the EAHCA in 1975. Moreover, by incorporating both involvement and progress, the requirement that students have access to the general education curriculum extends well beyond the concepts of mainstreaming and inclusion that developed following 1975 and focused mainly on placement in the regular classroom.

FIGURE 5–1 Cycle of ensuring access to the general education curriculum

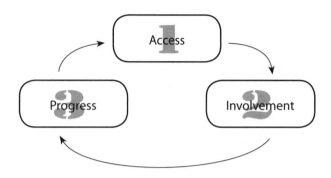

IDEA '04 includes a new provision not found in IDEA '97 that has the potential to bring about improved accessibility of the general education curriculum for students with disabilities—the establishment of a National Instructional Materials Access Center, which will maintain a catalog of print instructional materials prepared in accordance with the National Instructional Materials Accessibility Standard (NIMAS) [20 U.S.C. § 1474(e)(2)]. The NIMAS standard, which is "to be used in the preparation of electronic files suitable and used solely for efficient conversion into specialized formats" [*id*. at § 20 U.S.C. § 1474(e)(3)(B)], will help students with print and other disabilities have greater access in a more timely fashion to the print materials that are part of the general education curriculum. IDEA '04 also establishes a process for the preparation, delivery, and purchase of digitized instructional materials for states and school districts that choose to utilize the voluntary NIMAS standard [*id*. §§ 1412(a)(23); 1413(a)(6)].

Involvement in the General Education Curriculum
Both IDEA '97 and IDEA '04 contain three requirements pertaining to a student's individualized education program (IEP) that specifically mention involvement in the general education curriculum—the requirements concerning present levels of performance, annual goals, and supplementary aids and services, program modifications, and supports for personnel. IDEA '04 maintains the major focus of the provisions found in IDEA '97 while at the same time introducing a number of changes. The provisions appearing in IDEA '04 are as follows:

- The IEP must include a statement of the child's present levels of academic achievement and functional performance, including how the child's disability affects the child's involvement and progress[5] in the general education curriculum.
- The IEP must include a statement of measurable annual goals, including academic and functional goals, designed to meet the child's needs that result from the child's disability to enable the child to be involved in and make progress in the general education curriculum.
- The IEP must include a statement of the special education and related services and supplementary aids and services, based on peer-reviewed research to the extent practicable, to be provided to the child, or on behalf of the child, and a statement of the program modifications or supports for school personnel that will be provided for the child to be involved in and make progress in the general education curriculum.

[20 U.S.C. §§ 1414(d)(1)(A)(i)(I), (II), (IV)]

These provisions pertain to the IEP, which can be viewed as the central mechanism, both legally and educationally, for ensuring access to the general education curriculum. These three requirements translate into important educational obligations for school districts by laying out specific steps that must be taken by the IEP team in order to enable the student to be involved in the general education curriculum in a meaningful way.

The first provision relates to the child's present levels of performance. Before IDEA '97, the IEP team had to state the student's current levels of educational performance. IDEA '97 and IDEA '04, however, add the requirement that the statement describe the specific effect of the student's disability on his/her involvement and progress in the general education curriculum. Such specification is an important first step in the design of an appropriate educational program for the student. IDEA '04 goes beyond IDEA '97 in requiring not only the levels of the student's educational performance but also the level of his/her "functional performance," acknowledging "that for some children, functional performance is also a critical element that should be measured" (Sen. Rep. No. 108-185, 2004).

The second provision requires the IEP to include annual goals that will enable the child to be involved in and progress in the general education curriculum, as appropriate to the needs of the child. IEP goals lay the foundation for a student's educational program and provide a road map for the teacher. Before IDEA '97, IEP goals had to be based on the specific needs of the individual student; however, the goals did not necessarily relate to the general education curriculum (U.S. Department of Education, 1995). As with the first provision, IDEA '04 extends the requirement to include "functional goals" in addition to academic goals, again with the intent of recognizing the importance of functional performance for some students with disabilities (Sen. Rep. No. 108-185, 2004).

IDEA '04 also introduces another change by eliminating the requirement in IDEA '97 for the inclusion of short-term objectives or benchmarks. The report of the Senate Health, Education, Labor and Pensions (HELP) Committee notes that short-term objectives and benchmarks have contributed to the large paperwork burden associated with IEPs and that elimination of this requirement should facilitate a greater focus on the goals themselves (Sen. Rep. No. 108-185, 2004). The elimination of short-term objectives and benchmarks, however, does not apply to students who are taking part in alternative assessments aligned with alternative achievement standards [20 U.S.C. § 1414(d)(1)(A)(i)(I)(cc)]. (See discussion of alternative achievement standards under the No Child Left Behind section later in this chapter.)

The third provision specifies that the IEP team must consider the supplementary aids and services, program modifications, and supports provided for school personnel that will enable the student to be involved in and progress in the general education curriculum. This provision, underscoring the fact that mere physical access to the regular classroom without appropriate support is no longer sufficient under the law, has the potential to lead teachers to consider ways to adapt their instructional practices to enable the student to participate in the general education curriculum. The legislative history leading up to IDEA '97 explained:

> The new emphasis on participation in the general education curriculum . . . is intended to produce attention to the accommodations and

adjustments necessary for disabled children to access the general education curriculum and the special services which may be necessary for appropriate participation in particular areas of the curriculum (Sen. Rep. No. 105-17, 1997).

IDEA '04 also extends the language of IDEA '97 by specifying that determination of the necessary supplementary aids and services, program modifications, and supports for school personnel should be based on peer-reviewed research, thereby enhancing the quality of supports provided.

Progress in the General Education Curriculum

As described earlier, access to the general education curriculum consists of three interrelated phases forming a cycle, the third of which is progress. Three aspects of progress in the general education curriculum[6] can be delineated: (1) progress toward IEP goals, (2) participation in state and districtwide assessments, and (3) establishment of state-level performance goals and indicators.

The following provisions in IDEA '04 pertain to the first aspect of progress in the general education curriculum, progress toward IEP goals:

- The IEP must include a description of how the child's progress toward meeting the annual goals will be measured and when periodic reports on the progress the child is making toward meeting the annual goals (such as through the use of quarterly or other periodic reports, concurrent with the issuance of report cards) will be provided. [20 U.S.C. § 1414(d)(1)(A)(i)(III)]
- The IEP must be reviewed periodically, but not less frequently than annually, and revised as appropriate to address any lack of expected progress toward the annual goals and in the general education curriculum, where appropriate. [*id.* §§ 1414(d)(4)(A)(i), (ii)(I)]

As with the majority of the requirements pertaining to involvement in the general education curriculum, these two requirements also focus on the IEP, and each translates into specific educational obligations for school districts. The first does not explicitly mention the general education curriculum; however, because IEP goals must address the child's involvement and progress in the general education curriculum (as appropriate to the needs of the child), the measurement of progress toward the attainment of these goals and the reporting of this progress to parents will also be connected to the general education curriculum. The Senate HELP Committee stated that although IDEA '04 eliminated the requirement for short-term objectives and benchmarks, the reauthorization also heightened the reporting requirements regarding progress toward IEP goals.[7] According to this committee, "These progress updates must provide parents with specific, meaningful, and understandable information on the progress children are making" (Sen. Rep. 108-185, 2004).

The following provisions in IDEA '04 pertain to the second aspect of progress in the general education curriculum, the participation of students with disabilities in state and districtwide assessments:

- All children with disabilities must be included in all general State and districtwide assessment programs, including assessments described under NCLB, with appropriate accommodations and alternate assessments where necessary and as indicated in their respective IEPs. [20 U.S.C. § 1412(a)(16)(A)]
- The IEP must include a statement of any individual appropriate accommodations that are necessary to measure the academic achievement and functional performance of the child on State and districtwide assessments; if the IEP team determines that the child will take an alternate assessment, the IEP must state why the child cannot participate in the regular assessment and why the particular alternate assessment selected is appropriate. [*id.* § 1414(d)(1)(A)(i)(VI)]
- States and districts must report, and make available to the public, information concerning the number of children with disabilities participating in regular assessments, in regular assessments with accommodations, and in alternate assessments, as well as the performance of children with disabilities on regular assessments and alternate assessments compared with the achievement of all children, including children with disabilities, on those assessments.[8] [*id.* § 1412(a)(16)(D)]

The requirements pertaining to the participation of students with disabilities in state and districtwide assessments were introduced in IDEA

'97 in order to increase accountability for the performance of students with disabilities and thereby improve their educational results. As part of the IDEA reauthorization process completed in 1997, the Department of Education (1995) stated: "When schools are required to assess students with disabilities and report on the results, schools are more likely to focus on improving results for students with disabilities, and students are more likely to have *meaningful access to the general curriculum*" (p. 12; *emphasis added*).

IDEA '04 not only maintains the emphasis of IDEA '97 on assessments and accountability, but also aligns IDEA with NCLB by stating that the IDEA mandate for the inclusion of students with disabilities in state and districtwide assessments includes assessments described under NCLB. In addition, while IDEA '97 included the phrase "individual modifications in the administration of State or districtwide assessments" [20 U.S.C. § 1414(d)(1)(A)(v)], IDEA '04 changed the corresponding wording to read, "individual appropriate accommodations" [20 U.S.C. § 1414(d)(1)(A)(i)(VI)]. In the field of special education, an accommodation is generally thought of as an alteration that does not change the content of the curriculum or lower standards. In contrast, a modification is generally considered a change that creates a substantial alteration in the content of the curriculum or lowers standards (for example, teaching less content or different content; Nolet & McLaughlin, 2000).

The participation of students with disabilities in state and districtwide assessments raises complex educational and psychometric issues with which states and districts must grapple in administering appropriate testing accommodations and alternative assessments. Testing accommodations that are appropriate can be thought of as a "corrective lens" through which "to correct for distortions in a student's true competence caused by a disability unrelated to the construct being measured" (McDonnell, McLaughlin, & Morison, 1997, pp. 173, 176). There is the risk, however, that the accommodations may over- or undercompensate for such distortions and thereby interfere with the validity of the inferences being drawn from the assessment scores. Although decisions about the use of appropriate accommodations with respect to physical disabilities may be somewhat straightforward, according to the National Research Council (McDonnell et al., 1997), "Most students with disabilities have cognitive impairments that presumably are related to at least some of the constructs tested" (p. 170). Unfortunately, there is little research examining the effects of specific accommodations on the validity of inferences made from the assessment scores of students with different types of disabilities (McDonnell et al., 1997; Heubert & Hauser, 1999; Sireci, Li, & Scarpati, 2003). IDEA '04 further indicates that states and local school districts should, to the extent feasible, use "universal design principles" in the development and administration of state and districtwide assessments [20 U.S.C. § 1412(a)(16)(E)]. According to the National Center on Educational Outcomes, "'Universally designed assessments' are designed and developed from the beginning to allow participation of the widest possible range of students, and to result in valid inferences about performance for all students who participate in the assessment" (Thompson, Johnstone, & Thurlow, 2002).

An alternative assessment is a different measure of the educational progress of students who cannot take part in the regular assessment, even with the help of accommodations. An alternative assessment, for example, may be a portfolio of the student's work. As with the use of accommodations, educational and psychometric issues arise with respect to the use of alternative assessments (see, for example, Quenemoen, Rigney, & Thurlow, 2002). IDEA '04 includes a new provision specifying that alternative assessments must be aligned with the state's content and achievement standards; if the state has adopted alternative academic achievement standards as permitted under the implementing regulations for NCLB, the alternative assessments must measure the achievement of children with disabilities against those standards [20 U.S.C. § 1412(a)(16)(C)(ii)]. (See the discussion of alternative achievement standards under the following No Child Left Behind section.)

Finally, the following provisions in IDEA '04 pertain to the third aspect of progress in the general education curriculum, the establishment of performance goals and indicators by states. Specifically, states must:

• Establish performance goals for children with disabilities that are the same as the State's definition of adequate yearly progress, including the State's objectives for progress by children with disabilities, as specified under NCLB, address graduation rates and dropout rates, as well as other factors that are consistent, to the extent appropriate, with any other goals and standards for children established by the State.

- Establish performance indicators to assess progress toward achieving the performance goals, including measurable annual objectives for progress by children with disabilities under NCLB.
- Provide annual reports on the progress of the State, and of children with disabilities in the State, toward meeting the performance goals. [20 U.S.C. §§1412(a)(15)(A)-(C)]

These three requirements pertain to obligations on the part of states. As noted with respect to the participation in assessment provisions, these requirements concerning performance goals and indicators are intended to increase accountability for the educational performance of students with disabilities. The first provision, requiring performance goals for students with disabilities to be consistent to the maximum extent appropriate with goals and standards for all children, also underscores the intent of both IDEA '97 and IDEA '04 to raise the level of expectations for the educational performance of students with disabilities. Moreover, it can be seen that IDEA '04 connects the first two provisions to NCLB (See "Accountability" under the following NCLB section).

In summary, IDEA '97 and IDEA '04 lay out specific obligations incumbent on states and districts to ensure that students with disabilities have access to, are involved in, and make progress in the general education curriculum. For many of these obligations, the IEP serves as the central mechanism, both legally and educationally, for ensuring access to the general education curriculum. The next section will discuss the impact of certain provisions in the No Child Left Behind Act of 2001 on the accessibility to the general education curriculum for students with disabilities.

NO CHILD LEFT BEHIND ACT

Four years after the 1997 reauthorization of IDEA, Congress passed the No Child Left Behind Act, the purpose of which was "to ensure that *all* children have a fair, equal, and significant opportunity to obtain a high-quality education and reach, at a minimum, proficiency on challenging State academic achievement standards and State academic assessments"

(20 U.S.C. § 6301; *emphasis added*). Although NCLB applies to all students, including students with disabilities, and IDEA applies only to students with disabilities, both statutes share the goal of raising expectations for the educational performance of students with disabilities and increasing accountability for their educational results. In several places in the law, NCLB makes explicit reference to IDEA.[9] Moreover, as noted earlier, IDEA '04 aligns a number of requirements in IDEA with those in NCLB.

This section will examine various requirements in NCLB that have implications for providing access to the general education curriculum for students with disabilities. NCLB, which was enacted prior to IDEA '04, uses the earlier phrase found in IDEA '97, "general curriculum," rather than "general education curriculum" as used in IDEA '04. The relevant provisions of NCLB will be discussed under the three rubrics of access, involvement, and progress.[10] In these discussions, "general education curriculum" will be used, unless the words are a direct quote from NCLB.

Access to Challenging Content and Achievement Standards

IDEA, as noted, requires that students with disabilities have access to the general education curriculum—that is, the same curriculum as that provided to students without disabilities—but does not elaborate further on the meaning of the term "general education curriculum," leaving the details to be filled in by states and school districts. NCLB focuses attention on the general education curriculum by requiring that states develop "challenging" academic standards for both content and student achievement for all children in at least mathematics and reading/language arts and, by the beginning of the 2005–2006 school year, science [20 U.S.C. §§ 6311(b)(1)(A)-(C)].[11] The obligation to develop challenging content standards should help states define the general education curriculum. Moreover, the requirement for states to adopt challenging achievement standards has the potential to raise the level of the general education curriculum. The development of standards is thus a point of intersection for the two statutes: IDEA requires that students with disabilities have access to the general education curriculum, according to their individualized needs, while NCLB helps to define and raise the level of the general education curriculum.

It is significant that the applicability of a state's challenging academic standards to all students under NCLB is inclusive of students with disabilities. In the appendix to the statute's implementing regulations, the DOE states,

> Too often in the past, schools and LEAs have not expected students with disabilities to meet the same grade-level standards as other students. The NCLB Act sought to correct this problem by requiring each State to develop grade-level academic content and achievement standards that it expects all students—including students with disabilities—to meet. (67 F.R. 71710, 71741)

Thus, IDEA and NCLB converge with respect to expectations for the educational performance of students with disabilities: IDEA requires that students with disabilities have access to the same curriculum (according to their individualized needs) as students without disabilities so that they can meet the educational standards that apply to all children; NCLB establishes the expectation that students with disabilities can meet the same standards as students without disabilities.

Access to a High-Quality Curriculum

In addition to the mandate for states to develop challenging content and achievement standards, NCLB also refers, in a number of places, to the use of a high-quality curriculum, further emphasizing the high level expected of a state's general education curriculum. For example, NCLB discusses the shared responsibility of schools and parents to develop a school-parent compact that describes "the school's responsibility to provide *high-quality curriculum* and instruction . . . that enables the children served under this part to meet the State's student academic achievement standards" [20 U.S.C. § 6318(d)(1); *emphasis added*; see also *id.* §§ 6311(b)(8)(D), 6312(c)(1)(O)]. Thus, NCLB raises the level of the general education curriculum by requiring that a state develop "challenging" content and achievement standards, and that it establish a "high-quality" curriculum.

Involvement in the General Education Curriculum

IDEA, as noted, requires that students with disabilities be involved in the general education curriculum. Several provisions in NCLB have implications for such involvement—namely, (1) teacher qualifications, (2) professional development and (3) special programs and services. (Professional development is the only one included here.)

Professional development

A second area that can be identified as having the potential to facilitate the involvement of students with disabilities in the general education curriculum is professional development. NCLB, for example, calls for professional development that is aligned with state content and achievement standards as well as assessments [20 U.S.C. § 7801(34)(A)(viii)]. Such alignment has the effect of linking professional development activities to an understanding of the general education curriculum, an important step for teachers who will be helping students with disabilities to be involved in the general education curriculum. In addition, professional development, to the extent appropriate, is to include training in the use of technology that can improve the quality of teaching in the curricula and core academic subjects [*id.* § 7801(34)(A)(xi)]. The provision of training for teachers in technology is crucial in helping teachers to integrate technology into their instructional practices. Such integration can also play a significant role in helping students with disabilities have access to and participate in the general education curriculum (Rose & Meyer, 2002). IDEA '04 similarly discusses professional development training that incorporates the integration of technology into curricula and instruction [*id.* § 1454(a)(2)].

NCLB further specifies that professional development should, among other pedagogical activities, "provide instruction in methods of teaching children with special needs" [20 U.S.C. § 7801(34)(A)(xiii)] and "provide training in how to teach and address the needs of students with different learning styles, particularly students with disabilities" [*id.* § 6623(a)(3)(B)(ii)]. Moreover, NCLB also encourages the development of programs to train and hire regular and special education teachers, including the hiring of special education teachers who will team-teach classes that include students with and without disabilities [*id.* § 6623(a)

(2)(C)(i)]. IDEA'04 similarly emphasizes the need to recruit, train, and retain highly qualified special education personnel as well as prepare regular education teachers who provide instruction for students with disabilities.[12] Professional development that is instructive to regular education teachers in promoting an understanding of the needs of students with disabilities in their classroom can help teachers provide more effective instruction to these students. Professional development that trains special education teachers to team-teach with regular education teachers is also important. When regular and special education teachers work together, they can pool their resources and expertise toward the goal of involving students with disabilities in the general education curriculum.

Progress in the General Education Curriculum

A major focus of NCLB is the area of assessments and accountability. As noted earlier, IDEA '04 aligns the requirements in IDEA pertaining to assessments and accountability with some of the provisions in NCLB.

Assessments

NCLB requires states to institute "high-quality, yearly student academic assessments" that are the same for all children and are aligned with the state's content and achievement standards [20 U.S.C. §§ 6311(b)(3) (A), (C)(i)-(ii)]. The implementing regulations add that the assessments must "be designed to be valid and accessible for use by the widest possible range of students, including students with disabilities" [34 C.F.R. § 200.2(b)(2)]. These assessments must include, at a minimum, mathematics and reading/language arts (also science, beginning in the 2007–2008 school year) and are to be the primary measure to determine the annual performance of the state, districts, and schools in helping all children meet the state's achievement standards [*id.* § 6311(b)(3)(A)].

Beginning in the 2005–2006 school year, students must be tested in each of grades 3 through 8 [*id.* § 6311(b)(3)(C)(vii)] and at least once in grades 10 through 12 [34 C.F.R. § 200.5(a)(2)(ii)]. Moreover, because state standards help define the general education curriculum, the assessments under NCLB will also be based on the general education curriculum. These standards have implications for the provision of access to the general education curriculum for students with disabilities. If students are to be evaluated by means of tests that are based on the general education curriculum, the students must first be taught the material that comprises this curriculum. Therefore, the assessment provisions of NCLB also have the potential to impact access to and involvement in the general education curriculum for students with disabilities. As noted, IDEA '04 requires that students with disabilities participate in assessments mandated under NCLB.

NCLB requires *reporting* on the results of the assessments and disaggregation by students with disabilities as compared to students without disabilities. NCLB also provides for an exception to the requirement for disaggregation when "the number of students in a category is insufficient to yield statistically reliable information or the results would reveal personally identifiable information about an individual student" [20 U.S.C. § 6311(b)(3)(C)(xiii)]. The implementing regulations add that each state must determine what constitutes the minimum number of students that would provide statistically reliable information [34 C.F.R. § 200.7(a)(2)]. IDEA '04 similarly requires reporting on the assessment results of students with disabilities as compared to the achievement of all children so long as the number of children with disabilities participating is large enough to yield statistically reliable information and reporting will not reveal personally identifiable information [20 U.S.C. § 1412(a)(16)(D)(iv)].

As noted with respect to IDEA, assessing students with disabilities and reporting on the assessment results is intended to hold educators accountable for the educational performance of these students. NCLB, however, goes beyond IDEA by also requiring that an individual report of each student's performance be provided to parents, teachers, and principals in "a language that parents can understand" [*id.* § 6311(b)(3)(C)(xii)], thus including an additional layer of accountability that extends to parents.

NCLB further requires that state assessments provide for the participation of students with disabilities (as defined under IDEA) with *accommodations* [20 U.S.C. § 6311(b)(3)(C)(ix)(II)]. The implementing regulations for NCLB add that the accommodations are to be determined by the student's IEP team [34 C.F.R. § 200.6(a)(1)(i)]. The references to IDEA and the IEP team again show the intended coordination between the two statutes. In addition, it is significant that neither NCLB nor IDEA '04 addresses the issues concerning the validity of inferences drawn from scores on assessments on which students receive accommo-dations.[13] As noted, there has been little research on the effect of specific accommodations on the validity of inferences made from the scores of students with different types of disabilities.

Accountability

NCLB requires that each state develop a statewide system of account-ability to measure whether schools and districts are making "adequate yearly progress" (AYP) toward enabling all students, including stu-dents with disabilities, to meet or exceed the proficiency level on the state assessments no later than twelve years after the end of the 2001–2002 school year [20 U.S.C. §§ 6311(b)(2)(A), (F)]. Moreover, AYP also requires states to establish measurable annual objectives, applied sepa-rately to students with disabilities,[14] which will specify the minimum percentage of students who must meet or exceed the state's proficiency level on the state assessments [*id.* § 6311(b)(2)(G)(iii); see also *id.* § 6311(b)(2)(C)(v)]. As noted, IDEA '04 states that performance goals should be the same as the state's definition of AYP and that performance indicators should include measurable annual goals under NCLB. NCLB further specifies that in order for a school or district to make AYP, not less than 95 percent of students with disabilities[15] must participate in the assessments through regular assessments, regular assessments with accommodations, or by means of alternative assessments [*id.* § 6311(b)(2)(I)(ii)]. The regulations add that if a student takes the same assess-ment more than once, the score from the first administration should be used to determine AYP [34 C.F.R. § 200.20(c)(3)].

In spite of these stringent requirements, it is important to note that NCLB does not attach "high-stakes" consequences—such as the denial of a high school diploma—to testing results for individual students. There are, however, serious consequences for schools and districts, which can weigh heavily on school personnel. As part of a state's accountability system, the district must identify for improvement those schools that have failed to make AYP for two consecutive years [20 U.S.C. § 6316(b)(1)(A)]. In addition, the district must allow all students, including students with disabilities, who are enrolled in a school that has been identi-fied for school improvement (i.e., did not make AYP for two consecutive years), the option of transferring to another public school within the dis-trict that has not been identified for school improvement [*id.* §§ 6316(b) (1)(E)-(F)]. The regulations add that for students with disabilities cov-ered under IDEA or Section 504, "the public school choice option must provide a free appropriate public education" [34 C.F.R. § 200.44(j)]. If the school continues to fail to make AYP after being identified for school improvement, the district must identify the school for "corrective action" and subsequently for "restructuring" [*id.* §§ 6316(b)(7)-(8)].[16]

The expectation underlying NCLB is that holding schools account-able for the educational performance of students with disabilities will ultimately lead to improvement in the provision of educational services for these students as well as improved results. At the same time, how-ever, it is also possible that the stringent accountability requirements of NCLB may, in certain respects, have a negative impact on students with disabilities. For example, being identified as a school that has failed to make AYP can lower the morale of both teachers and students, including students with disabilities, especially in light of the fact that sanctions are applied to schools without regard to factors that might contribute to low performance (e.g., lack of resources). Moreover, although NCLB does not attach high stakes for the individual student, such as denial of a high school diploma, many states on their own have done so, with potentially negative consequences for students with disabilities.

SUMMARY

Since passage of the EAHCA in 1975, significant improvements have been made in the quality of education provided to students with disabil-ities. Increased numbers of students with disabilities have been attend-ing public schools and participating in classes with students without disabilities. Moreover, attention has shifted from mainstreaming and inclusion to the meaningful participation of students with disabilities in the regular class. IDEA '97 has played a major role in this evolution, with one of the most important innovations being the requirement that students with disabilities have access to the general education curriculum. Four years after the passage of IDEA '97, Congress passed NCLB, which shares the goal of raising expectations for the educational performance of students with disabilities and increasing accountability for their educational results. IDEA '04 has maintained the focus on access to the general education curriculum, while at the same time introducing a number of changes, several of which were intended to align IDEA with NCLB.

This paper has discussed the legal provisions in IDEA '97, IDEA '04, and NCLB associated with access to the general education curriculum, as well as the translation of these provisions into educational obligations for states and school districts. A theoretical framework has been utilized that conceptualizes the overall right of students with disabilities in IDEA to have access to the general education curriculum as comprising three interrelated stages that form an ongoing cycle: access, involvement, and progress. The educational obligations of states and school districts extend to each of these stages. The first stage, "access," requires that the general education curriculum be accessible to students with disabilities. The second stage, "involvement," requires that students with disabilities participate in the general education curriculum in an ongoing and meaningful way. The third stage, "progress," requires that students with disabilities be able to demonstrate progress in the general education curriculum through improved educational performance.

The first stage of the cycle involves the accessibility of the general education curriculum to students with disabilities. The implementing regulations for IDEA '97 described the general curriculum as the same curriculum as that provided to students without disabilities but did not elaborate further on the meaning of the term. The requirement in NCLB that states adopt challenging academic content and achievement standards, as well as the emphasis on a high-quality curriculum, should help states to define and raise the level of the general education curriculum. IDEA '04 includes new provisions pertaining to the establishment of the National Instructional Materials Accessibility Standard and the National Instructional Materials Access Center that should help students with print and other disabilities have greater access in a more timely manner to the print materials that are part of the general education curriculum.

With respect to the second stage, involvement in the general education curriculum, IDEA '04 maintains, for the most part, the obligations on the part of school districts that were introduced in IDEA '97. These obligations, centering around the IEP, include specification in the IEP of how the student's disability affects his/her involvement and progress in the general education curriculum; IEP goals that enable the student to be involved in and progress in the general education curriculum; identification in the IEP of supplementary aids and services, program modifications or supports for personnel that help the student to be involved in and progress in the general education curriculum; explanation of the extent to which the student will not participate in the regular class; and inclusion of the regular education teacher on the IEP team. These requirements are intended to engage students with disabilities as actual participants rather than passive observers in the regular education class. IDEA '04 also includes a focus on functional performance and functional goals and eliminates the requirement for short-term objectives and benchmarks, except for those students who are taking assessments aligned with alternative achievement standards.

In addition, a number of provisions in NCLB have the potential to facilitate greater involvement in the general education curriculum—namely, the requirement that teachers be highly qualified; professional development that focuses on, for example, strategies for providing instruction to students with disabilities in regular education classes; and programs/services such as Reading First and supplemental educational services. While NCLB is silent regarding the qualifications of special education teachers, IDEA '04 specifically requires that these teachers be highly qualified.

Finally, with respect to the third stage, progress in the general education curriculum, both IDEA '97 and IDEA '04 include requirements concerning progress toward IEP goals, participation in state and districtwide assessments, and the establishment of state performance goals and indicators. In the area of assessments, NCLB mandates that states establish high-quality, yearly academic assessments for all students, including students with disabilities (with accommodations or by means of alternative assessments), and that these assessments must be aligned with state content and achievement standards. Implementing regulations for NCLB also allows for the development of alternative achievement standards for students with the most significant cognitive disabilities, whose performance is based on an alternative assessment. IDEA '04 aligns IDEA with NCLB with respect to assessments by stating that the IDEA mandate for the inclusion of students with disabilities in state and districtwide assessments includes assessments required under NCLB. Moreover, IDEA '04 refers to the use of alternative achievement standards in several places in the statute that pertain to access to the general education curriculum.

NCLB also requires the establishment of a system of accountability to measure whether schools and districts are making "adequate yearly progress" toward enabling all students, including students with disabilities, to meet or exceed the proficiency level on the state assessments within twelve years. The implementing regulations for NCLB modify the manner of the inclusion of the performance of students with the most significant cognitive disabilities by permitting the use of alternative achievement standards in determination of AYP, provided that the number of proficient or advanced scores based on the alternative achievement standards counted toward AYP at the district and state level does not exceed 1.0 percent of all students assessed. IDEA '04 aligns IDEA with NCLB with respect to accountability by stating that performance goals should be the same as AYP and that performance indicators should include measurable annual goals under NCLB.

The accountability system called for under NCLB is intended to increase accountability for the educational performance of all students, including students with disabilities. At the same time, there is also the possibility that the stringent accountability requirements in NCLB, including the threat of sanctions, may in some instances have a negative effect on students with disabilities. For example, the sanctions are applied without taking into account factors such as a lack of resources and may adversely affect the morale of teachers and students, including students with disabilities. In addition, many states on their own have decided to attach high-stakes consequences for individual students, which can have significant consequences for students with disabilities.

In conclusion, through a discussion of the interrelationship between IDEA and NCLB, this paper has presented a comprehensive analysis of the concept of access to the general education curriculum. It is significant that IDEA '04 has maintained the majority of the provisions pertaining to access to the general education curriculum found in IDEA '97, while at the same time following in the direction of NCLB with respect to requirements pertaining to highly qualified personnel, assessments, and accountability. The provisions in IDEA '04 concerning access to the general education curriculum have the potential to lead to increased expectations and improved educational outcomes for students with disabilities.

NOTES

1. FAPE is defined as "special education and related services that (A) have been provided at public expense, under public supervision and direction, and without charge; (B) meet the standards of the State educational agency; (C) include an appropriate preschool, elementary, or secondary school education in the State involved; and (D) are provided in conformity with the individualized education program required under [the law]" [20 U.S.C. § 1401(9)].

2. LRE refers to the education of students with disabilities to the maximum extent appropriate in a setting together with students without disabilities [20 U.S.C. § 1412(a)(5)(A)].

3. The DOE is currently in the process of preparing its implementing regulations for IDEA '04, having completed its period for comments and recommendations on February 28, 2005 (69 F.R. 77968, 77969).

4. For a discussion of this congressional preference, see, e.g., *Oberti v. Board of Educ.*, 995, F.2d 1204, 1214 (3d Cir. 1993); *Daniel R.R. v. State Board of Educ.*, 874 F.2d 1036, 1044 (5th Cir. 1989); *Roncker v. Walter*, 700 F.2d 1058, 1063 (6th Cir. 1983).

5. Although the language used by IDEA in these requirements refers to both involvement and progress, the requirements are included here under the rubric of involvement.

6. In addition, the implementing regulations for IDEA '97 require that when a student with a disability is placed in an "interim alternative educational setting," the setting must be selected so as to enable the child to continue to progress in the general curriculum [34 C.F.R. § 300.522(b)(1)].

7. As with the elimination of short-term objectives and benchmarks, in an effort to help reduce the paperwork associated with IEPs, IDEA '04 authorizes the U.S. secretary of education to approve no more than fifteen proposals from states to develop a comprehensive multiyear IEP, not to exceed three years, designed to coincide with the natural transition points for the child [20 U.S.C. § 1414(d)(5)(A)].

8. States are required to report on the performance of students with disabilities only "if the number of children with disabilities participating in those assessments is sufficient to yield statistically reliable information and reporting that information will not reveal personally identifiable information about an individual student" [20 U.S.C. § 1412(a)(16)(D)(iv)].

9. For example, NCLB mandates that, in order to receive Title I funds, the plan of a state or district must be coordinated with the requirements of IDEA [20 U.S.C. §§ 6311(a)(1), 6312(a)(1)].

10. NCLB is a vast statute with many components. This paper includes only select provisions that relate specifically to access to the general education curriculum for students with disabilities.

11. Content standards are to "specify what children are expected to know and be able to do; contain coherent and rigorous content; and encourage the teaching of advanced skills" [20 U.S.C. § 6311(b)(1)(D)(i)]. Achievement standards are to be aligned with a state's content standards and describe at least two levels of high achievement (proficient and advanced), as well as a third level of achievement (basic) [*id.* § 6311(b) (1)(D)(ii)].

12. Although IDEA '04 eliminated the requirement found in IDEA '97 for states to develop a comprehensive system of personnel development, IDEA '04 replaced the State Improvement Grant program with the State Personnel Preparation and Professional Development Grant program, in which states receive funds to provide professional development training for regular and special education teachers and administrators [20 U.S.C. § 1454(a)(1)].

13. The regulations do state that assessments should "be designed to be valid and accessible for use by the widest possible range of students, including students with disabilities" [34 C.F.R. § 200.2(b)(2)].

14. Disaggregation is not required when the number of students in the category is so small that the results would not be statistically reliable or would reveal identifiable information about the students [20 U.S.C. § 6311(b)(2)(C)(v)].

15. The 95 percent rule does "not apply in a case in which the number of students in a category is insufficient to yield statistically reliable information or the results would reveal personally identifiable information about an individual student" [20 U.S.C. § 6311(b)(2)(I)(ii)].

16. Corrective action may include such measures as replacing staff, implementing a new curriculum, appointing an outside expert, or extending the school year or school day [20 U.S.C. § 6316(b)(7)(C)(iv)]. Restructuring may include reopening the school as a public charter school, replacing all or most of the school staff, or turning over operation of the school to the state or a private contractor [*id.* § 6316(b)(8)(B)].

REFERENCES

Heubert, J. P., & Hauser, R. M. (Eds.), National Research Council, Committee on Appropriate Test Use. (1999). *High stakes: Testing for tracking, promotion, and graduation.* Washington, DC: National Academy Press.

Hitchcock, C., Meyer, A., Rose, D., & Jackson, R. (2002). Providing new access to the general curriculum: Universal design for learning. *Teaching Exceptional Children, 35,* 8–17.

Hocutt, A. M. (1996). Effectiveness of special education: Is placement the critical factor? *The Future of Children, 6*(1), 77–102.

H.R. Rep. No. 105–95. (1997).

Individuals with Disabilities Education Act Amendments of 1997, 20 U.S.C. §§ 1400 *et seq.* (amended 2004); 34 C.F.R. §§ 300.1 *et seq.* (2003).

Individuals with Disabilities Education Improvement Act of 2004, P.L. No. 108-446, 118 Stat. 2647. (2004). (Amending 20 U.S.C. §§ 1400 *et seq.*).

McDonnell, L. M., McLaughlin, M. J., & Morison, P. (Eds.), National Research Council, Committee on Goals 2000 and the Inclusion of Students with Disabilities. (1997). *Educating one and all: Students with disabilities and standards-based reform.* Washington, DC: National Academy Press.

No Child Left Behind Act, 20 U.S.C. §§ 6301 *et seq.* (2002); 34 C.F.R. §§ 200.1 *et seq.* (2003).

Nolet, V., & McLaughlin, M. J. (2000). *Accessing the general curriculum: Including students with disabilities in standards-based reform.* Thousand Oaks, CA: Corwin Press.

Quenemoen, R., Rigney, S., & Thurlow, M. (2002). *Use of alternate assessment results in reporting and accountability systems: Conditions for use based on research and practice* (Synthesis Report 43). Minneapolis, MN: University of Minnesota, National Center on Educational Outcomes. Retrieved June 7, 2004, from http://education.umn.edu/NCEO/OnlinePubs/Synthesis43.html.

Rose, D. H., & Meyer, A. (2002). *Teaching every student in the digital age: Universal design for learning.* Alexandria, VA: Association for Supervision and Curriculum Development.

Sen. Rep. 105-17. (1997).

Sen. Rep. 108-185. (2004).

Sireci, S. G., Li, S., & Scarpati, S. (2003). *The effects of test accommodations on test performance: A review of the literature* (Center for Educational Assessment Research Report no. 485). Amherst, MA: School of Education, University of Massachusetts. Commissioned by the Board on Testing and Assessment of the National Research Council of the National Academy of Sciences. Retrieved June 7, 2004, from http://education.umn.edu/nceo/OnlinePubs/TestAccommLitReview.pdf.

Thompson, S. J., Johnstone, C. J., & Thurlow, M. L. (2002). *Universal design applied to large scale assessments* (Synthesis Report 44). Minneapolis, MN: University of Minnesota, National Center on Educational Outcomes. Retrieved March 25, 2005, from http://education.umn.edu/NCEO/OnlinePubs/Synthesis44.html.

U.S. Department of Education. (1995). *Individuals with Disabilities Education Act amendments of 1995: Reauthorization of the Individuals with Disabilities Education Act (IDEA).* Washington, DC: Author.

U.S. Department of Education, Office of Elementary and Secondary Education. (Dec. 2, 2002). *Title I—Improving the academic achievement of the disadvantaged: Analysis of comments and changes.* 67 F.R. 71710, 71739–71771.

U.S. Department of Education, Office of Elementary and Secondary Education. (Mar. 20, 2003). *Title I—Improving the academic achievement of the disadvantaged: Notice of proposed rulemaking.* 68 F.R. 13796–13801.

U.S. Department of Education, Office of Elementary and Secondary Education. (Dec. 9, 2003). *Title I—Improving the academic achievement of the disadvantaged: Back-*

ground and analysis of comments and changes. 68 F.R. 68698–68701, 68703–68708.

U.S. Department of Education, Office of Elementary and Secondary Education. (Jan. 16, 2004). *Improving teacher quality state grants (Title II part A): Non-regulatory guidance.* Retrieved June 7, 2004 from http://www.ed.gov/programs/teacherqual/guidance.pdf.

U.S. Department of Education, Office of Special Education and Rehabilitative Services. (Dec. 29, 2004). Notice of request for comments and recommendations on regulatory issues under the Individuals with Disabilities Education Act (IDEA), as amended by the Individuals with Disabilities Education Improvement Act of 2004. 69 F.R. 77968, 77968–77969.

Wagner, M., Blackorby, J., Cameto, R., Hebbeler, K., & Newman, K. (1993). *The transition experiences of young people with disabilities.* Palo Alto, CA: SRI.

Note: This paper is an abridged version of a paper that was previously published as:

Karger, J. (2005). What IDEA and NCLB suggest about curriculum access for students with disabilities. In D. H. Rose, A. Meyer, and C. Hitchcock (Eds.), *The universally designed classroom: Accessible curriculum and digital technologies* (pp. 69–100). Cambridge, MA: Harvard Education Press.

Karger, J. (2005). Access to the general curriculum for students with disabilities: A discussion of the interrelationship between IDEA and NCLB (updated for 2004). Wakefield, MA: CAST.

The original report was written with support from the National Center on Accessing the General Curriculum (NCAC), a cooperative agreement between the Center for Applied Special Technology (CAST) and the U.S. Department of Education, Office of Special Education Programs (OSEP), Cooperative Agreement No. H324H990004. Although the U.S. Department of Education reviewed this document for consistency with the IDEA and NCLB, the contents of this document do not necessarily reflect the views or policies of the U.S. Department of Education, nor does mention of other organizations imply their endorsement of this report.

CHAPTER SIX

Saving Resources . . .
And Saving Children

Testimony to the U.S. Senate Committee on Appropriations,
Subcommittee on Labor, Health, Human Services,
Education and Related Agencies, July 25, 2001

DAVID H. ROSE

EDITORS' NOTE

*In the summer of 2001, the U.S. Senate Appropriations Subcommittee
on Labor, Health, Human Services, Education and Related Agencies convened a hearing on how educational technology could improve education for all. In his opening statement, the subcommittee chairman, Senator
Tom Harkin of Iowa, remarked:*

> *Five or ten years ago people would argue about whether technology
> helps students learn. "All these computers are expensive," they'd say.
> "Are they really worth the money? Will they really make a difference in
> student achievement?"*
>
> *Well, I'm glad to say we've gotten past that debate. They key is not
> whether technology can help students, but how it's used. When technol-
> ogy is used well, it can transform education, open minds to new worlds
> of learning, and brighten a child's future.*

*In fact, the debate about whether technology can help students would
continue for several years. However, as Senator Harkin anticipated, the*

question was becoming irrelevant as technology became more prevalent in students' lives via multimedia cell phones, social networking Web sites, and so forth. By the end of the decade, printed books, not computers, would stand in the dock: Are they really worth the money? Will they really make a difference in student achievement?

Harkin continued:

> *Technology can get students excited about school. It can give them instant access to the Internet. It can help them visualize concepts in ways that textbooks can't possibly match. It can open up a whole new world for students with disabilities. And it can give all students the twenty-first-century skills they need to succeed in a technology-based workplace.*

In this dramatic statement, the senator quite intuitively articulated the three principles of universal design for learning—the need for multiple means of representation, action and expression, and engagement.

David Rose's remarks to the committee on the affordances of UDL came three years before the IDEA reauthorization in 2004 and months before the passage of NCLB in 2001. However, they provide valuable insight into the pressing issues of the time. In particular, members of the larger education community—including publishers, researchers, advocates, and others—were wrestling with the issue of how best to leverage the dynamic promise of digital materials while still ensuring copyright protection to curriculum developers. IDEA 2004 put into place the National Instructional Materials Accessibility Standard (NIMAS), a trailblazing initiative to facilitate the timely conversion of textbooks and ancillary materials into accessible versions for qualifying students with print disabilities. IDEA requires publishers to provide digital source files of printed materials in a uniform format based on the standard. NIMAS represents an important first step in the eventual development of UDL curricula by facilitating the provision of accessible instructional materials.

Mr. Chairman, and members of the subcommittee, it is an honor to be asked to testify at this important hearing on education and technology. My name is David Rose and I am the co-executive director of CAST, the Center for Applied Special Technology and principal investigator of the National Center for Access to the General Curriculum, an OSEP (Office of Special Education Programs)-funded cooperative agreement. I welcome the opportunity to speak with you today. The fact that I have been asked to testify on the educational technology needs of students with disabilities demonstrates that Congress understands the critical importance of education technology for all learners.

Members of this committee were central to the passage of numerous pieces of landmark legislation over the past thirty years, including Section 504 of the Rehabilitation Act of 1973, the Individuals with Disabilities Education Act of 1975, Section 508 of the Rehabilitation Act of 1988 and 1998, and the Americans with Disabilities Act in 1990. Because of these laws, many things formerly thought to be impossible for individuals with disabilities are now commonplace.

Now, individuals with disabilities have a right to a free appropriate public school education, and can expect to find physically accessible educational buildings. Tragically, however, most curricula—the materials and methods for learning found inside these newly accessible buildings—are in fact not available or accessible to students with disabilities.

This moment in history, when innovative new educational technologies are proliferating, presents a unique and urgent opportunity to right this injustice. If we seize this opportunity, we will see people with disabilities making the contributions to our society envisioned and supported by past landmark legislation. Further, the strategic appropriation of funds at this time will result in more effective use of educational dollars and a subsequent reduction in the number of people entering SSI (Supplemental Security Income) and SSDI (Social Security Disability Insurance) programs because they are not qualified to work in the jobs of the future. Very significant benefits will accrue not only to children with disabilities, but to all children.

I will describe three key areas in educational technology significant for students with disabilities: assistive technology, digital curricula, and universal design. In each area, I offer specific recommendations for Congress.

ASSISTIVE TECHNOLOGIES

Most current successes of technology for individuals with disabilities are examples of "adaptive" or "assistive" technologies. Assistive technologies are applications (either hardware or software) designed specifically to assist disabled individuals in overcoming barriers. Examples include:

- Matthew, a third grader with physical disabilities who cannot speak or use his arms or legs, uses electronic switches to drive a wheelchair and operate his computer to write and communicate.
- Katherine, a sixth grader who is blind, uses screen reader technologies to navigate the Internet and do her social studies homework.
- Nina, who has a brain injury that causes her to be aphasic, uses an electronic augmentative communication device to speak to her friends and collaborate on schoolwork.

Even more spectacular assistive technologies are under development, including devices that can be implanted in the brain for hearing, for vision, for control of paralyzed muscles. These essential uses of technology for individuals with disabilities will require sustained federal support. There is simply not enough profit in developing for these "low incidence" students to attract the investments of the private sector.

Recommendations Regarding Assistive Technologies

1. Congress should continue to fund IDEA Part D research and technology development to ensure that new assistive and augmentative technologies are developed, particularly those that interface with new learning technologies (see the next section, "Digital Curricula") and those that support cognitive as well as sensory and physical access.
2. Congress should support, through technical assistance grants or contracts, the training of assistive technology specialists so that every school district has access to trained individuals who can teach children to use these powerful technologies in a timely fashion, can assist their parents in understanding and advocating for their use, and can assist teachers and administrators in successful classroom implementation of assistive technologies.

DIGITAL CURRICULA

That recommendation notwithstanding, it is dangerous to view assistive technology as the sole focus of educational technology for students with disabilities. Such an orientation places the emphasis of intervention on the individual rather than the learning environment. Developing powerful technologies to overcome barriers must be balanced by designing environments with fewer barriers. The lesson of the Americans with Disabilities Act is that small affordances built in everywhere, like curb cuts and ramps, are as critical for access as are assistive technologies like motorized wheelchairs.

The same is true for educational materials and methods. We need to use the new technologies not only to overcome existing learning barriers but also to design learning environments with fewer barriers right from the start. In the Concord, New Hampshire, public schools, teachers and parents are engaged in the painstaking task of digitizing many of their printed curricular materials. They are working to create digital versions of the printed materials used in their schools. Why are they going to all this trouble? They are doing this work because digital versions of the books are much better for students with disabilities. The difference is not in the content—the digital versions have exactly the same content. The difference is in the way that content is displayed.

In print versions the content is permanently on paper. Its display is fixed, unchangeable, "one size fits all." In digital versions, content is presented dynamically by the computer. As a result, content can be displayed in many different ways, adjusting to many different learners.

Imagine, for example, a digital version of Harper Lee's *To Kill a Mockingbird* for a tenth-grade classroom:

- Sarah, a student with low vision, can display the text in a very large font so she can see it.
- Bill, a student who is blind, can have the computer display the text as spoken words or have the computer print it on a braille printer.
- Jennifer, a student with severe physical disabilities, can change the display (e.g., turn the pages) with a single blink of her eye.
- Michael, a student with dyslexia, can click on a difficult word to have the computer read it aloud or link it instantly to a context-based definition.

In these ways, digital versions of traditional curricular materials can effectively reduce barriers to learning, thereby reducing the costs associated with expensive adaptations and pull-out programs.

With digital curricula, we can reduce barriers and we can do much more. In a recently completed research study (with technology developed under support from the U.S. Department of Education's Office of Special Education Programs), researchers at CAST (Center for Applied Special Technology) digitized books being used to teach reading and embedded research-based strategies for improving reading comprehension into the new flexible, digital texts. Nearly all of the 109 students in the study had learning disabilities and were performing at least two grade levels below their peers. Because of the digital texts, the level of access and support for reading comprehension could be adjusted closely to each child—providing the foundation for highly efficient learning.

The results were stunning—the students who used the digital texts found them more accessible, enjoyable, and empowering than traditional books, and they learned reading comprehension strategies much more effectively, showing highly significant improvements (achieving a half year's progress after reading only three novels) on later standardized tests of reading comprehension. The control group, comparable learning-disabled students who used traditional printed books, showed no significant progress at all. Further, where this approach was used, students exhibited fewer behavioral problems because they were engaged in the learning activity.

Where can schools get these kinds of digital books? Local solutions are far too inefficient. While many schools across the country, like Concord, have begun to digitize their own books, the duplication of effort wastes valuable resources. And it will get worse. As more schools engage in digitizing printed curriculum, more resources will be poured into a redundant, inefficient effort. Schools and national publishers also face a bewildering and contradictory array of local requirements and formats.

A new piece of proposed legislation, the Instructional Materials Accessibility Act of 2001, is critical. This bill provides for the establishment of a single national electronic file format to be used by publishers when creating electronic versions of texts. A consistent standard will greatly facilitate the timely and efficient conversion of textbooks into digital versions that are accessible to students with print disabilities: for example, braille, large print, digital audio, and other specialized formats like those that I have been describing. The proposed bill further calls for a national electronic file repository—a central and efficient solution to replace a hodgepodge of local ones. [Editors' note: These proposals were incorporated into IDEA 2004, and the National Instructional Materials Accessibility Standard took effect in 2006.]

OSEP, under part D of IDEA, is supporting efforts that further the development of digital curriculum. For example, OSEP funds the National Center on Accessing the General Curriculum housed at CAST. Research, design, development, dissemination, and training relating to digital curriculum materials urgently need expanded support.

Recommendations Regarding Digital Curricula

1. Congress should support the points proposed in the Instructional Materials Accessibility Act, including standardized file formats and a national repository of available digital curricular content.
2. Congress should support dissemination and training for teachers, administrators, and parents.
3. Congress should support ongoing research and development in the design, development, and release of digital curricula infused with the best research-based accommodations and enhancements for individuals with disabilities and their peers.

UNIVERSAL DESIGN OF LEARNING TECHNOLOGIES

Making traditional books and printed materials accessible via new technology is a necessary but not sufficient step if all learners are to find the opportunities they deserve. In effect, we are still using new technologies to do old things. My colleagues on this panel have been describing ways to use powerful new technologies to do *new* things—to engage all students in active experimentation at a level impossible in traditional classrooms, to communicate about learning with other students all over the world, to evaluate their own learning, to construct problem solutions in social groups, to create and edit new kinds of media well beyond the limits of writing text. These technologies prepare students for their future.

Unfortunately, the design of most of these learning technologies does not consider students with disabilities. As a result, innumerable new barriers for students with disabilities are being created inadvertently every day. These powerful new learning technologies are in their infancy, as yet unformed. Once formed, disseminated, and in use, these technologies will have to be retrofitted, or new assistive technologies designed, to overcome the new barriers being designed while we are discussing these issues.

An analogy well known to members of this panel will illustrate my point. Several decades ago, the new technology of television was inaccessible for viewers who were deaf. Eventually, decoder boxes to display captions improved access to television for deaf viewers. The cost of this retrofitted technology, several hundred dollars per television, still excluded many people. Legislation requiring televisions to include caption display technology led to the development of small decoder chips costing pennies apiece that were then included on all new televisions. The beneficiaries of this high-quality, efficient technology include not only those who are deaf but also hearing individuals in gyms and noisy airports, spouses retiring at different times, and individuals learning English as a second language.

The concept of building accessibility into learning technology from the start is an example of what is called universal design. Well-executed universal design leads to less-expensive solutions and better outcomes for all learners. At this moment in history, with rapid proliferation of learning technologies, it is imperative that we make universal design an urgent high priority.

The recent history of Section 508 illustrates the potential national problem if we wait. Most government Web sites were originally created with little or no awareness of disability access options. The mandate to make such sites accessible has led to enormous expense in retrofitting these designs—adding electronic "ramps" after the designs were completed. Had the knowledge of universal design approaches been available, time and dollars could have been saved, and more people could have enjoyed access to these important sites from the beginning.

To ensure that learning technologies work for all learners, Congress can take the same kind of leadership as it did in legislating 508 for the workplace. In this case, the application would be to the "learning place."

Recommendations Regarding Universal Design of Learning Technologies

1. Congress should require that any educational technology developed, maintained, procured, or used by the federal government be universally designed.
2. Congress should require that all educational programs administered or supported by the federal government use universally designed educational technology.
3. To ensure rapid dissemination of universally designed educational technologies, Congress should support the development of research-based guidelines for school districts, publishers, parents, and administrators on how to evaluate and select universally designed educational technologies.
4. Congress should provide funding for continued research and development in designing, implementing, and integrating better universally designed educational technologies.

SUMMARY

I commend the Congress for its leadership and its commitment to students with disabilities. Fundamental to this commitment, and to all of the things I have recommended, is the leadership implicit in IDEA. I strongly support the commitment to fund this foundational legislation for our future. In the innovative area of educational technology it is essential not only to provide support under Part B of IDEA, it is also essential to fund discretionary programs for technology research, training, and dissemination—those under Part D. Without that support we will miss the opportunity, just at this propitious moment, to turn the power of educational technology in a direction that will leave none of our children behind. In specific, I have made recommendations in three areas:

1. *Assistive technologies.* These individual technologies are essential to overcome the barriers that students with disabilities face. Congress should support their continued development into areas where barriers remain, including cognitive as well as sensory and motor issues, and should fund technical assistance to school districts so that they can be effective consumers of these powerful technologies.

2. *Digital curricula.* Most existing classroom technologies are still print based, making it very difficult to use assistive technologies, and even more difficult to individualize the curriculum in ways that are necessary for students with disabilities. Congress should provide legislation requiring that all curricula be made available in digital format so that it can be easily customized and made accessible for all students and fund a central place where teachers and parents can locate these resources.

3. *Universal design of learning technologies.* As new technologies are developed for schools, they should be made accessible to all of the students in the school, right from the start. Congress should support efforts to make guidelines for the universal design of such technologies, to research and develop such technologies, and to provide training and technical support to schools and parents. Congress should also provide leadership by requiring, purchasing, maintaining, and disseminating such technologies in all of its programs.

The overarching recommendation that I make to you is that we extend the same kinds of protections now afforded to physical spaces and to information in the workplace to a new area, the most important space for our future—the learning space. Our future as a culture depends on us to make learning spaces, those most precious spaces in the lives of our children, accessible and supportive of every single child. I believe that if we make the learning spaces of our schools accessible to all of our children, we will save both the short-term costs of poorly educating our children in the present and the long-term costs of *not* educating them for their future. This approach will save resources, but most importantly, it will save children.

CHAPTER SEVEN

Universal Design for Learning

Policy Challenges and Recommendations

KIM MOHEREK SOPKO

EDITORS' NOTE

In late 2008, Project Forum of the National Association of State Directors of Special Education convened a working group of some forty experts from across education policy and practice at the local, state, and national level to examine the state of UDL, identify challenges for scaling up the field, and make policy recommendations. A face-to-face meeting in December followed three months of online discussions—with nearly a hundred individuals participating in those discussions.

The Higher Education Opportunity Act of 2008 was passed while the forum was being planned and answered a major question going into the forum: How, for the purposes of a policy forum, should UDL be defined? Framing the discussion with the statutory definition clarified and reinforced for participants the importance of the "learning" in UDL. This reinforcement helped participants recognize that guaranteeing a high-quality education requires much more than providing physical or representational access to learning environments and tools, though that is essential, too. It requires a whole-curriculum approach that addresses representation, action and expression, and engagement for all learners across general and special education.

This chapter is an abridged version of the full report, which can be accessed online at www.projectforum.org.

Universal design for learning (UDL) is a growing practice across the nation, one that is increasingly referenced in education policy briefs, research literature, teacher professional development, and books and articles for educators. Several states and state universities have some type of UDL initiative under way. The Center for Applied Special Technology (CAST)[1] developed the theoretical framework and guidelines of UDL that promote the proactive design of curricula (including learning goals, instructional methods and materials, and assessments) that simultaneously customize learner supports while minimizing curriculum barriers, thereby expanding learning opportunities for all individuals. This framework provided a strong foundation for the definition of UDL included in the 2008 reauthorization of the Higher Education Act (HEA), which is called the Higher Education Opportunity Act (HEOA).[2]

> Universal design for learning (UDL) is a scientifically valid framework for guiding educational practice that—
>
> (A) provides flexibility in the ways information is presented, in the ways students respond or demonstrate knowledge and skills, and in the ways students are engaged; and
> (B) reduces barriers in instruction, provides appropriate accommodations, supports, and challenges, and maintains high achievement expectations for all students, including students with disabilities and students who are limited English proficient. [HEOA, P.L. 110-315, § 103(a)(24)]

The inclusion of UDL in the reauthorization of the HEA demonstrates its escalating importance in the education field. UDL concepts and practices are not yet broadly integrated into all education policy. Policy has been slow to catch up to this quickly growing practice. To address that disparity, Project Forum at the National Association of State Directors of Special Education (NASDSE) held a policy forum calling upon educators, including representatives of early childhood, related and pupil services, local and state administrators, institutions of higher education (IHEs), and national organizations, to first identify challenges to UDL implementation and then develop policy recommendations to address those challenges. Project Forum conducted this policy forum as part of its cooperative agreement with the U.S. Department of Education's Office of Special Education Programs (OSEP) in December 2008.

BACKGROUND

UDL is implemented at a variety of levels—individual classrooms, school buildings, local education agencies (LEAs),[3] and IHEs—but without consistent policies to support implementation. There is a multitude of materials, technical assistance, and professional development available from CAST[4] and other centers (e.g., Center for Implementing Technology in Education,[5] Family Center on Technology and Disability[6]) to support front-line educators and administrators in their implementation of UDL. Recently [in 2008] the U.S. Department of Education released its *Tool Kit on Teaching and Assessing Students with Disabilities: Universal Design for Learning,*[7] which provides a collection of resources on UDL to help policy makers, educators, and parents identify and implement policies and practices related to UDL. Programs with promise or evidence of effective UDL practices can be found throughout the nation from early childhood through postsecondary education, but there remains much opportunity for growth and acceptance of UDL as a national best practice.

Since 2006, the National UDL Task Force,[8] consisting of more than twenty-five national education and disability organizations, has been working to improve instruction and assessment for all students by incorporating UDL into policy and to promote UDL through grants, technical assistance, and a communication campaign. The work of this task force was instrumental in the addition of UDL to the HEOA. The task force also has provided recommended legislative language[9] for reauthorization of the Elementary and Secondary Education Act.[10]

Currently there is no direct reference to UDL in federal K–12 legislation, including No Child Left Behind (NCLB) and the Individuals with Disabilities Education Act (IDEA). However, there are references to universal design in IDEA. The act references the Assistive Technology Act, which defines universal design as a concept or philosophy for designing and delivering products and services that are usable by people with the widest possible range of functional capabilities, which include products and services that are directly accessible (without requiring assistive technologies) and products and services that are interoperable with assistive technologies. [29 U.S.C. 3002 § 3(19)]

IDEA refers to the use of universal design principles in developing and administering assessments [34 CFR § 300.160(g)], and authorizes activities to support the research, development, dissemination, and use of technology with universal design principles so that technology is accessible and maximizes access to and participation in the general education curriculum [34 CFR § 300.704(b)(4)]. Universal design principles are important, but not sufficient without integration of UDL since UDL extends the concept of universal design to the field of education and provides a research-based framework for designing curriculum.

In addition, IDEA 2004 includes a new standard, the National Instructional Materials Accessibility Standard (NIMAS), that states must adopt in a timely manner for the purposes of providing instructional materials to blind persons or other persons with print disabilities [34 CFR § 300.172(a)(1)] to maximize access to the general education curriculum. The references to universal design and accessibility in IDEA lay the groundwork for explicitly integrating UDL into K–12 general education and special education policy.

In the HEOA, universal design for learning has been explicitly defined and is integrated into the programs that are part of the law. The law states that recipients of "teacher quality partnership grants" and "teach to reach grants" must offer preparation programs that enable teachers to understand and use "strategies consistent with the principles of *universal design for learning*" [P.L. 110-315, § 202(d)(1)(A)(ii)], and "to integrate technology effectively into curricula and instruction, including technology consistent with the principles of *universal design for learning*" [P.L. 110-315, §204(a)(G)(i)]. In addition, UDL should be incorporated into evaluation and performance measures for each preparation program. In reference to model demonstration projects to provide technical assistance or professional development for postsecondary education faculty, staff, and administrators, the act indicates the following:

A grant, contract, or cooperative agreement awarded under this subpart shall be used to carry out one or more of the following activities:

(A) TEACHING METHODS AND STRATEGIES.—The development of innovative, effective, and efficient teaching methods and strategies, consistent with the principles of universal design for learning . . . . [P.L. 110-315, §762(b)(2)(A)]

Additionally, HEOA calls for the establishment of a national technical assistance center that will develop and provide "training modules for higher education faculty on exemplary practices for accommodating and supporting postsecondary students with disabilities across a range of academic fields, which may include *universal design for learning*" [P.L. 110-315, §777(4)(B)(ii)].

This language in the HEOA may serve as an impetus for change that can lead to the integration of UDL into other education policies and practices. The UDL policy forum participants expressed support for this forward movement, and this proceedings document describes challenges to UDL implementation, policy recommendations, and action plans to address those challenges.

METHODOLOGY

Outcomes and recommendations from CAST's UDL Summit[11] held in 2007 provided a basis and direction for the UDL policy forum. Project Forum collaborated with CAST to conduct the multiphase forum in order to identify challenges for UDL implementation. The forum consisted of the following phases:

- First, a virtual forum process was conducted starting with a live webinar using iVocalize, which served as the kick-off event for a facilitated virtual discussion on challenges to UDL implementation. Approximately ninety participants joined the webinar the day it was presented, October 6, 2008.
- Immediately following the webinar, approximately one hundred participants entered into a virtual discussion on the challenges to UDL implementation at www.sharedwork.org,[12] which Project Forum and CAST facilitated through November 3, 2008. SharedWork.

org served as an asynchronous, informal communication vehicle to promote dialogue and understanding across many stakeholders interested in UDL over an extended time frame. Participation was voluntary and open to all interested parties.

- Finally, for the face-to-face portion of the forum, Project Forum and CAST generated a list of approximately fifty invitees, some of whom had also attended CAST's 2007 UDL Summit. The majority of these invitees also participated in the virtual forum to identify challenges. The invitees included a variety of stakeholders who were knowledgeable about UDL at the building, local, state, and federal levels and who were familiar with UDL policy. The participants represented parents, local school administrators, state education administrators, and IHE faculty—including early childhood representatives, researchers, national organizations, technical assistance providers, and the U.S. Department of Education. The face-to-face forum was held December 1–3, 2008, in Alexandria, Virginia.

Project Forum used the definition of UDL from the HEOA and provided the following definition of the word *policy* to help participants collaborate effectively to develop policy recommendations:

For the purpose of this policy forum, *policy* is a principle, plan, or course of action based on a combination of basic decisions and commitments pursued by a government, organization, or individual.

The expected outcomes of the forum were to:

- identify challenges to UDL implementation across federal, state, district, and school levels, particularly in the areas of content standards; instructional methods, materials, and assessments; and technology use and support;
- develop policy recommendations for federal, state, district, and school policy makers and administrators to support UDL implementation across the areas of content standards; instructional methods, materials, and assessments; and technology use and support; and
- share concrete examples of how state and local policies on UDL can support strategies to improve performance indicators such as grad-

uation, drop-out, assessment, least restrictive environment, transition, and postschool outcomes.

The face-to-face forum began with a panel presentation and continued for one and a half days to refine challenges identified in the virtual forum and develop policy recommendations and action plans to address the challenges for UDL implementation.

UDL PANEL PRESENTATION

The policy forum opened with a panel of forum participants sharing their perspectives on UDL implementation, policies that support it, and needed changes. The panelists were Patricia Ralabate (National Education Association), representing a national perspective; Margo Izzo (Ohio State University), representing a higher education perspective; Jeff Diedrich (Michigan Integrated Technology Supports), representing a state perspective; and Mary Forde (Greenwich Public Schools, Connecticut), representing a local perspective. Nancy Reder (NASDSE) served as the moderator. The panelists introduced UDL as the topic of discussion while reviewing its current status and shared their perspectives of UDL implementation across the education field. Summaries of the panel members' presentations and discussion with forum attendees follow.

A National Perspective

The National UDL Task Force has been working collaboratively to develop policy briefs and fact sheets, provide recommended legislative language for upcoming reauthorization of federal education laws, and communicate the importance of UDL to national organizations. The task force is also collaborating with OSEP and the Office of Elementary and Secondary Education (OESE) to jointly model collaboration to support UDL. Information about UDL has been included in partner organizations' annual conferences, and some are providing professional development on UDL. The task force believes UDL is applicable to all students and recommends funding for UDL research. A main challenge faced at the national level is promoting UDL as an effective practice for all students, not as only a special education practice. An additional challenge is the inclusion of UDL in legislative language at the national policy level.

A Higher Education Perspective

More than thirty institutions of higher education have received funds from the U.S. Department of Education, Office of Postsecondary Education (OPE), to ensure that students with disabilities receive a quality higher education. During the technical assistance workshop coordinated by OPE, UDL was defined and suggested as an appropriate activity to improve teaching methods and strategies. The following example was given in materials provided at that workshop (held April 8, 2008):

> Some projects have held summer institutes for college faculty and disability support coordinators to provide them with recommendations regarding making their curriculum more accommodating based on universal design for learning.

Despite the preparation of more than eighty grant applications, and the award of over $6 million to twenty-three IHEs during FY 2008, UDL is often confused with a wide range of acronyms and terminology, such as RTI (response to intervention), inclusion, and PBS (positive behavioral supports). Clarity of these terms and how they interconnect is needed across all departments in colleges of education in order to prepare future teachers.

Many faculty within colleges of education regularly model UDL principles and a few teach courses specific to UDL, but there is limited, if any, policy to support UDL implementation within individual IHEs. Teacher preparation programs often incorporate many examples for ways students can engage in the content and express what they learn through multiple assessment methods, but the majority of faculty across the university continues to teach how they were taught—primarily through lecture. While many universities are using course management systems, some of these systems do not adequately align to the principles of UDL, as evidenced by numerous accessibility complaints filed by both faculty and students with disabilities.

Additionally, UDL may be represented conceptually in university mission and goal statements, but the term itself is not often used. A main challenge faced at the higher education level is the lack of clear terminology for UDL and inclusion of UDL within policy, mission statements, course design, instructional methods, and assessment. However, the passage of the HEOA may help address these challenges since it defines UDL and provides for its implementation in higher education.

A State Perspective

UDL emerged in Michigan largely as a result of the 2006 state board of education policy on universal education.[13] Viewing UDL as a significant paradigm shift in education, a group of diverse stakeholders met in 2007 to plan strategies for UDL implementation. At the state level, through collaboration with CAST, stakeholders are working to describe, in practical terms, what UDL does and does not look like and how UDL can be incorporated in the frame of the State Performance Plan (SPP) and Annual Performance Report (APR). Michigan benefits from the advocacy of its state director of special education and the state board of education, which has included UDL in board policy regarding grant applications by requiring applicants to describe how they will meet the needs of the broadest range of students, largely through the framework of UDL. Further, the application of this board policy has also impacted teacher certification standards. Challenges faced at the state level include the theory-to-implementation gap, lack of exemplars, and a system that in many respects perpetuates the continued division between general education and special education. To address these issues, Michigan has recently initiated the design and implementation of Michigan's Integrated Improvement Initiatives (MI3). MI3 supports the adoption, coordination, and implementation of research-based strategies. A key component is using research available through the National Implementation Research Network (NIRN).[14] In early 2008, MI3 received a state implementation and scale-up of evidence-based practices (SISEP) grant to assist with the effective implementation and scale-up of evidence-based practices statewide. An intended state outcome for the work with SISEP is the "ongoing development of a learning community, among

Michigan Department of Education–funded initiatives, for the purpose of effective installation and implementation fidelity of quality evidence based interventions," according to panelist Jeff Diedrich. UDL became the focus of this work.

A Local Perspective

Greenwich Public Schools, an LEA in Connecticut, revised its teacher evaluation process so administrators could consider how teachers use UDL in their classrooms and emphasize that UDL is good teaching. This LEA is also revising its report cards to reflect UDL so that communications with families incorporate a UDL philosophy. Greenwich stresses that UDL is about instruction, not technology, but that technology can support UDL. The LEA does not have specific written policy about UDL, but engages in conversations to support inclusive education and promote the collaboration of general and special education to integrate UDL into schools to support all students. This perspective is also integrated into new teacher orientation. Challenges faced at the local level include convincing high school teachers of the importance and value of UDL, helping teachers acquire materials that incorporate UDL, and collaborating with IHEs to link UDL practices at both the high school and postsecondary education level.

Summary of Panel Presentation

Clear and succinct terminology and in-depth understanding of the principles and practice of UDL and how they can benefit every student is needed at all levels. UDL also needs to be viewed as a general education practice, not a special education practice. Panel members recommended

- continuing to highlight the principles and strategies of UDL while there is a huge effort for course redesign in higher education;
- encouraging collaborative efforts between IHEs and states with the provision of coaches to work with classroom teachers;
- providing opportunities to share information with and collaborate with textbook and instructional material designers; and
- training teachers so they may choose appropriate materials to support UDL implementation.

CHALLENGES TO UDL IMPLEMENTATION

Participants in the virtual forum identified a variety of challenges that were summarized into five groups: (1) awareness and outreach, (2) leadership/systems, (3) data collection and assessment, (4) technology and learning/funding, and (5) professional development. After a brief review of the challenges identified through the virtual forum, the participants at the face-to-face forum engaged in discussion, consolidation, refinement, and identification of ten top challenges. They identified the top ten challenges for UDL implementation:

1. Engage and excite educators at all levels: pre-service, in-service, mentors, coaches, and higher education faculty.
2. Create and facilitate community capacity (including leadership) to promote the principles of UDL.
3. Communicate and ensure that all stakeholders understand the problems UDL addresses and the benefits/solutions UDL offers.
4. Integrate UDL and technology within school cultures and communities.
5. Find intersections among standards to infuse UDL and measure growth and progress of teachers (but not as a formal evaluation tool).
6. Identify and provide supports needed for the effective implementation of UDL that include existing practices and initiatives as well as newly available tools and resources to encourage and sustain engagement of educators and families.
7. Reexamine our current systems through two lenses: those that impede the implementation of UDL and those that encourage the collaboration and cooperation needed to implement UDL (e.g., inclusion).
8. Collect and apply appropriate and functional data (including technology use) to inform and support users (i.e., students, educators, administrators, parents/community, evaluators, publishers, and legislators).
9. Ensure multiple methods of assessments are developed using UDL principles while maintaining reliability and validity.
10. Provide incentives for commercial enterprises and the content/curriculum developers to broaden usability for all.

In summary, participants identified challenges as effectively communicating; gaining excitement from the field; examining current systems; motivating leaders and policy makers to build or increase capacity; using data to inform and support UDL implementation; ensuring that assessment methods incorporate UDL; and providing incentives for development of curricula, software, and textbooks that integrate UDL.

POLICY RECOMMENDATIONS

Editors' note: Forum participants developed recommendations to address the challenges they identified. The following were perceived to have a "high level of impact" and were suggested without controversy by the group.

- Require every personnel preparation grant in general and special education to include instruction on UDL implementation and teach UDL in a manner that reflects the principles of UDL.
- The secretary of education should convene a technical review board or working group (Office of Special Education and Rehabilitative Services, Office of Special Education Programs, Office of Elementary and Secondary Education, Office of Postsecondary Education, Institute of Education Sciences, etc.) to develop and publicize a reasonable set of features/recommendations for educational publishers/developers that support implementation of UDL based on the principles outlined in the *UDL Guidelines*, Version 1.0.[15]
- Build a consortium from which will evolve a national knowledge network that impacts the development and implementation of content standards, professional development standards, and accreditation standards based on UDL principles.
- Establish a federal competitive grant program to transform existing practices to reflect the UDL framework in the following areas: standards, instructional methods, curriculum, accountability/assessment systems, and professional development, beginning with a needs assessment and including evaluation and national dissemination of what works.
- Encourage local school boards to adopt policies requiring curriculum adoption committees to consider UDL principles in evaluating

and selecting curricula, and include a broad representation of stakeholders in discussions of curriculum adoption.

- Develop and fund mechanisms for reviewing assessment tools and practices through the lens of UDL at state education agency (SEA), local education agency (LEA), and building levels.
- Ensure continuity between assessment and instruction by aligning use of UDL principles.
- Build and facilitate community capacity through activities such as
  - funding UDL research
  - developing a UDL model demonstration/data collection and evaluation center (similar to Positive Behavior Support Center)
  - creating state and LEA consortia to develop model UDL initiatives (including IHEs, SEAs, LEAs, associations)
  - designing funded priorities for pre-service, in-service, and leadership grants that incorporate UDL
- Include as part of state educator/teacher certification the requirement that continuing education address effective use of technology, instructional techniques, and strategies consistent with principles of UDL.
- Embed UDL in a comprehensive professional development system that includes
  - pre-service program accreditation
  - university-wide accreditation
  - state licensure/certification (i.e., teachers, administrators, related and pupil services personnel, school boards, and others)
- Identify and fund projects that demonstrate successful incorporation and implementation of the principles of UDL.
- Provide greater detail in procurement and development for formative and summative assessments that incorporate principles of UDL.

In addition, participants addressed their concerns for the addition of language in federal legislation (such as NCLB and IDEA) to explicitly integrate UDL concepts and principles into education programs through these authorizing statutes and subsequent appropriations bills. However, participants agreed to table specific discussion about legal language and focus their limited time in this forum on recommendations and action plans in which significant progress could be made, with the understanding that the National Task Force on UDL has already proposed language to integrate UDL into NCLB.[16]

Editors' note: Forum participants developed specific action plans for some of the recommendations, outlining immediate steps that could be taken to support UDL implementation. Time limitations at the forum prevented further work.

CONCLUDING REMARKS

Participants at this policy forum demonstrated excitement about and commitment to ensuring that UDL becomes integrated as a best practice in the field of education. Participants recommended that UDL as a practice and its many benefits be marketed across the nation to educators; administrators; parents; policy makers; curriculum, software, and text developers and publishers; and students. To effectively market UDL, it is important to develop a national knowledge network supported by a technical review board convened by the U.S. secretary of education to develop and publicize features and recommendations that support UDL implementation and that impact not only educational software and materials, but also content standards, professional development standards, and accreditation standards. Additionally, it would be beneficial to include in federal and state grants some type of agreement or assurance that the program described in the grant application incorporates UDL principles in its goals and activities. By working simultaneously on marketing UDL, developing policy that supports UDL implementation, and conducting research and data that demonstrate its effectiveness as a practice, there is greater likelihood for the integration of UDL principles in all aspects of education, leading to greater student motivation and learning.

Editors' note: The forum concluded on December 3, 2008, and this report was issued, with input from the participants, in April 2009.

NOTES

1. http://www.cast.org.
2. The HEA was reauthorized in 2008 by the Higher Education Opportunity Act of 2008. The law is available online at http://frwebgate.access.gpo.gov/cgi-bin/getdoc. cgi?dbname=110_cong_public_laws&docid=f:publ315.110.pdf
3. See http://www.projectforum.org/docs/UDLImplementationinSixLEAs.pdf for a summary of UDL implementation from six local education agencies.
4. http://www.cast.org/research/udl/index.html.
5. http://www.cited.org/index.aspx.
6. http://www.fctd.info/.
7. U.S. Department of Education. (2008). *Tool kit on teaching and assessing students with disabilities: Universal design for learning.* Available at http://www.osepideasthat work.org/UDL/index.asp.
8. See http://www.advocacyinstitute.org/UDL/organizations.shtml for a list of participating organizations.
9. Refer to http://www.advocacyinstitute.org/UDL/NCLB.shtml.
10. In its most recent reauthorization, the ESEA was called the No Child Left Behind Act (NCLB) and is often referred to by this name.
11. http://www.cast.org/publications/bycast/UDL_Summit_Summary_All_Invitees_11_29_07.pdf.
12. SharedWork.org is a Web site maintained by the IDEA Partnership at the National Association of State Directors of Special Education, a project funded by the U.S. Department of Education Office of Special Education Programs for the purpose of connecting stakeholders in the national Communities of Practice (CoP) and participating states' CoP and Practice Groups to develop their shared work.
13. http://www.michigan.gov/documents/UnivEdBrochureFINAL_incl_152066_7._Glossary_03-02-06a.pdf.
14. http://www.fpg.unc.edu/~nirn/.
15. CAST. (2008). *Universal design for learning guidelines version 1.0.* Wakefield, MA: Author. Available at http://www.cast.org/publications/UDLguidelines/version1. html.
16. Refer to http://www.advocacyinstitute.org/UDL/NCLB.shtml.

Note: This report was prepared for Project Forum at the National Association of State Directors of Special Education. Project Forum is a cooperative agreement funded by the Office of Special Education Programs of the U.S. Department of Education. For more information, go to www.projectforum.org. The report was supported by the U.S. Department of Education (Cooperative Agreement No. H326F050001). However, the opinions expressed herein do not necessarily reflect the positions of the U.S. Department of Education, and no official endorsement by the department should be inferred.

CHAPTER EIGHT

Universal Design for Learning

Implementation in Six Local Education Agencies

KIM MOHEREK SOPKO

EDITORS' NOTE

In 2007, Project Forum, an initiative through the National Association of State Directors of Special Education, surveyed its members to determine local education agencies (LEAs) that were effectively implementing the principles of UDL. Project Forum identified six LEAs in five states—Indiana, Iowa, Kentucky, Massachusetts, and Ohio—for more extensive interviews on UDL implementation. This chapter is Project Forum's summary of the interviews highlighting the practical applications, benefits, and challenges to UDL implementation.

While none of the districts mentioned specific policies on UDL, all of the districts acknowledged the benefit of UDL implementation for all students and the desire to continue the expansion of UDL guided practice. As a result of this research, Project Forum recommends ways to incorporate UDL into federal and state policies.

U niversal design for learning (UDL) affords opportunities for all individuals to gain knowledge and skills by providing rich support for learning and reducing barriers that can inhibit access to learning. Just as universal design in architecture anticipates the needs of individuals with disabilities and builds structures accordingly, universal design for learning anticipates special needs of students and creates curriculum, instruction, and assessments that are specifically designed to facilitate access. In the process, all students benefit.

While UDL is an overall practice, not a method for individualizing services for students, educators must consider the individual needs of students when implementing instructional practices and assessments. The UDL theoretical framework designed by CAST (the Center for Applied Special Technology) includes three principles to enable every student to access and participate in all facets of learning. The three principles are multiple and flexible means of

- *representation* to provide students various ways of acquiring information and knowledge;
- *action and expression* to provide students alternatives for performing learning tasks and demonstrating what they know; and
- *engagement* to tap into students' interests, challenge them appropriately, and motivate them to learn.

The Center for Universal Design (CUD) at North Carolina State established seven principles of universal design to provide guidance for environmental, product, and communication design:

1. equitable use
2. flexibility in use
3. simple and intuitive use
4. perceptible information
5. tolerance for error
6. low physical effort
7. size and space for approach and use

Project Forum and CAST integrated CAST's theoretical framework of UDL and the CUD's principles of universal design as a conceptual framework to structure interview questions to learn about and summarize local level implementation of UDL. Conceptually, UDL assumes that the physical structure of buildings, classrooms, equipment, and materials as well as the technology infrastructure follow standard universal design guidelines. With that as a foundation, UDL provides a framework and guidelines for building a curriculum that is also universally designed for learning. UDL is equitable, flexible, simple, intuitive, and perceptible.

UDL ensures that individuals with a wide range of diverse abilities can access and use educational curricula, instruction, and assessments through the same or equivalent means regardless of their knowledge, skills, and experiences. It supports flexible models of skilled performance; choices of content, tools, learning context, and rewards; adjustable levels of challenge; opportunities for practice with supports; flexible opportunities for demonstrating skill and knowledge; and ongoing, relevant feedback. UDL also provides multiple examples of perceptible information through various modes of communication (pictorial, verbal, tactile) that are compatible with available assistive technology (AT). By considering universal design principles while incorporating the UDL theoretical framework of representation, action and expression, and engagement, educators can effectively implement UDL practices for the benefit of all students.

This document summarizes UDL implementation information from six local education agencies in five states. Project Forum at the National Association of State Directors of Special Education (NASDSE) produced this document as part of its cooperative agreement with the U.S. Department of Education Office of Special Education Programs (OSEP).

METHODOLOGY

Project Forum first conducted a minisurvey of state directors of special education to identify states with local education agencies (LEAs) that are effectively incorporating UDL principles as defined in this document. Nine state directors responded positively to the minisurvey, identifying potential LEA representatives to interview. Based on these responses, six LEAs identified in five states (IN, IA, KY, MA, OH) were contacted regarding interviews. Interview participants varied in number and roles for each LEA. In four of the LEAs, there was one interview participant, in one LEA there were two participants, and in another LEA there were five participants. There was one interview session for each LEA. In the LEAs with multiple participants, the responses were a team effort rather than individual perspectives. Participants agreed on the primary speaker's response to the question and would occasionally elaborate on the answer. The professional roles of participants included school principals, project directors, teachers, a superintendent, a special education director, an IT specialist, and regional education agency staff. They were interviewed to gather information about UDL practices, successes, and challenges in their LEA.

FINDINGS

Policies and Practices

How UDL practices started in the LEAs

UDL was generally introduced to the LEAs by an outside source such as a regional education center/agency or a state-funded project. One interviewee reported the LEA superintendent was aware of UDL, brought CAST into the state for a large presentation on UDL, and encouraged but never required schools to begin a UDL initiative. On average, UDL was introduced to the LEAs five years ago and the LEAs have been developing the practices since then. While some interviewees reported that UDL was initially presented as an initiative to support special education programs, most quickly realized it was good practice that would benefit all students. Most interviewees believed the introduction of UDL with the clear opportunity for individuals and teachers to take hold of the practices without a district mandate was an effective approach to begin the incorporation of UDL into the LEA. One interviewee believed UDL practices in her system would be more effective if they were presented as a top-down mandate, but added that the LEA had experienced regular changes in superintendents over an eight-year period.

Policy around UDL

None of the LEAs has a clear policy specific to UDL. However, one LEA has written goals and includes these goals in its continuous improvement plan. Other interviewees reported that UDL provides a framework for curriculum and is implemented as a good practice that benefits all children. In general, these LEAs are implementing UDL as a best practice, communicating about it, and encouraging its use without a formal written policy.

Systemic Issues

Structure

All of the LEA respondents reported that their school buildings and classrooms are accessible. No significant physical building structural changes have been made to implement UDL practices and LEAs work with the buildings they have available, making adaptations and accommodations as they can. Types of changes that have occurred include changing class periods as block scheduling is implemented, changing storage methods of materials, and building small learning communities.

Technology and infrastructure use

All of the school buildings have an upgraded (within the last six years) technology infrastructure to support computer use with Internet connections. The LEAs vary in the amount of technology incorporated into their schools to support UDL. The ratio of students per computer ranges from 1:2.5 to 1:6, with computers available in classrooms as well as computer labs. One LEA interviewee reported that a school's computer lab is not as updated as the rest of the school, but is driven more by the computer teacher, who is comfortable with the current level of technology in the lab.

Most interviewees reported that teachers use computers from 15 to 60 percent of the day for instruction and administration (e.g., recording attendance, grades, or e-mail). One LEA interviewee reported computer use is constant because of the availability of Smart Boards in classrooms. The frequency of computer use for instruction varies by the teacher, but as UDL practices and technology become more integrated in the schools, teachers reportedly tend to increasingly use computers for instruction. Interviewees reported that students use computers 10 to 80 percent of their school day for curriculum-based activities, researching, and word processing. In one LEA, students in kindergarten through second grade use the computer 20–25 minutes per day to participate in the Waterford Early Reading Program. In another LEA, student use of computers increases by school level; e-lockers (designated places on the school network for storage of student documents and projects) are available and e-portfolios (a collection of student work stored on the school network to monitor student progress) are created at the secondary grade levels. This LEA also provides computer-based credit options as an independent study program at the secondary level. Students regularly prepare PowerPoint presentations and use word processing software on the computers. The computer is an essential component for integrating UDL practices in these LEAs.

The integration and use of Smart Boards in the classrooms varies by LEA based on the number of Smart Boards available. One LEA has a Smart Board in every classroom; another has them in every special education classroom and is starting to add them to other classrooms. The other four LEAs have a few Smart Boards available.

Digital materials

No LEA has a schoolwide digital curriculum in its entirety, but some have posted the state content standards and courses of study on LEA Web sites. As LEAs adopt new textbooks, they strive to include digitized materials provided by the book publishers, and many use United Video Streaming as another source of digital materials. Some of the LEAs have centralized digital materials and software through their schools' media centers or another central location in the LEA and have implemented a bar code system so teachers may check out materials as needed. LEAs also post digital materials on their network for specific grade levels or subject areas. Teachers may also find effective supplemental digital materials to use, and most LEAs encourage teachers to investigate appropriate materials and provide recommendations to the administration and curriculum committees on which materials to adopt. LEAs do not yet have complete, accessible databases of digital materials available, but some are developing them because they believe these databases would be useful tools for teachers.

Commonly used digitally accessible materials in LEAs include Kidspiration, Inspiration, Read-Write-Gold, United Video Streaming, Read 180, and E-Reader. Interviewees made no strong recommendation for a particular program because not all teachers consistently use them, so data are lacking. Digital materials are primarily used to support literacy skills (reading and writing) and may also include Co-Writer, Lexia SOS, or Read Naturally. Additional materials mentioned by interviewees include Clicker, Waterford, Type to Learn, Go Solve, Classroom Suite, Encyclomedia, Fast Forward, Fast Math, Go Solve, and Board Maker. In addition, scanners are available at least in every school building in all LEAs and are sporadically used by teachers to scan/digitize text.

Practical Application

Curriculum and instruction

All interviewees reported that many teachers are applying UDL practices, but consistency among teachers is lacking. Teachers generally have become more flexible with how information is presented, how students demonstrate knowledge, and ways students are engaged, but there is variability within the schools and throughout the LEAs. Overall, the use of UDL makes teachers consider individual learning styles and strengths to ensure equitable and flexible opportunities for all students. Some interviewees reported that administrators had developed a culture of risk taking, creativity, and flexibility to encourage teachers to apply UDL and continue to work creatively to ensure that curriculum, instruction, and assessments are accessible for all students.

The variety of teaching methods reportedly used to support UDL practices include small groups, flexible grouping (often based on learning styles of students rather than on student areas of weakness), and incorporation of low-tech assistive technology devices (e.g., highlighters, pencil grips, sensory-integration seat supports) as well as more advanced AT devices (e.g., digital cameras, Alpha Smart with cowriters, Smart Boards, and clickers). Teaching methods are shifting away from a one-size-fits-all approach and toward multiple opportunities for creativity and flexibility. A specific example provided was the study of the novel *Huckleberry Finn*. Teachers took students to a local park where three rivers converged (similar to details in the novel), and the teachers dressed up, read, and acted as characters in the novel. The follow-up activity included reflection on the experience and its correlation to the novel that students were able to complete by writing in a journal, drawing, and/or taking photographs. This type of activity demonstrates flexibility with many opportunities to address a variety of learning styles.

Another creative teaching and learning method reported was the use of digital cameras and LCD projectors for presentations. One LEA holds an annual community science fair for senior students, and there is increased variation in the presentation and delivery formats of the student projects as UDL is integrated.

Teachers adjust their teaching primarily based on informal observations of student participation, motivation, intrigue, excitement, and learning, but may also use log sheets and surveys. In one LEA, teachers have individual conversations with students about learning styles so they may appropriately adjust their teaching methods. Two different LEAs use a UDL observation or self-assessment checklist to make instructional decisions and assess teachers' use of UDL practices.

Assessments

While formal assessments are still commonly used, especially to address accountability in the LEA and state, teachers are becoming more creative and flexible to ensure assessments are accessible and usable by all students, that ongoing and relevant feedback is provided, and that assessment is an embedded and continuous process. Teachers are moving away from pencil-and-paper assessment measures and affording more flexible opportunities for students to demonstrate knowledge (e.g., writing songs, painting pictures, writing stories, acting out skits, and creating video and/or audio projects). Most interviewees reported teachers feel limited due to the statewide testing/accountability measures and believe students will suffer if those types of assessments are not included in the classroom practices as students will not be familiar with the assessment format. Since statewide testing and accountability measures do not yet incorporate UDL, teachers reportedly feel efforts to design and implement UDL assessments are undermined.

LEAs are incorporating Web-based assessments into their programs. Read 180 provides a continuous Web-based assessment within its program design. AIMS Web provides periodic one-minute assessments in reading and math to chart a student's growth in those skill areas. Measures of Academic Progress provides one question at a time to identify a student's instructional level in reading and math, while also providing support and ideas for flexible grouping. E-portfolios are used in one LEA to monitor student progress. Some LEAs are using Web-based, high-stakes testing. In one LEA, the effectiveness of its online high-stakes testing improved once testing was centralized and responses were collected on one server.

Supports and Influences

The LEA interview teams were asked what was critical to have in place to make UDL work. While many indicated money and time are always valuable assets, lack of these resources alone was not a limiting factor for integrating UDL practices in their schools. Common responses included support from administration; effective technology; a state-level vision; collaboration within the district and among teachers and staff within individual schools; regional education center staff and administration belief in UDL as a best practice; and support from regional education centers that included introducing concepts, technology, and AT devices as well as training. One key UDL influence component is a supportive administrator with motivated, creative teachers who are willing to take risks, believe in the usefulness of UDL, and expand concepts and practices by working collaboratively within the school and across the district. In contrast, one LEA interviewee believes a top-down policy supported by funding is needed for effective UDL implementation.

Other interviewees indicated that the championing of UDL by general education staff was essential for the effective integration of UDL in the schools. Most also commented that it is important to implement the change to UDL slowly so that people can internalize the practices that led them to embrace the concept rather than quickly forcing change and requiring the practices.

Several interviewees described a collaborative structure that facilitates and supports the integration of UDL practices. For instance, in one LEA, the elementary and secondary curriculum directors and the special education director worked collaboratively to learn about UDL and then promoted and supported the use of UDL for all students. Another LEA created instructional service delivery/design teams that became a core group in school buildings to develop action plans related to inclusion and UDL, and it continues to bring those core groups together at the district level several times a year to collaborate. From those core groups, the teams created one core district-level team to focus specifically on UDL. Another LEA provided time for teachers to plan UDL practices collaboratively, which increased collegiality and the expansion of UDL practices across the schools.

Professional development

Professional development in support of UDL practices varies among the LEAs interviewed. One LEA incorporated the theme of UDL throughout its in-service program for second-year teachers and another developed a core district team to bring UDL training and information back to the school buildings. Another LEA provides AT training with a focus on UDL. Two LEAs received training through other projects such as Project Focus or the Promoting Achievement Through Technology and Instruction for all Students (PATINS) Project. Another LEA received training from its Center for Leadership. Training is provided through multiple ongoing training strands, through a consortium, as after-school courses with in-service credit, and/or as summer institutes. Some regional educational agencies provide individual consultations and workshops on specific UDL-related topics upon request. In one LEA, a learning center that is a partnership between community businesses and institutes of higher education offers a summer academy for teachers. Most of the training is introductory information based on teacher needs and is generally more focused on AT and technology in general than on UDL as a practice. Training is provided on how to use new computer software programs and AT equipment with a discussion of how technology and AT are tools to support UDL; however, no training specific to UDL in regard to curriculum, instruction, and assessment is offered.

In general, teachers are training and mentoring each other on UDL principles and practices. In one LEA, teachers who began implementing UDL practices quickly found another teacher who was savvy with technology and began working collaboratively. Teachers in another LEA are presenting information about UDL in college courses as well as providing workshops on UDL in other venues.

Interviewees reported that recognition of innovative practices, which may include UDL, is provided through acknowledgment of teacher efforts at staff and school board meetings, in school newsletters and Web pages, and through community newspaper publicity. Some teachers may receive minigrants or small rewards such as gift certificates, flash drives, or laptop bags, but these rewards and incentives are driven primarily by building principals. One LEA developed its own UDL marketing logo and slogan and provided teachers with notepads, water bottle holders, and other paraphernalia to spread the word about UDL.

Coordinators

Interviewees reported that technology specialists/coordinators are available within the district and usually at individual schools. In some schools, a teacher receives a stipend to provide technology support. Most of the technology support is not instructionally based and therefore does not focus on or specifically support UDL in the classroom. The technology specialists/coordinators provide technology training to teachers only so they can use computers, software programs, and other technology at a basic level.

In all LEAs, there was a reported increase in teacher technology ability over the years, primarily with the use of e-mail and Web pages and Microsoft Office products. However, as more programs were integrated, such as Read and Write Gold, teachers also increased their skills in using technology for instruction.

Five of the LEAs have no specific UDL coordinator. One LEA has a supplemental UDL coordinator position in each building, and this person's role is to communicate and collaborate with the LEA's Center for Leadership regarding UDL. Having these building-level coordinators strengthens ownership of UDL at the teacher level.

Interviewees were not aware of any state-level UDL coordinators, but believed state personnel with other responsibilities also address UDL. Interviewees believed if there were a state-level UDL coordinator, his or her role would be to coordinate professional development, access funds through grant writing, coordinate online testing, help identify technology and software needs, support teachers in the use of technology, and ensure UDL best practices are implemented. However, one interviewee believed that having a specific UDL coordinator "makes UDL sound like a separate thing or program when it is not—we are trying to help people understand that it is a framework, not a project."

Funding systems, resources, and other supports
Funds to support UDL practices come from a variety of sources; however, the funds are directed primarily toward the technology aspect of UDL implementation, not the creation of universally designed curricula. One LEA reported that it started with a state grant and sought matching funds from special education, technology, building-level, and other funding pools. Two LEAs used some special education funds to support UDL practices. Funds are also used from Title I and a general technology fund. In one LEA, a philanthropic organization provided a great deal of financial support. Another LEA used a local tax fund for financial support of technology and training. LEAs also obtain grant funds, but the frequency and amount of these funds vary significantly, and most LEAs do not consistently or actively seek grants for UDL implementation at this time. LEAs have learned that some vendors will provide discounts on technology, especially if the LEA offers to be a demonstration site, so they have used this opportunity to save money while informing others about UDL.

Interviewees reported that parents have been made aware of UDL as an instructional framework, and many are highly receptive to the concepts and practice. Some of the parent-teacher organizations have purchased equipment to support UDL in the schools. In some LEAs, parents participate on the special education advisory board, continuous improvement council, or other school committees and learn about and support UDL through those mechanisms. At this time, these LEAs do not pursue additional community buy-in specific to UDL, but strive to make the community aware and continue to collaborate with the community to support education in general.

There is variation in how much LEAs tap into CAST as a resource. Five of the interviewed LEAs are aware of CAST and, at a minimum, have visited the CAST Web site. Some use tools and activities developed by CAST and have participated in training offered by that organization. Two LEAs have used the book *Teaching Every Student in the Digital*

Age: Universal Design for Learning by David H. Rose & Anne Meyer (ASCD, 2002) as the core of initial training; one LEA gives every teacher a copy of the book.

Benefits

According to the interviewees, UDL provides benefits to students, teachers, and administrators. They reported an increase in student learning, student performance, and high-stakes/accountability test scores. Additionally, they believe that due in part to the use of UDL, student behavior improves and students demonstrate a greater love of learning, are more engaged, have fun, and show excitement in learning.

Interviewees reported that teachers are more attuned to individual students, better able to address individual learning styles, and more energized and excited about teaching. The teachers also collaborate and discuss academics, including sharing ideas and strategies to support learning, more often. There are higher-quality interactions between teachers because they discuss teaching strategies and student outcomes more than before using UDL. Interviewees reported that administrators benefit because there are fewer discipline issues to address, fewer referrals to special education, a reduced number of upset parents, a reduced number of grievances from teachers, and improved student test scores.

Challenges

Interviewees indicated that time and money are barriers, but stated that these resources are barriers for any improvements, such as those that result from the adoption of UDL. Interviewees commented that additional funding and release time for teachers to attend professional development and stay current with technology usage would be helpful. Some LEAs struggle to balance what the students need and what the LEA can afford. Interviewees reported that these challenges do not prevent the implementation of UDL practices.

The interviewees expressed concern about keeping and expanding UDL practices when there is turnover in local-level administrative positions, especially the superintendent. A few interviewees discussed the philosophical challenge of changing belief systems regarding good instructional practice. UDL requires teachers to think differently and change their belief systems and practices, which is a challenge because teachers often need to experience success before making a change. Some interviewees believe that the motivation and momentum carried by other teachers who regularly implement UDL practices positively influence resisters as UDL benefits become evident. Another challenge is educating others to understand UDL as a framework for good instructional practice and not simply the incorporation of technology in the classroom.

Some LEAs struggled with their technology infrastructure and support initially, but work with what they have. Some interviewees indicated funding to maintain and update technology on a regular basis is needed, and others indicated funding to purchase more technology, especially Smart Boards, is needed. As teachers use technology, they need more knowledge and information on how to incorporate its use in the classroom to support UDL principles. Interviewees reported that high-quality professional development specific to UDL in the classroom is needed as well as technology training and support.

Future Directions

All LEAs involved in the interviews have plans to continue and expand the implementation of UDL practices in their schools. They are operating at varying levels regarding UDL implementation. Some referred generally to a vision and policy, while others were more specific about technology needs or expansion plans. One interviewee would like to organize a UDL policy across the district and cement a good framework to guarantee that good instructional practices remain in the district as administrators and school board members change. Another commented that he strives to ensure UDL is viewed as a continuum in his district and continues to grow, but at a pace that allows for demonstration of positive outcomes and thereby results in administrative support. Another aims to integrate UDL into curriculum meetings to strengthen the implementation of UDL practices. Interviewees from one LEA were more specific about technology and indicated that they want to have laptops and wireless access; add amplification systems for art, music, and physical education rooms; and update old systems to make them more teacher-friendly. Additionally, another LEA recently completed a UDL rubric to conduct self-assessments and obtain a baseline of implementation so they can create an effective professional development plan and have useful information for school action plans.

RECOMMENDATIONS

Respondents in this study provided the following advice for other LEAs that plan to implement UDL practices:

- Ensure that a commitment to student learning through good instructional practices exists.
- Start small and work with your teacher leaders and those interested in UDL to spread the implementation.
- Implement UDL for all students from the very beginning (i.e., not only for students who receive special education services).
- Develop a vision statement to decide where you are going and what you want UDL to look like.
- Use the available resources from state-funded projects, regional education agencies, and the community.
- Provide appropriate professional development and follow-up and encourage peer coaching/mentoring.
- Be sure you have an administrator and key teachers on board who believe in and support UDL practices.
- Allow UDL to grow at a pace that demonstrates effectiveness.
- Get involved in CAST training and resources.
- Begin implementation at elementary schools and expand into secondary schools.

CONCLUSION

Based on interviewee responses, LEAs are at various stages of implementation of UDL practices. All interviewees believe UDL is best practice and highly beneficial for all students. All expressed a positive approach to implementing UDL and addressing any challenges. They are pleased with the benefits for the students and observe changes such as improved test scores, greater interest in learning, and higher motivation and excitement about learning and school. All but one interviewee indicated it is best to begin the process of buy-in and implementation at the teacher level and allow it to develop from the bottom-up instead of from a top-down mandate.

A few interviewees expressed a perspective that technology is what makes UDL effective, but others indicated it is the flexibility and creativity of teachers that makes it effective. Overall, the LEAs support the theoretical principles of UDL by encouraging teachers to plan creatively and take risks in order to provide multiple and flexible means of presentation, expression, and engagement to benefit all students; finding funds to purchase and update technology; and providing time for teachers to collaborate and plan lessons that integrate UDL practices.

Based on background research and information gained from these interviews, Project Forum recommends the following to support the expansion of UDL for the benefit of all students:

- Convene a national forum to share information and experiences and develop recommended strategies or processes for UDL implementation in LEAs.
- Place a greater focus on marketing UDL as a best practice.
- Incorporate terminology that supports UDL practices in future federal and state law and policy.
- Ensure that high-stakes accountability measures incorporate principles of UDL.
- Create mechanisms to provide instructionally based technology support.
- Showcase LEAs that are effectively incorporating UDL practices at national conferences and meetings and through other means.
- Create and integrate courses on UDL in education curriculum at institutes of higher education.
- Educate parents and community members about UDL practices and its benefits.
- Make funding available for technology and professional development to ensure UDL practices become a consistent practice through all levels of education.

REFERENCES

Rose, D., & Meyer, A. (2002). Teaching every student in the digital age: Universal design for learning. Alexandria, VA: Association for Supervision and Curriculum Development.

Note: This report was prepared for Project Forum at the National Association of State Directors of Special Education. Project Forum is a cooperative agreement funded by the Office of Special Education Progress of the U.S. Department of Education. For more information, go to www.projectforum.org.

The report was supported by the U.S. Department of Education (Cooperative Agreement No. H326F050001). However, the opinions expressed herein do not necessarily reflect the positions of the U.S. Department of Education, and no official endorsement by the department should be inferred.

CHAPTER NINE

Universal Design Concept Pushed for Education

CHRISTINA A. SAMUELS

EDITORS' NOTE

In 2007, Education Week *ran a front-page feature on the work of the National UDL Task Force. As the article explains, the task force, which had formed the previous year, represents a remarkable coalition of organizations spanning general education, special education, and advocacy groups—remarkable because, by the task force participants' own reckoning, these groups rarely agree on how to address the stickiest issues of education policy. Yet all see UDL as a unifying framework, one that could help meet everyone's goal of raising achievement for all students through better curriculum design. In this case, the task force came together to recommend language on UDL around issues of standards and assessment.*

Coincidentally, the article appeared the same week as the first National UDL Summit in Washington, D.C., in which some one hundred leaders in education policy, publishing, research, technology development, professional development, and practice gathered to review the state of the field and recommend an agenda for growing it.

The same design principles that brought braille panels to public elevators and curb cuts to city sidewalks should be imported to the classroom and used to transform lessons and textbooks, says a coalition of education groups. Called universal design for learning, or UDL, the philosophy advocates creating lessons and classroom materials that are flexible enough to accommodate different learning styles. The coalition has drafted language it wants to have included in federal education law. A requirement for states to "develop a comprehensive plan to address the implementation of universal design for learning" is in the draft bill for reauthorizing the No Child Left Behind Act (NCLB) released in August [2007] by the House Education and Labor Committee. UDL is also supported in a reauthorization measure sponsored by Senator Joseph I. Lieberman, I-CT, and cosponsored by Senators Norm Coleman, R-MN, and Mary L. Landrieu, D-LA. Much of the Senate bill includes language taken verbatim from the coalition's materials.

According to the tenets of UDL, lessons should be designed with accessibility in mind, instead of retrofitting existing materials in an attempt to accommodate students with learning differences. While the early days of UDL focused on helping students with disabilities, supporters say it has benefits for any student, including those who are learning English, gifted students, or students who simply learn better through methods other than a teacher's lecture. Sometimes, accommodating different learning styles can be achieved through the use of technology. For instance, computer devices can "read" a book aloud to a student who is blind. However, low-tech methods can be valid applications of UDL as well. An example of a simple application is allowing a student to create a poster that visually depicts the main ideas in a classroom reading assignment, rather than asking the student to write a book report, if he or she has difficulty with written language. Developing alternative methods for students to show they've mastered a concept is an integral part of UDL.

Support for the concept has linked several education and disability-rights organizations, even those that have been in disagreement over other aspects of the No Child Left Behind law. Some groups call for softening or eliminating some of the sanctions imposed on schools when students in any of various subgroups, including students with disabilities, do not make adequate yearly progress under the law. Other groups fear that removing such sanctions would mean students with disabilities might not get access to rigorous instruction.

But twenty-eight organizations have put aside those differences and come together in support of UDL, including the National Education Association, the National School Boards Association, the Council for Exceptional Children, and a host of groups that work to help children with specific disabilities. "I don't see how it can fail to be compelling," said Ricki Sabia, the associate director of the national-policy center of the National Down Syndrome Society, in New York City, and one of the main drivers behind including UDL language in the reauthorized federal school law. "There's only one thing in NCLB that we're all in agreement on."

The school boards association supports UDL because it can help all students, said Reginald M. Felton, the director of federal relations for the Alexandria, Virginia–based group. "Everyone realizes if both the special education and regular education communities can talk about the same goals, they have a lot more chance of being successful," he said.

The education groups are currently working to include more of the coalition's UDL language in the House education committee's draft reauthorization bill, including a precise definition of the educational philosophy. Universal design for learning does not represent an educational package or a simple set of techniques, according to practitioners. Rather, it offers a variety of solutions to different problems, and can be compared to accessibility in the physical environment. Some sidewalk-design elements, such as curb cuts, were originally meant to accommodate people who use wheelchairs. Television closed-captioning was intended to aid people who are deaf.

Over time, those accommodations have become useful to people who do not have mobility or hearing problems, advocates point out. And both are so common now that they're practically invisible, said David H. Rose, a cofounder of the Center for Applied Special Technology (CAST), in Wakefield, Massachusetts. Founded in 1984, CAST has spearheaded the development of classroom materials based on universal design principles. Removing barriers from learning materials seems just as logical when people take the time to think about the idea, Mr. Rose said. But instead, he said, people have tended to depend on the use of technology so students can access existing lessons or materials, rather than rethinking the lessons to make them more readily accessible in the first place. CAST itself first focused solely on creating so-called assistive technology to allow students with disabilities to work with existing lesson plans. But the center's experts learned that making classroom materials accessible doesn't always mean students are learning the lessons teachers are trying to impart, Mr. Rose said.

"The view was more like, you fix this kid so they can fit in better," Mr. Rose said. "The more we did it, the more we could see it wasn't working." For example, highlighting key words in a text for a student isn't helpful if those words represent the lesson students are supposed to be learning on their own. True universal design requires that educators think deeply about what each lesson is about. Those goals then guide how UDL is implemented, Mr. Rose said. CAST's mission still includes developing software and hardware solutions for meeting the needs of students with disabilities, Mr. Rose said. But the organization also offers classes and consulting services that teach educators how to rethink their lessons and customize them for students with different needs.

Some states have already moved to implement UDL on their own. For four years, Indiana has provided grants to schools that write detailed proposals for how they would use UDL principles in their classrooms. School staff members also have to spend time learning about UDL, and at the end of each school's grant, report on their achievements. Vicki Hershman, the state project director of the program that oversees the grants, said educators at first saw UDL as a way to get technology dollars for their schools. Now, they understand that the intent is to transform the way lessons are developed and taught. She agrees with the goal of having UDL language written into the No Child Left Behind law. "The UDL project supports all the other general education and special education initiatives we have going on," Ms. Hershman said. Under the grant program, one school developed a Civil War module for middle school students that included audiotapes and text-to-speech software. Another school that received a grant created a fourth-grade lesson on long division that included an opportunity for students to work together in small groups to create a rap song about division, using free Web-based software.

Michigan is in the early stages of trying to start its own statewide UDL initiative, said Jeff Diedrich, who oversees the adaptive technology division for the state department of education. The state is proceeding slowly, though, Mr. Diedrich said. Proponents don't want to present UDL as a product that can be purchased, or as a fad initiative that quickly fades. "I'm seeing UDL get more and more attention, but it's a danger that once something reaches the status of a buzzword, it's on the way out," Mr. Diedrich said. "But if you can start people thinking about the curriculum as having a disability, instead of the student having a disability, it'll be worth it."

This article originally appeared in *Education Week*, 27(10), 1 and 12. Reprinted with permission.

CHAPTER TEN

Assistive Technology, NIMAS, and UDL

From Some Students to All Students

DAVID H. ROSE, TED S. HASSELBRING, SKIP STAHL,
AND JOY ZABALA

EDITORS' NOTE

In this chapter, four of the leading names in educational technology design, especially as it relates to students with disabilities, take up the sometimes confusing subject of just exactly how universal design for learning and assistive technology relate to one another: comparing and contrasting the two initiatives. The article attempts to correct a common misunderstanding that UDL is purely a technology initiative or that, in some way, is meant to replace assistive technology. The authors argue that UDL and AT are complementary initiatives that support the learning of all individuals.

The original text of this article, written in 2005, discusses UDL through the filter of a technology initiative; however, as has been noted elsewhere in this book, UDL addresses the whole curriculum—the goals, methods, materials, and assessments that can either open up or shut off learning opportunities for individuals. A UDL curriculum may or may not include new digital technologies, though when designed well, digital technologies can make the curriculum work better for all learners. The technology is just a means to an end. UDL starts from the premise that curriculum should adapt to learner differences rather than placing that expectation on diverse learners. So rather than simply assist learners in making do with an inadequate and inaccessible curriculum, UDL aims to address the source of inaccessibility itself: the curriculum, not the learner. Clearly for many students with disabilities, assistive technologies are absolutely necessary in order to participate and succeed in a universally designed curriculum.

New technologies are transforming education, and in no domain more dramatically or successfully than in the education of students with disabilities. Although the existing benefits of technology for students with disabilities are already widely recognized, the potential benefits are likely to be even more profound and pervasive than present practices would suggest. To ensure full realization of technology's potential for students with disabilities, the Office of Special Education Programs (OSEP) has funded a series of assistive and instructional technology-related programs including, at the time this original version of this article was written, two national centers with a strong focus on technology: the National Assistive Technology Research Institute (NATRI; 2001–2006) at the University of Kentucky and the National Center on Accessing the General Curriculum (NCAC; 1999–2005) at CAST. While both centers focused on the role of technology, their work was neither duplicative nor competitive. Rather, each researched a distinct role for technology in improving education for students with disabilities. The question of how these two approaches could enhance and even support one another for the further benefit of students with disabilities was fundamentally important.

In this chapter researchers from both centers provide a framework for further discussion of this significant issue by articulating the points of commonality and difference between AT and UDL. Some individuals may see AT and UDL as identical or, conversely, antithetical. We believe that neither view is accurate but instead that AT and UDL, while different, are completely complementary—much like two sides of the same coin. Advances in one approach prompt advances in the other, and this reciprocity will evolve in ways that will maximize their mutual benefits, making it essential that both approaches are pursued vigorously and distinctively. Through a better understanding and melding of AT and UDL, the lives of individuals with disabilities will ultimately be improved.

TWO ROLES FOR TECHNOLOGY: ASSISTIVE TECHNOLOGY AND UNIVERSAL DESIGN FOR LEARNING

When most people imagine the role of technology for students with disabilities they think of AT. Relatively low-tech AT (like canes, wheelchairs, and eyeglasses) has been in place for a century, but the high-tech AT that has emerged over the last two decades has had a particularly dramatic impact on education, and has also captured the imagination of the public (Behrmann & Schaff, 2001; Edyburn, 2002). These newer technologies include diverse items such as electronic mobility switches and alternative keyboards for individuals with physical disabilities, computer-screen enlargers and text-to-speech readers for individuals with visual disabilities, and calculators and spell-checkers for individuals with learning disabilities. The enormous power of such computer-based technologies to assist individuals with disabilities in overcoming barriers to educational access, participation, and progress is evident in the research base (Crealock & Sitko, 1990; Hebert & Murdock, 1994; MacArthur & Haynes, 1995; MacArthur, Haynes, Malouf, Harris, & Owings, 1990; Raskind & Higgins, 1999; van Daal & Reitsma, 1993; von Tetzchner, Rogne, & Lilleeng, 1997; Xin & Rieth, 2001).

In contrast to AT, universal design for learning, in its emergence from the universal design movement in architecture and product development, is relatively new. One indication of this newness is the lack of clarity about what constitutes "universal design" in the education arena, and a lack of differentiation among a number of approaches that address individual differences and disabilities. For example, there is frequent confusion about the relationship between UDL and AT, in large part because both approaches take advantage of modern technology (Bowser & Reed, 2000; Hitchcock & Stahl, 2003). UDL has goals similar to those of AT, including the overarching goal of increasing the access, participation, and progress of students with disabilities in our schools. However, the approaches differ in important ways. The UDL approach is to create products and/or environments that are designed, from the outset, to accommodate individuals with a wider range of abilities and disabilities than can be accommodated by traditional applications. Rather than retrofitting ramps to existing buildings, the universal design movement in architecture educated architects in how to design buildings that are inherently accessible (Story, Mueller, & Mace, 1998). Such buildings tend to be more accommodating and flexible for all users. In a related fashion, UDL seeks to educate curriculum developers, teachers, and administrators in how to design curricula and learning environments that from the outset make learning accessible to the widest range of students. The focus of UDL, then, is the learning environment rather than any particular student. Its purpose is to identify potential barriers to learning in a curriculum or classroom and to reduce such barriers through better initial designs, designs with the inherent flexibility to enable the curriculum itself to adjust to individual learners (Rose & Meyer, 2002).

Thus, although both the AT and UDL approaches may use modern technology to improve education for students with disabilities, the technology tools have a different site and mechanism of action. In AT, modern technology is employed at the level of the individual student to help him or her overcome barriers in the curriculum and living environments. With UDL, modern technology targets the curriculum itself; that is, technology is used to create curriculum and environments that, by design, lack traditional barriers to learning.

Distinctions Between AT and UDL

UDL and AT can be thought of as two approaches existing on a continuum. At the ends of this continuum, the two approaches are easily distinguishable. Toward the middle of the continuum, such easy distinctions are muddied, and there are greater points of interaction and commonality. Here we emphasize the interactions, because any comprehensive solution is likely to require attention to AT, UDL, and their effective integration. However, some crucial distinctions must also be understood.

Assistive technology is technology that increases, improves, or maintains the functional capabilities of students with disabilities. Usually it is specifically designed to assist individuals with disabilities in overcoming barriers in their environment and in increasing their opportunities for independence. Because the intended consumers are usually individuals, specifically individuals with disabilities, AT can be carefully engineered, fitted, and adapted to the specific strengths and weaknesses of each person. In that regard AT is unique, personal (travels with the individual), customized, and dedicated.

Universal design is a process for designing general (i.e., used by everyone) products or structures in such a way as to reduce barriers for any individual (either with or without disabilities) and to increase opportunities for the widest possible range of users. Because the intended consumers are groups of individuals (i.e., a whole community), universal designs are engineered for flexibility, designed to anticipate the need for alternatives, options, and adaptations. In that regard, universal designs are often malleable and variable rather than dedicated. They are not unique or personal, but universal and inclusive, accommodating diversity.

The term *universal design for learning* emphasizes the special purpose of learning environments—they are not created to provide information or shelter but to support and foster the changes in knowledge and skills that we call learning. While providing accessible spaces and materials is often essential to learning, it is not sufficient. Success requires that the components of pedagogy—the techniques, methods, scaffolds, and processes that are embedded in classrooms and curricula—are also accessible, and that the measure of their success is learning. The UDL framework is based in the neuroscience of learning, and its principles emphasize three key aspects of pedagogy: the means of representing information, the means for the expression of knowledge, and the means of engagement in learning (Rose & Meyer, 2002).

The Importance of Interaction and Integration of AT and UDL

In practice, universal design and AT often work in concert to achieve optimal and practical results (Hitchcock & Stahl, 2003). The following examples illustrate the value of integrating universal design and AT in architecture and the classroom, respectively.

Integration of assistive technology and universal design in architecture

Consider the problem of mobility for the person with a physical disability. On the one hand, mobility can be viewed as primarily an individual problem—individual physical limitations create a unique, personal need for adaptation or enhancement. Such a view underscores the need for *assistive* solutions, solutions that are designed to help the individual to overcome his limitations, usually through application of technology. Electronic wheelchairs, wheeled walkers, and the like are examples. The advantage of such solutions is that they can be precisely tailored to the specific needs of the individual—adaptive seating for support, individual switch placement for control, and so forth.

On the other hand, mobility can also be viewed as an *environmental* problem—limitations in the design of the environment create physical barriers to mobility. A building that offers only stairs for moving between floors or rooms creates barriers for many individuals, including those who are using wheelchairs or wheeled walkers for mobility. Such a view underscores the need for a properly designed environment—one that provides alternatives like ramps and elevators. The advantage of such solutions is that they are universal, that is, they benefit not only a specific individual facing a mobility barrier, but also many individuals, including *nondisabled* people, who are using baby carriages, carts, strollers, or pulling their luggage on wheels.

In reality, both the individual view and the environmental view are essential. If we focus only on the design of AT, we will inherit an environment that is so poorly designed and barrier ridden that mobility will be limited for many individuals, creating a need for AT that is prohibitively extensive and expensive. The next generation of wheelchairs, for example, will be able to surmount barriers like stairs—a great advance—but they will cost many times more than existing wheelchairs, will be too cumbersome for many environments, and will still face barriers like spiral staircases, ladders, and so on.

On the other hand, if we focus on universal designs at the exclusion of AT, we will fail to consider the customized adaptations that many people need and will build environments that are too complex and expensive. Many next-generation buildings, for example, will include ubiquitous moving walkways, but these will not adapt sufficiently for all individuals and will be prohibitively expensive and cumbersome for many buildings. Assistive technologies make universal designs more effective.

The most powerful and cost-effective solutions are ones that integrate these two approaches, yielding universal designs that are aware of the requirements of AT (e.g., buildings whose ramps have corners and inclines that are accessible to power wheelchairs) and AT that is aware of the affordances of universally designed buildings (e.g., wheelchairs that incorporate infrared switches to activate universally designed door and elevator buttons). Such integrated designs are not only more economical and ecological, they reflect the fact that disabilities are defined by the interaction between the environment and the individual.

Integration of AT and UDL in the classroom

Consider the problem that mastering a history concept poses for a student with a reading disability. Most history curricula pose significant barriers to such a student, especially the predominance of text. Most of the content is presented in text, and most of the assessment requires writing. This problem, too, can be viewed and solved in two different ways.

From an AT perspective, the problem can be considered an individual problem—it is clearly the individual student's reading disability that interferes with his or her ability to master the history content and demonstrate knowledge. This view fosters solutions that address the individual's weaknesses—remedial reading classes, special tutoring, and AT, for example. Of these, AT is particularly valuable because it provides independent means for the student to overcome his or her limitations— for example, by using a spell-checker or audio version of the digital history book.

A UDL perspective, on the other hand, sees the problem as an environmental problem— the history curriculum's overreliance on printed text raises barriers to engagement and mastery for many students. This view fosters solutions targeting limitations in the curriculum rather than limitations in the student. Imagine a multimedia curriculum that provides digital, universally designed media that offer diverse options for viewing and manipulating content and expressing knowledge. Within such a flexible curriculum fewer students face barriers; digital text can speak aloud to reduce decoding barriers for students with dyslexia; digital images or video provide an alternative representation that reduces barriers in comprehension for students with language-based disabilities while providing descriptions and captions for students who are blind or deaf; and keyboard alternatives may reduce barriers in navigation and control for students with physical disabilities. These UDL solutions have the advantage of enhancing learning for many different kinds of students (Rose & Meyer, 2002).

In reality, both kinds of solutions are needed (Hitchcock & Stahl, 2003). In an educational setting, the disadvantage of exclusively using AT is that it is not integrated with the learning goals of a given lesson. If that is the case, AT may not be helpful, or may even interfere, from an educational standpoint. For example, a spell-checker would be a valuable AT for a student with learning disabilities in many situations, but in a lesson on spelling it would be counterproductive. The proper use of a spell-checker must be determined contextually, with an eye toward the goals of the lesson rather than merely the student's general access to technologies (MacArthur, Graham, Haynes, & De la Paz, 1996).

At the same time, a purely UDL solution has the disadvantage that some built-in accommodations, particularly for students with low-incidence disabilities, are cumbersome, inefficient, or prohibitively expensive when included as an element of the basic curriculum. It is not necessary or advantageous to provide a screen reader or alternative keyboard with every piece of curriculum—students are better served by individual AT that has been adapted and fitted precisely to their own capacities and that can be used across many different pieces of curriculum without further adaptation or change of settings.

It is essential that universally designed curricula incorporate common assistive technologies and accommodate their features in the design process. For example, a UDL curriculum that is not aware of the requirements for keyboard equivalents in order to interface properly with single-switch access devices and alternative keyboards cannot provide universal access. Similarly, assistive technologies must be aware of the features built into universally designed curricula so that they are complementary and expansive rather than redundant. A text-to-speech technology that does not recognize common tagging features (like links or long descriptions) cannot provide adequate access to curricular materials.

In the past, there have been all too few examples of universally designed curricula, and even fewer examples of optimal linkages between such curricula and AT. We believe the future will bring many more. The next section provides a contemporary example of the kinds of progress that we anticipate.

CURRENT LINKAGE BETWEEN UDL AND AT

New developments in policy and practice are illuminating the educational landscape ahead and shaping the operational linkage between AT and UDL. One illustrative example is the recent inclusion of the National Instructional Materials Accessibility Standard (NIMAS) as part of the IDEA reauthorization in 2004.

We begin this section by examining the policy supporting this new legislation and the technological efficiencies it is designed to implement. We then discuss how the increased, timely availability of alternative accessible versions of textbooks, a development supported by NIMAS, promises to have a significant impact on the educational use of AT and relates to the integration of AT and UDL. Last, we address how this state of affairs may impact the education of students with disabilities now and in the future.

Constraints on the Availability of Accessible Textbooks

As noted earlier, traditional print-based textbooks so prevalent in most classrooms pose barriers for many students with disabilities. While many students who are educated in general education classrooms can take advantage of the resources available in textbooks, these same resources are largely unavailable to students who cannot see the words or images on a page, cannot hold a book or turn its pages, cannot decode the text, or cannot comprehend the syntax that supports comprehension. These students may all require different supports to extract meaning from information that is book bound, and many require the retrofitting of print-based materials.

Two problems constrain the availability of accessible textbooks. The first is a problem of policy, the second a problem of technology.

Policy

Copyright laws provide publishers with the protection under which they produce, format, and distribute instructional materials. The content found in most textbooks used in K–12 classrooms is owned by individual or organizational rights holders who, not themselves publishers, grant fee-based permission to curriculum publishers to reproduce and use their materials. These permissions allow publishers to combine proprietary content with their own materials and distribute a product in an agreed-upon format or formats: print, audiobook, digital, and so on. The original format for most K–12 textbooks is print, and traditionally it is this format for which publishers have secured and purchased copyright permissions. Unfortunately, when this is the case, legal agreements may prevent publishers from providing more accessible versions of the materials as commercial products.

However, students with disabilities and those supporting them have a legal means to acquire accessible versions of print textbooks by virtue of an existing copyright exemption. In September 1996, President Bill Clinton authorized Section 121 of the United States Code, amending Chapter 1 of Title 17 and establishing a limitation on exclusive rights in copyrighted works. This legislative adjustment, commonly referred to as the Chafee Amendment (originally introduced by Sen. John Chafee, R-RI), was specifically designed to create a legal conduit that would significantly enhance the flow of accessible, alternative-format works to the blind or other persons with disabilities. The Chafee Amendment copyright exemption was the culmination of efforts by disability advocates and the publishing community to create a mechanism that would obviate the need to seek, on a case-by-case basis, permission of the copyright holder every time a print work needed to be transformed into an alternative format for use by a person with a disability.

This exemption was designed as a relief valve for publishers and individuals with disabilities, allowing for the carefully monitored transformation of inaccessible materials into specialized formats for use by qualifying students (Perl, 2003*)*.

Unfortunately, under current copyright law, only students with qualifying print disabilities may be provided with accessible braille, audio, or digital text versions of print materials without directly seeking permission from (and giving compensation to) the copyright holder. If the most conservative interpretation of the Chafee Amendment guidelines is applied, less than 5 percent of the nearly 6 million students who receive IDEA services and support would qualify to receive accessible instructional materials. In practice, there has been some flexibility in interpreting the Chafee Amendment guidelines; nevertheless, the fact that the Chafee Amendment provides the only legal means of distributing accessible versions of proprietary materials to students with disabilities imposes a significant limitation when it becomes the basis for a compliance mandate in such expansive legislation as the IDEA.

The language in the 2004 IDEA reauthorization includes a proposed modification to the copyright exemption that would allow publishers to provide digital files to *authorized* third parties specifically for the creation of accessible versions of textbooks for students with qualifying disabilities. This provision would include curriculum publishers within the Chafee exemption. While this modification would not expand access to these materials to a broader range of students than is currently identified under existing copyright law, it would significantly facilitate the flow of textbook files from producers to converters to users.

The significance of the inclusion of NIMAS in the IDEA as a mandate for both states and publishers cannot be overstated. It reflects widespread agreement among educators, disability advocates, and publishers, and it creates a precedent-setting national agenda by recognizing that instructional materials themselves, rather than the students using them, are in need of improvement. However, the fact that the right to accessible versions of print materials is extended to only a subset of IDEA-eligible students necessitates a more comprehensive alternative approach.

Technology

Beyond its application to IDEA-eligible students, the Chafee exemption created a new avenue for compliance with other federal mandates, including Section 504 of the Rehabilitation Act and the Americans with Disabilities Act. After passage of the Chafee Amendment in 1996, special educators, disability service providers, advocacy organizations, and new not-for-profits created specifically to take advantage of the copyright exemption began to actively transform print materials into accessible alternative versions. As these localized operations became more sophisticated and learned to exploit the potential of desktop computer technologies, textbooks became the content most often transformed. As a result, it is now common to find alternative-format materials produced in schools and districts, postsecondary institutions, and regional education service centers nationwide. Not surprisingly, as more educational institutions have become equipped to create alternative-format materials, students, their families, and their advocates have increased their awareness of and, subsequently, their requests for this content.

A variety of stakeholders—educators, national advocacy organizations, curriculum publishers, and others—have realized that the copyright exemption, originally designed to address individual instances of print inaccessibility, is increasingly being relied upon as the cornerstone for large-scale content transformation. This creates a problem because much like the architectural retrofitting referenced earlier, large-scale content transformation can be costly and time consuming and often results in an academic experience that is not equal to that provided to nondisabled students. Because the creation of these alternative editions begins with retrofitting and transforming an existing print version, each one represents a custom product. There is no economy of scale, no consistent quality control, no guarantee of efficient or timely delivery, and no guarantee of a consistent or harmonious interface with changing assistive technologies.

NIMAS: Integrating Policy and Technology

In the late 1980s, the Instructional Materials and Solutions Forum (convened by the American Foundation for the Blind) brought together approximately forty national stakeholder organizations to address, among other things, the need for a scalable technological solution that would make the process of providing accessible, alternative versions of curriculum materials more efficient, consistent, and timely. This initiative ultimately resulted in the creation of the National File Format Technical Panel in 2002 by the U. S. Department of Education, Office of

Special Education Programs (Rose & Stahl, 2003). Charged with identifying the technical specifications for the NIMAS, the agreement reached by the technical panel in the fall of 2003 resulted in the identification of a technological format for source (publisher-provided) files that will facilitate the efficient and consistent production of quality alternative formats. The inclusion of this recommendation in the reauthorization of IDEA reinforces the technical consensus with a national mandate for adoption (NCAC, 2003; Rose & Stahl, 2003).

The National File Format Technical Panel recommended that the NIMAS version 1.0 be an application of an XML-based (eXtensible Markup Language) standard. The panel recommended the DTBook element set, a component of the ANSI/NISO Z39.86 standard. This recommendation aligned the NIMAS with the work being done concurrently by the DAISY Consortium (www.daisy.org), the Open eBook Forum (www.openebook.org; now International Digital Publishing Forum), and the IMS Global Learning Consortium (www.imsproject.org), thus ensuring cross-industry standards conformance.

The curriculum publishing community agreed to make available digital files containing all of the elements of the print textbooks (a combination of XML and PDF files), and further agreed to identify the XML components according to the NIMAS 1.0 standard. As a result of this consensus, third-party conversion organizations (Recording for the Blind & Dyslexic, American Printing House for the Blind, National Braille Press, etc.) and school districts will receive consistent, valid, and well-formatted digital source files from which to create accessible and student-ready versions. This will cut the conversion time—and therefore the distribution time—significantly. The promise of the NIMAS standard is that alternative versions will be made available to students at the same time that print versions are made available to their nondisabled classmates.

While this agreement will significantly streamline the conversion process by eliminating existing incongruities in publisher files, its true impact will likely be as a precedent-setting designation of the critical importance of separating content from its presentation. XML-based files remain malleable, their baseline component labeling (tags) can be extended to encompass a wide range of presentation needs, and content stored in this format can ultimately be transformed not only into accessible alternative versions, but into new, universally designed, enhanced learning editions as well.

The NIMAS standard is both a policy advance (an advance that ensures equitable access to educational materials for all students) and a technology advance (an advance in the publishing workflow that will lead to more efficient distribution for publishers and consumers alike). While NIMAS is not yet broadly based enough to be called a true universal design, it is clearly the foundation for future universal designs.

CURRENT INTEGRATION OF UDL AND AT: ACCESSIBLE CURRICULUM CONTENT INCREASES THE EFFICACY OF ASSISTIVE TECHNOLOGY

The increased availability of flexible and inherently accessible core curriculum materials under NIMAS will probably lead to an increased awareness of AT and a broadening of its use. The reason is that accessible information is not necessarily optimized for every potential user and, therefore, may prompt the use of AT. Consider, for example, familiar technological solutions for everyday tasks: word processing for writing and revision, spell-checking for editing, e-mail for communication, financial software to reconcile our bank balances. Each requires the interplay between an application program (word processor, e-mail, or spreadsheet software) and the files that contain the information being rendered (word processing document, e-mail message, or financial worksheet). These software applications may each be customized to fit the individual needs of a user, and AT is simply the magnification of that customization to accommodate needs that are not inherently addressed by the application itself.

To take another example, a Web page can be built to ensure the highest degree of accessibility according to the World Wide Web Consortium's Web Access Initiative Standards (www.w3.org/wai). But the capabilities of the browser—Internet Explorer, Netscape, Mozilla, Opera, Safari, or others—supply the transformational energy needed to realize this accessibility. Assistive technology acts on accessible instructional materials in an identical fashion, and, much as there is a direct correlation between the capabilities and use of browsers and the availability and functions of Web pages, a similar relationship exists between AT and the materials it acts upon.

What will be the effect of NIMAS, a foundation for universal design, on AT? The availability of a universal file format will optimize AT in a number of ways. For example:

- All publishers will be producing a common format for access, greatly reducing the complexity of design for interfacing AT.
- Every state and district will optimally accept and use materials in a common format, greatly reducing the complexity of training and support for the personnel who will administer and use AT.
- Every student who needs them will get high-quality digital accessible materials in a timely fashion, rendering their AT more effective for classroom learning with their peers.

Complementarily, the availability of high-quality AT in the classroom will render these new materials immediately useful for students and their teachers, and will allow teachers, special educators, and AT professionals to concentrate on learning rather than production of accessible materials. While either universally designed materials or AT in isolation can be helpful, it is at the intersection of the two that information access, and ultimately learning, becomes most individualized and appropriate.

The intrinsic flexibility of digital alternative-format versions of textbooks supports transformations not previously possible. For example, accessible alternative versions of textbooks can be transformed into braille files ready to be sent to an embosser for the creation of printed braille. Alternatively, digital textbook files can be formatted for a refreshable braille display, or for display on a computer screen with instantaneous onscreen braille-to-text and text-to-braille conversion capabilities. This application allows teachers of the visually impaired, the majority of whom are sighted, to quickly and efficiently locate a paragraph, sentence, phrase, or even single word reference in a document—something that is very difficult to do with print braille. Similarly, subsections of a document can be translated to braille onscreen and either sent to a refreshable display print or an embosser, or translated into synthetic speech and saved as a portable audio (MP3) format. The alternative format (in this example, digital) provides the flexibility and the inherent transformative potential; the AT, refreshable braille display, synthetic speech, MP3 player, and so on allow the user (or those teaching them) to customize the experience for optimal benefit.

The schools, districts, and even states that have begun to incorporate flexible digital versions of textbooks into their educational practice have increased their understanding of the importance and potential of AT devices and software. Because the emphasis on alternative format materials is on core curriculum resources, this awareness (and growing expertise) is extending well beyond special education and into general education classrooms. As a result, it is not as unusual as it once was to encounter a workshop on supported reading software during an institute for language arts teachers, and many schools are equipped with portable smart keyboards for word processing and text downloading; even MP3 players are no longer anomalies in the classroom—and they are not being used solely to store music.

THE FUTURE OF ACCESSIBILITY: MOVING FROM *SOME* STUDENTS TO *ALL* STUDENTS

Existing copyright constraints limit the distribution of accessible alternative-format materials, and thus fail to address the needs of all students with disabilities. But the establishment of the NIMAS and its inclusion in the IDEA reauthorization does create the foundation for that solution. The scope of current local efforts to use technology to create accessible alternative versions of core textbooks has highlighted the need while simultaneously exposing the inaccuracies and inefficiencies inherent in an uncoordinated approach. It has also illuminated the weaknesses in the present system, establishing the impetus necessary to promote widespread change.

The most effective approach to providing accessible versions of print textbooks entails the creation of a free market distribution model. In this model publishers would create alternative and accessible versions of print textbooks for direct distribution to states, districts, schools, and students at the same time that the print versions are made available. In this model, accessible (likely digital) versions could serve a broad range of students' needs, well beyond the needs identified in the narrow exemption from copyright laws granted by Chafee. The free market approach could eliminate the delay in the development and distribution of accessible digital versions that currently exists. However, for a free market system to become established, a number of conditions must be met.

First, education consumers (states, districts, schools) must demonstrate a willingness to pay for the value represented in the publishers' production and delivery of fully accessible instructional materials. If the growing array of state textbook adoption legislation—that is, legislation mandating the provision of accessible versions that go beyond requiring digital text files to the inclusion of graphical elements and easy-to-use navigation—is an indicator, the demand is beginning to be established.

Second, publishers must be able to reclaim the rights that have been exempted under the Chafee Amendment in order to facilitate production investments, including the acquisition of all rights required for reproduction and distribution of materials in digital formats. While nontrivial, obtaining these rights is made much more enticing if the intellectual property holders and the publishers perceive that adequate compensation is viable.

Third, the workflow that produces print textbooks has to be adjusted to accommodate the creation of digital versions, not as a deflection of core product development and manufacturing efforts but as a naturally occurring variation in the product cycle. Many of the large curriculum publishing companies have begun to move in this direction—some as a direct result of the NIMAS consensus—by establishing a digital workflow that can result in a number of published products, print textbooks and digital versions among them.

Fourth, third-party conversion entities must prepare to meet an increased demand for their expertise. As commercial publishers move to establish a capacity to produce accessible digital versions for sale on the open market, organizations and companies that now perform the final step in the alternative-format conversion, creating braille, digital audio, or otherwise accessible editions, will find an increased demand for their skills as subcontractors or codevelopers with curriculum materials producers.

None of these four conditions is felt to be unattainable, and the benefits to intellectual property holders, content developers, content conversion experts, and students with disabilities are readily apparent. Accessible digital versions would be provided to students with disabilities (who need them) and students without disabilities (who might prefer them). Intellectual property holders and content developers would be assured of adequate compensation and digital rights management. Content conversion experts would see their expertise in the development of alternative versions of instructional materials expand beyond the limited market in which they now exist into the broader educational enterprise. The NIMAS establishes an extensible foundation for moving this vision forward. This vision is moving toward a true universal design for learning.

BEYOND ACCESS—TOWARD THE LEARNING ENTERPRISE

While the stated purpose of determining the NIMAS specification was to facilitate the timely provision of accessible materials to students with disabilities, it is important to keep in mind that it is the nation's educational system within which these alternative versions will be provided. With that emphasis, the extent to which alternative, accessible versions of textbooks created from NIMAS-compliant source files enhance student *achievement* is a significant and very relevant question.

The answer to that question will require more research—research on outcomes (Edyburn, 2003). To date, flexible and accessible digital versions of core curriculum print textbooks have simply not been sufficiently available to measure their impact within the context of large-scale academic achievement. What is known, however, is that students with a wide range of disabling conditions—those who currently qualify as persons with print disabilities and those who do not—can benefit from universally designed instructional solutions (Rose & Meyer, 2002).

A recent extensive summary of research in this area has been prepared by NCAC at www.cast.org/ncac (Strangman, Hall, & Meyer, 2003). Among many studies in this area are the following:

- Students with language-related disabilities showed positive effects for word recognition, comprehension, and fluency when using digi-

tal texts with syllable- or letter name–level synthetic speech transformations (Elbro, Rasmussen, & Spelling, 1996).
- Students with attentional, organizational, and learning disabilities have shown increased academic gain when exposed to technology-supported concept mapping strategies (Anderson-Inman, Knox-Quinn, & Horney, 1996; Herl, O'Neil, Chung, & Schacter, 1999).
- Students who are deaf or hard of hearing show consistent academic gains when provided with the sequential text highlighting and supportive captions available with digital instructional materials (Andrews & Jordan, 1997; McInerney, Riley, & Osher, 1999).
- Students with low cognitive abilities demonstrate increased functional skills when exposed to flexible technologies that maximize their strengths while helping to compensate for their weaknesses (Carroll, 1993; Wehmeyer, Smith, Palmer, Davies, & Stock, 2003).

The true promise of NIMAS is that it provides a flexible but sturdy foundation for curricula that embody UDL and capitalize on ATs to make that learning accessible to everyone. Realization of the promise of NIMAS will be apparent as a cultural shift for students with disabilities: the shift from a focus on *access* to a focus on *learning*. That critical shift will depend upon the continued evolution of an optimal interplay between UDL and AT.

THE FUTURE OF ASSISTIVE TECHNOLOGY AND UNIVERSAL DESIGN FOR LEARNING

We expect a continuing dialogue along the continuum of universal design for learning and assistive technologies. As UDL matures, it will advance by incorporating many features now provided only by assistive technologies, in the same way that text-to-speech, spell-checking, and calculators can routinely be built into office word processing or that captioning is built into every television. As assistive technology matures, it will advance by assuming increasing connectivity with universal designs, taking advantage of the common structures (e.g., XML semantic tagging in a universally designed Web site) to provide highly individualized solutions that are not only oriented to sensory and motor abilities but also to cognitive and linguistic ones. During this period of AT and UDL maturation and advancement, we must make every effort to ensure that these two fields develop symbiotically. When UDL and AT are designed to coexist, learning for all individuals is enhanced.

In a world where we are very aware that understanding human behavior requires knowledge of the complex interaction between both cultural and individual development, we should not be surprised to find that fostering human learning will require access solutions that are optimal interactions between what is universal and what is individual.

REFERENCES

Anderson-Inman, L., Knox-Quinn, C., & Horney, M. A. (1996). Computer-based study strategies for students with learning disabilities: Individual differences associated with adoption level. *Journal of Learning Disabilities, 29*(5), 461–484.

Andrews, J. F., and Jordan, D. L. (1997, February). *Special education technology for the next century.* Proceedings of the 1997 CSF/CEC and TAM Conference on Special Education and Technology, San Diego, California.

Behrmann, M., & Schaff, J. (2001). Assisting educators with assistive technology: Enabling children to achieve independence in living and learning. *Children and Families, 42*(3), 24–28.

Bowser, G., & Reed, P. (2000). Considering your child's need for assistive technology. *LD Online.* Retrieved May 20, 2009, from http://www.ldonline.org/ld_indepth/technology/bowzer_reed.html.

Carroll, J. M. (1993). Creating a design science of human-computer interaction. *Interacting with Computers, 5*(1), 3–12.

Crealock, C., & Sitko, M. (1990). Comparison between computer and handwriting technologies in writing training with learning disabled students. *International Journal of Special Education, 5*(2), 173–183.

Edyburn, D. L. (2002). Models, theories, and frameworks: Contributions to understanding special education technology. *Special Education Technology Practice, 4*(2), 16–24.

Edyburn, D. L. (2003). 2002 in review: A synthesis of the special education technology literature. *Journal of Special Education Technology, 18*(3), 5–28.

Elbro, C., Rasmussen, I., & Spelling, B. (1996). Teaching reading to disabled readers with language disorders: A controlled evaluation of synthetic speech feedback. *Scandinavian Journal of Psychology, 37,* 140–155.

Hebert, B. M., & Murdock, J. Y. (1994). Comparing three computer-aided instruction output modes to teach vocabulary words to students with learning disabilities. *Learning Disabilities Research & Practice, 9*(3), 136–141.

Herl, H. E., O'Neil, H. F. Jr., Chung, G. K. W. K., & Schacter, J. (1999). Reliability and validity of a computer-based knowledge mapping system to measure content understanding. *Computers in Human Behavior, 15*(3–4), 315–333.

Higher Education Opportunity Act, Pub. L. No. 110-315, 2008.

Hitchcock, C., & Stahl, S. (2003). Assistive technology, universal design, universal design for learning: Improved learning opportunities. *Journal of Special Education Technology, 18*(4). Retrieved May 20, 2009, from: http://jset.unlv.edu/18.4T/hitchcock/first.html.

MacArthur, C. A., Graham, S., Haynes, J. A., & De la Paz, S. (1996). Spelling checkers and students with learning disabilities: Performance comparisons and impact on spelling. *Journal of Special Education, 30,* 35–57.

MacArthur, C. A., & Haynes, J. B. (1995). Student assistant for learning from text (SALT): A hypermedia reading aid. *Journal of Learning Disabilities, 28*(3), 50–59.

MacArthur, C. A., Haynes, J. A., Malouf, D. B., Harris, K., & Owings, M. (1990). Computer assisted instruction with learning disabled students: achievement, engagement, and other factors that influence achievement. *Journal of Educational Computing Research, 6*(3), 311–328.

McInerney, M., Riley, K., & Osher, D. (1999). *Technology to support literacy strategies for students who are deaf.* Washington, DC: American Institutes for Research.

National Center on Accessing the General Curriculum (2003). National file format initiative at NCAC. Wakefield, MA: Author. Retrieved May 20, 2009, from http://www.cast.org/ncac/index.cfm?i=3138.

Perl, E. (2003). *Federal and state legislation regarding accessible instructional materials.* Wakefield, MA: National Center on Accessing the General Curriculum. Retrieved May 20, 2009, from http://www.cast.org/ncac/index.cfm?i=3122.

Raskind, M. H., & Higgins, E. L. (1999). Speaking to read: The effects of speech recognition technology on the reading and spelling performance of children with learning disabilities. *Annals of Dyslexia, 49,* 251–281.

Rose, D. H., & Meyer, A. (2002). *Teaching every student in the digital age: Universal design for learning.* Alexandria, VA: Association for Supervision and Curriculum Development.

Rose, D. & Stahl, S. (2003). The NFF: A national file format for accessible instructional materials. *Journal of Special Education Technology, 18*(2), 5–28.

Story, M. F., Mueller, J. L., & Mace, R. L. (1998). *The universal design file: Designing for people of all ages and abilities.* Raleigh: North Carolina State University, Center for Universal Design.

Strangman, N., Hall, T., & Meyer, A. (2003). *Text transformations.* National Center on Accessing the General Curriculum. Retrieved July 16, 2009, from http://www.cast.org/ncac/index.cfm?i=4864.

van Daal, V. H. P., & Reitsma, P. (1993, September). The use of speech feedback by normal and disabled readers in computer-based reading practice. *Reading and Writing, 5*(3), 243–259.

von Tetzchner, S., Rogne, S. O., & Lilleeng, M. K. (1997). Literacy intervention for a deaf child with severe reading disorder. *Journal of Literacy Research, 29*(1), 25–46.

Wehmeyer, M. L., Smith, S. J., Palmer, S. B., Davies, D. K. & Stock, S. (2003). Technology use and people with mental retardation. In L. M. Glidden (Ed.), *International review of research in mental retardation*. San Diego: Academic Press.

Xin, J. F. & Rieth, H. (2001). Video-assisted vocabulary instruction for elementary school students with learning disabilities. *Information Technology in Childhood Education Annual*, 87–103.

Originally published as "Assistive technology and universal design for learning: Two sides of the same coin," in D. Edyburn, K. Higgins, R. Boone (eds), *Handbook of Special Education Technology Research and Practice*. Copyright 2004 Knowledge by Design, Inc. Reprinted with permission and edited for this volume.

CHAPTER ELEVEN

Response to Intervention and Universal Design for Learning

How Might They Intersect in the General Education Classroom?

NICOLE STRANGMAN, CHUCK HITCHCOCK, TRACEY E. HALL, GRACE MEO, AND PEGGY COYNE

EDITORS' NOTE

In 2006, CAST was asked by the K–8 Access Center, a project supported by the U.S. Department of Education under the Ideas That Work initiative, to write a paper discussing the intersection of UDL and response to intervention. This paper has been edited for this book to include brief descriptions of RTI and UDL and a discussion of how the two interact.

In the discussion of how RTI and UDL interact, the authors highlight key similarities: both recognize the importance of instruction on educational outcomes, that children respond differently to curriculum, and that assessment should be used to inform instruction. The authors also suggest that incorporating a UDL framework into instructional practice can better inform a teacher's decision-making process within RTI.

As these complementing initiatives continue to flourish in schools and classrooms, educators and policy makers should recognize how their integration can improve implementation and support better outcomes for students.

R esponse to intervention (RTI) and universal design for learning (UDL) represent innovative approaches to addressing the needs of students with disabilities. In recent years, RTI (also referred to as "response to instruction," "response to treatment," and "responsiveness to intervention") and UDL have both received increased attention from the education, policy, and disability communities. Both of these strategies are important to improve the ability of students with disabilities to participate and progress in the general education curriculum. The purpose of this paper is to provide an introduction to RTI and UDL and to explore their possible intersection in the classroom. It is structured into three sections: the first provides a basic overview of RTI; the second provides a basic overview of UDL; and the third shares ideas for the possible synergism of these two approaches in the general education classroom. The first two sections are descriptive; the third is largely theoretical.

As a result of its federal approval (Individuals with Disabilities Education Improvement Act, 2004), response to intervention has recently garnered great attention as a means to identify students with learning disabilities (LD). (Note that the legislation does not require the use of RTI for LD identification.) Within the context of LD identification, RTI aptly may be described as an operational definition for LD and an alternative to IQ-achievement discrepancy, which the federal government previously recognized as the primary operational definition of LD (U.S. Office of Education, 1977). Although the use of RTI for LD identification is a major emphasis within IDEA 2004, RTI may be more broadly defined as an approach that uses students' response to high-quality instruction to guide educational decisions, including decisions about the efficacy of instruction and intervention, eligibility for special programs, design of individual education programs, and effectiveness of special education services (Batsche et al., 2005). Thus, RTI has the potential to influence how and when LD is identified, as well as the nature of early intervention and instruction.

THE PROCESS OF RESPONSE TO INTERVENTION

RTI is used to identify students with LD and to determine early intervention. This is accomplished through evaluation of student response to targeted, high-quality instruction that has been demonstrated as effective for most students (Batsche et al., 2005). In this sense, RTI emphasizes "student outcomes instead of student deficits" (Kavale, Holdnack, & Mostert, 2005) and makes a clear connection between identification and instruction (Vaughn & Fuchs, 2003). Whereas IQ-achievement discrepancy is focused on identifying LD (Kavale et al., 2005), RTI informs both LD identification and the design of early intervention and instruction (Batsche et al., 2005). Moreover, it has been argued that RTI can be used for all students, not just those with LD. RTI also prescribes the use of research-validated interventions to help ensure that students have access to appropriate learning experiences. It is focused on providing early and more immediate support for student needs by screening students as early as kindergarten (Fletcher, Coulter, Reschly, & Vaughn, 2004; Vaughn & Fuchs, 2003).

The process of RTI involves: (1) screening for at-risk students; (2) monitoring of responsiveness to instruction; and (3) determination of the course of action (Fuchs & Fuchs, 2006; Kavale, Holdnack, & Mostert, 2005). Steps 2 and 3 are iterative. The process begins with the selection of a subgroup of at-risk students (Fuchs & Fuchs, 2006). Initially, students are monitored for their responsiveness to general education instruction; that is, instructional approaches validated as effective for most students and differentiated as needed to meet broad student needs (Batsche et al., 2005). Different courses of action can be taken depending on the number of students found not able to perform. If the number is sufficiently large, it is concluded that the instructional program is inadequate, and the overall program is modified. If instead only a small percentage of students fail to perform, such students are removed from the general program of instruction to participate in a targeted, empirically validated intervention.

Student responsiveness to intervention is used to determine further course of action. Students who are responsive to the intervention are reintegrated into the traditional program of instruction. Students determined to be unresponsive are promoted to the next "tier" of intervention, different in content or rigor. Their progress is again monitored and the course redetermined. Ultimately, failure to respond leads either to LD diagnosis and special education or to LD evaluation, depending on the RTI model (Fuchs & Fuchs, 2006; Fuchs, Mock, Morgan, & Young, 2003). Although some students may respond to an intervention, they still may be referred to special education if it is determined infeasible to maintain the intervention in the regular classroom (Batsche et al., 2005).

UNIVERSAL DESIGN FOR LEARNING

Universal design for learning is a new approach to curriculum (goals, materials, methods, and assessment) that is firmly grounded in the belief that every learner is unique and brings different strengths and weaknesses to the classroom (Rose & Meyer, 2002). Indeed, today's classrooms are incredibly diverse, housing students from different cultures, socioeconomic backgrounds, and disability groups. By contrast, traditional curricula are "one-size-fits-all," designed to meet the needs of the "typical" student. The result is a host of barriers for any student who falls outside of this narrow category, such as barriers that impede access, participation, and progress in the general curriculum (Hitchcock, Meyer, Rose, & Jackson, 2002).

Three UDL principles guide the design of flexible curricula by calling for the embedding of options that support differences in recognition, strategic, and affective networks:

- To support recognition learning, provide multiple, flexible methods of representation.
- To support strategic learning, provide multiple, flexible methods of action and expression.
- To support affective learning, provide multiple, flexible options for engagement. (Rose & Meyer, 2002)

Using these three principles, all aspects of the curriculum—goals, methods, materials, and assessments—are made flexible. With respect to assessment, for example, a range of media, formats, and response options are used so that a student's knowledge and skills are not confounded by his or her aptitude with the medium (Rose & Dolan, 2000). In addition, during testing students have access to the same supports that they have during instruction—unless those supports undermine the purpose of the assessment (Dolan & Hall, 2001; Rose & Meyer,

2002). Ideally, curriculum-based measurement is used to perform ongoing assessment, providing a window into the learning process as well as the effectiveness of instruction (Rose & Dolan, 2000).

RESPONSE TO INTERVENTION AND UNIVERSAL DESIGN FOR LEARNING

RTI and UDL differ from one another in that RTI is a process for making educational decisions based on an at-risk student's success or failure during specialized intervention, while UDL is a process for making curriculum design decisions to maximize success in the general curriculum. However, RTI and UDL share the objective of improving educational outcomes for students with disabilities and are similar in several important ways.

First, both RTI and UDL recognize that poor achievement does not necessarily reflect disability, but rather may reflect poor instruction. That is, in some cases the curriculum, not the student, may be deficient. RTI puts this belief into practice by prescribing that general education curricula incorporate research-validated instruction and intervention by making LD identification contingent on the program of instruction and by acknowledging that there are cases where changes should be made to general classroom instruction in place of student intervention (Batsche et al., 2005). UDL also encourages the use of research-validated instruction and intervention (Dalton, Pisha, Eagleton, Coyne, & Deysher, 2002; Murray & Hall, 2006) and emphasizes the notion of disabled curriculum by further stating that the curriculum, and not the student, must bear the burden of adaptation (Rose & Meyer, 2002).

Second, RTI and UDL both reflect the understanding that a curriculum that is effective for one student may not be effective for another student. With RTI, this is most readily apparent with the individualized approach to intervention that is part of the problem-solving method. With UDL, the curriculum is designed to incorporate a wide variety of options in its goals, materials, methods, and assessment so that the curriculum in its entirety is flexible and accommodating of individual student needs.

Third, RTI and UDL treat assessment as something that should inform instruction and intervention and consider once-a-year test scores insufficient to determine student ability. In RTI, students' responsiveness is commonly monitored over time and with respect to multiple interventions; in UDL, multiple, ongoing assessments are administered. The use of curriculum-based measurement as a means to inform teachers about the effectiveness of instruction and guide decision making regarding appropriate instruction and intervention is a key point of convergence of RTI and UDL. With effective implementation of curriculum-based measurement, interventions can be determined while instruction is still ongoing and before a student fails.

It is important to acknowledge that teachers need new knowledge and skills to successfully implement both RTI and UDL (Dalton, Schleper, Kennedy, & Lutz, 2005; Howard, 2003; Mastropieri & Scruggs, 2005; Rose & Meyer, 2002). Thus, professional development and ongoing support within the schools is important. In addition, technology may be an important tool. UDL solutions often make use of technology to increase flexibility and adaptability, with the added benefit of improving teacher support and student engagement (Pisha & Coyne, 2001). Thus, technology can be used to reduce some of the difficulties of implementation. Its inherent flexibility helps make the design of an adaptable curriculum much more feasible.

Although IDEA 2004 is largely focused on the use of RTI to identify students with LD, we believe that the greatest potential for synergism with UDL is around instruction. In particular, the UDL framework may be able to support more effective decision making within RTI, which remains a significant challenge in RTI. Indeed, RTI has been criticized as lacking a systematic decision-making process (i.e., few criteria for distinguishing between no response to instruction and marginal response to instruction, and little ability to predict which intervention will be effective for a particular student [Kavale, Holdnack, & Mostert, 2005]). Teachers often struggle with interpreting curriculum-based measurement data and using it to modify instructional programs effectively (Fuchs, Deno, & Mirkin, 1984; Fuchs, Fuchs, & Hamlett, 1989). Moreover, individualization, a central component of the problem-solving approach, is of great difficulty for teachers (Batsche et al., 2005; Gersten & Dimino, 2006).

The UDL framework offers a potential means to guide such decisions. For example, differences in recognition, strategic, and affective learning parameters offer a means for selecting effective interventions. The problem-solving approach to RTI is already an individualized approach that considers students in a case-by-case fashion. The UDL framework could help to guide analysis and decision making for each student as part of RTI by focusing attention on the individual learner's recognition, strategic, and affective strengths and challenges.

Another means by which to integrate RTI and UDL is to use UDL to design more flexible RTI interventions. Research has shown that instructional programs designed according to the UDL principles can be effective for a range of students (Dalton & Coyne, 2002; Dalton et al., 2002; Dalton et al., 2005). By designing interventions with flexible supports for recognition, strategy, and affect it may be possible to reduce the number of RTI tiers that are necessary and increase the number of students who respond.

Currently, some students identified as responders with RTI are not reintegrated into traditional instruction because they have been determined to require intervention that is too resource-heavy for the general education classroom. It may be possible to extend the ability of the general education curriculum to offer various nontraditional forms of instruction by integrating more technology, guided by the UDL principles and teaching methods. Technology can make it more practical and feasible to provide alternative means of instruction in the same classroom and, together with UDL, may better support the delivery of specialized RTI intervention in the general education classroom.

Beyond improving the efficiency of RTI, UDL might ultimately be used to limit its necessity by building the capacity of the general education curriculum to accommodate the diverse needs of students. This could help to reduce the numbers of students requiring intervention and/or special education. For example, UDL could be used to identify and minimize barriers in the general education curriculum that, if left unaddressed, might unnecessarily undermine student performance and increase the number of students selected for targeted intervention.

CONCLUSION

Access, participation, and progress for all students in the general education curriculum are sought-after goals of education. However, in spite of impressive reform (Individuals with Disabilities Education Improvement Act, 2004; Individuals with Disabilities Education Act, 2000; U.S. Department of Education, 2001), there remains a significant gap in the performance of students with and without disabilities (Blackorby et al., 2004; Frieden, 2004; National Center for Education Statistics, 2003).

The success of our efforts to provide students equal access, participation, and progress in the general education curriculum hinges on how we understand the curriculum or, more precisely, the "conception, design, and implementation of the general curriculum and the assumptions that underlie it" (Hitchcock, Meyer, Rose, & Jackson, 2005, p. 1). Response to intervention and UDL embody a new and important understanding about curriculum: poor performance may reflect curriculum disability rather than student disability. They also represent relevant and useful approaches for improving student learning based on manipulation of instruction. Response to intervention uses a tiered approach of specialized intervention to identify disability and investigate the effectiveness of alternative instructional approaches. Universal design for learning seeks to design curricula that are capable of meeting every student's needs through flexible and adaptive instruction.

These two approaches are still being developed, and RTI is a topic of current debate. By applying the UDL framework, it may be possible to target some of the key uncertainties about RTI, such as how to effectively individualize intervention and make instructional decisions. Beyond this, their synergism may enable achievement of a loftier goal: by simultaneously implementing RTI and using UDL to build the capacity of the general education curriculum, it may be possible to realize broadly effective general education curricula that anticipate students' difficulties and eliminate the need for intervention.

REFERENCES

Batsche, G., Elliott, J., Graden, J. L., Grimes, J., Kovaleski, J. F., Prasse, D., et al. (2005). *Response to intervention: Policy considerations and implementation.* Alexandria, VA: National Association of State Directors of Special Education.

Blackorby, J., Wagner, M., Cameto, R., Davies, E., Levine, P., Newman, L., et al. (2004). *SEELS: Engagement, academics, social adjustment, and independence: The achievements of elementary and middle school students with disabilities.* Washington, DC: Office of Special Education Programs, U.S. Department of Education. Retrieved May 20, 2009, from http://www.seels.net/info_reports/engagement.htm.

Dalton, B., & Coyne, P. (2002). Universally designed digital picture books to support beginning reading in children with cognitive disabilities. Presentation at the Annual Meeting of the National Reading Conference. San Antonio, Texas.

Dalton, B., Pisha, B., Eagleton, M., Coyne, P., & Deysher, S. (2002). *Engaging the text: Final report to the U.S. Department of Education.* Peabody, MA: Center for Applied Special Technology.

Dalton, B., Schleper, D., Kennedy, M., & Lutz, L. (2005). *Shared reading project: Chapter by chapter—thinking reader: Final report.* Wakefield, MA: Center for Applied Special Technology.

Dolan, R. P., & Hall, T. E. (2001). Universal design for learning: Implications for large-scale assessment. *IDA Perspectives, 27*(4), 22–25.

Fletcher, J. M., Coulter, W. A., Reschly, D. J., & Vaughn, S. (2004). Alternative approaches to the definition and identification of learning disabilities: Some questions and answers. *Annals of Dyslexia, 54*(2), 304–331.

Frieden, L. (2004). *Improving educational outcomes for students with disabilities.* Washington, DC: National Council on Disability. Retrieved July 16, 2009, from http://www.educationalpolicy.org/pdf/NCD.pdf.

Fuchs, D., & Fuchs, L. S. (2006). Introduction to response to intervention: What, why, and how valid is it? *Reading Research Quarterly, 41*(1), 93–99.

Fuchs, D., Mock, D., Morgan, P. L., & Young, C. L. (2003). Responsiveness-to-intervention: Definitions, evidence, and implications for the learning disabilities construct. *Learning Disabilities: Research & Practice, 18,* 157–171.

Fuchs, L. S. (2003). Assessing intervention responsiveness: Conceptual and technical issues. *Learning Disabilities: Research & Practice, 18,* 172–186.

Fuchs, L. S., Deno, S. L., & Mirkin, P. K. (1984). The effects of frequent curriculum-based measurement and evaluation on pedagogy, student achievement, and student awareness of learning. *American Educational Research Journal, 21,* 449–460.

Fuchs, L. S., Fuchs, D., & Hamlett, C. L. (1989). Monitoring reading growth using student recalls: Effects of two teacher feedback systems. *Journal of Educational Research, 83*(2), 103–110.

Gersten, R., & Dimino, J. A. (2006). RTI (response to intervention): Rethinking special education for students with reading difficulties (yet again). *Reading Research Quarterly, 41*(1), 99–108.

Hitchcock, C., Meyer, A., Rose, D. H., & Jackson, R. (2002). Providing new access to the general education curriculum. *Teaching Exceptional Children, 35*(2), 8–17.

Hitchcock, C., Meyer, A., Rose, D. H., & Jackson, R. (2005). Equal access, participation, and progress in the general education curriculum. In D. H. Rose, A. Meyer, & C. Hitchcock (Eds.). *The universally designed classroom: Accessible curriculum and digital technologies* (pp. 52–96). Cambridge, MA: Harvard Education Press.

Howard, J. B. (2003). Universal design for learning: An essential concept for teacher education. *Journal of Computing in Teacher Education, 19*(4), 113–118.

Individuals with Disabilities Education Act Amendments of 1997, 20 U.S.C. §§ 1400 *et seq.* (amended 2004); 34 C.F.R. §§ 300.1 *et seq.* (2003).

Individuals with Disabilities Education Improvement Act of 2004, P.L. No. 108-446, 118 Stat. 2647. (2004). (Amending 20 U.S.C. §§ 1400 *et seq.*)

Kavale, K. A., Holdnack, J. A., & Mostert, M. P. (2005). Responsiveness to intervention and the identification of specific learning disability: A critique and alternative proposal. *Learning Disability Quarterly, 28,* 2.

Mastropieri, M. A., & Scruggs, T. E. (2005). Feasibility and consequences of response to intervention: Examination of the issues and scientific evidence as a model for the identification of individuals with learning disabilities. *Journal of Learning Disabilities, 38,* 525–531.

Murray, E., & Hall, T. (2006). *Science writer: A universally designed thinking writer for Science.* Wakefield, MA: CAST.

National Center for Education Statistics. (2003). *Digest of Education Statistics, 2003.* Washington, DC: Author. Retrieved May 20, 2009, from http://nces.ed.gov//programs/digest/d03/.

No Child Left Behind Act of 2001. (2001). U.S. Office of Education. Retrieved May 20, 2009, from http://www.ed.gov/policy/elsec/leg/esea02/index.html.

Pisha, B., & Coyne, P. (2001). Smart from the start: The promise of universal design for learning. *Remedial and Special Education, 22*(4), 197–203.

Rose, D. H., & Dolan, R. P. (2000). Universal design for learning: Assessment. *Journal of Special Education Technology, 15*(4).

Rose, D. H., & Meyer, A. (2002). *Teaching every student in the digital age: Universal design for learning.* Alexandria, VA: Association for Supervision and Curriculum Development.

U.S. Office of Education. (1977). Assistance to states for educating of handicapped children: Procedures for evaluating specific learning disabilities. *Federal Register, 42*(25), 65082–65085. Washington, DC: Government Printing Office.

Vaughn, S., & Fuchs, L. S. (2003). Redefining learning disabilities as inadequate response to instruction: The promise and potential problems. *Learning Disabilities: Research & Practice, 18,* 137–146.

This report was produced under U.S. Department of Education Grant # H326K020003 with the American Institutes for Research. The views expressed herein do not necessarily represent the positions or policies of the U.S. Department of Education. No official endorsement by the U.S. Department of Education of any product, commodity, service, or enterprise mentioned in this publication is intended or should be inferred.

CHAPTER TWELVE

Developing Accessible Tests with Universal Design and Digital Technologies

Ensuring We Standardize the Right Things

ROBERT P. DOLAN AND TRACEY E. HALL

EDITORS' NOTE

This chapter discusses the importance of applying universal design as well as universal design for learning to large-scale assessment. It is argued that the application of these two frameworks, especially in a technology-based environment, will lead to more accurate and more efficient assessments.

The chapter begins with an overview of UDL and a description of how UDL principles can be applied to assessment. It then reveals the resesarch and practice that support universally designed assessments, with a specific focus on assessments that are administered in a computer-based environment. The chapter concludes with a discussion of the implications for schools, policy, and assessment research.

The efforts of the Kentucky Department of Education to develop an accessible online format for their statewide assessment, the Commonwealth Accountability Testing System (CATS), are a centerpiece of this chapter. The development of CATS Online as well as its positive impact on students are revealed. However, it should be noted that as of January 15, 2009, the Kentucky Department of Education discontinued the use of online testing due to budgetary constraints. Although CATS Online is not currently in use, it remains an illustrative example nonetheless. The success of Kentucky's online assessment demonstrates how the flexibility and support embedded in an online environment allow for more accurate measurement of student learning and serves as a valuable model for future development.

With the advent of standards-based reform in the early 1990s and the passage of the No Child Left Behind Act of 2001 (NCLB), the role of large-scale assessment in public education has expanded significantly. Accurate large-scale assessment is necessary to the success of standards-based reform efforts insofar as those efforts aim to improve student outcomes, especially for students with disabilities (AERA, APA, & NCME, 1999; Elmore & Rothman, 1999). Federal initiatives such as NCLB and the Individuals with Disabilities Education Act of 1997 (IDEA '97) have legislated that large-scale assessment must be accurate for students within both the general and special education curricula (Nolet & McLaughlin, 2000). Unfortunately, available research indicates that current methods of large-scale assessment are generally inadequate for students with disabilities (Elmore & Rothman, 1999; Hollenbeck, 2002; Olson & Goldstein, 1996; Sireci, Li, & Scarpati, 2003; Thurlow et al., 2000).

The challenge facing educators is how to standardize assessment of nonstandard individuals—that is, to ensure adequate individualization of test delivery without compromising comparability. To accurately reflect student learning, large-scale assessments must be designed such that they carefully isolate knowledge, skills, and abilities (KSAs) related to intended constructs. Unfortunately, many assessments measure not only the target KSAs but also those associated with other unintended constructs, such as KSAs related to accessing test material or generating a response (Abedi, Leon, & Mirocha, 2001; Helwig, Rozek-Tedesco, Tindal, Heath, & Almond, 1999; Parkes, Suen, Zimmaro, & Zappe, 1999).

For example, taking a paper-and-pencil math test requires physical capabilities such as holding a pencil and manipulating the test booklet, sensory capabilities such as sight and hearing, and cognitive capabilities such as organization and attention, all of which fall outside the targeted construct of math skill. These test requirements may not be a problem for many students, but they leave some students at a disadvantage, particularly students with disabilities. For students with learning disabilities, the problem of unintended constructs in assessment is pervasive. Difficulties with fundamental testing tasks, such as selectively attending to a test item and recording responses on a separate answer sheet, potentially undermine these students' performance. Since reading is a requisite skill across subject areas, students who lack strong literacy skills—such as phonemic awareness, phonics/word recognition, vocabulary, fluency, comprehension, and engagement—may also be unfairly disadvantaged during assessment (Ehri, 1994; Graham & Harris, 1996; Helwig et al., 1999; Liberman, Shankweiler, & Liberman, 1989; Stanovich, 1988; Swanson, 1999; Torgesen, 1993). These students' abilities to demonstrate proficiency with the subject or skill area being tested may be hampered by unintended constructs such as facility with the test medium or format. To state the problem differently, accurate assessment of student progress vis-à-vis learning standards is compromised by efforts to standardize the means for demonstrating learning.

Testing accommodations represent an attempt to reduce the influence of construct-irrelevant factors during assessment. However, as retrofitted solutions, they generally provide "too little, too late." First, accommodations such as the read-aloud and scribe rob students of their ability to progress independently through a test, and do not fully address many students' needs. Second, these accommodations often interfere with the intended constructs, and thus jeopardize the validity of claims drawn from test results. As such, accommodations fall short of the goal.

How can we ensure that large-scale tests provide adequate individualization of test delivery without compromising comparability? In this chapter, we discuss how the principles of the educational framework universal design for learning (UDL)—as well as universal design of assessment (UDA)—may help improve the accuracy and efficacy of assessments, especially when applied in technology-based settings.

In the first part of this chapter, we review the UDL principles and their application to assessment. We also consider the affordances of new technologies. In the second section, we examine the research and practice of universally designed assessment, including technology applications. Finally, we discuss the implications for schools, policy, and assessment research.

THE PROMISE OF UNIVERSAL DESIGN AND DIGITAL TECHNOLOGIES

Universal design for learning (Rose & Meyer, 2000, 2002) and universal design of assessment (Thompson, Johnstone, & Thurlow, 2002) represent two related and complementary approaches that could redefine how assessments are designed and delivered. Both draw inspiration from the universal design movement in architecture and product development founded by Ron Mace (1991) at North Carolina State University. Universal design's objective is to build innately accessible structures by addressing the mobility and communication needs of individuals with disabilities at the design stage, a practice that has spread to areas such as civic engineering and commercial product design. Designs that increase accessibility for individuals with disabilities make everyone's experience better. A good example from product development is television captioning. Captioning was first developed for people with hearing impairments, who had to retrofit their televisions by purchasing expensive decoder boxes to access the captions. But captioning later became a standard feature of every television. This universal design feature now benefits not only individuals with hearing impairments but also viewers without disabilities who use the technology to view television in noisy health clubs and restaurants, build English or Spanish language skills, and so forth (Rose & Meyer, 2002).

Universal design of assessment seeks to design tests that allow greater participation by students with disabilities by directly applying Mace's universal design principles (Thompson et al., 2002). Preliminary research findings suggest that students with disabilities—indeed all students—may perform significantly better on tests that apply universal design principles than on traditionally designed tests (Johnstone, 2003).

The educational framework of UDL extends universal design from a physical space to a pedagogical space. It guides the design of more flexible curricula, including more flexible assessments that offer multiple opportunities for recognizing, using, and engaging with curriculum content. Universal design for learning serves as a guide for minimizing learning barriers and maximizing learning opportunities by flexibly accommodating individual differences, following these three principles:

- To support individual differences in learning to recognize the world, provide multiple, flexible methods of presentation.
- To support individual differences in learning strategies for action, provide multiple, flexible methods of expression and apprenticeship.
- To support individual differences in what is motivating and engaging, provide multiple, flexible options for engagement. (Rose & Meyer, 2002)

By applying the principles of UDL to assessments, it should be possible to create more accurate assessments that incorporate widespread student needs into the original design. It should be possible to create tests that more accurately assess the knowledge and abilities of all students, including those with dyslexia and other learning, cognitive, or physical disabilities. In the process, the need for many accommodations that are used today as retrofit solutions will be reduced (Dolan & Hall, 2001; Dolan & Rose, 2000). While UDL curricula can be designed with traditional media and instructional approaches, technology is seen as a key enabler due to its inherent flexibility (Meyer & Rose, 2005). New media, such as digital texts and images, are potentially powerful educational tools because they are malleable and flexible, enabling content to be represented and accessed in multiple ways (Rose & Meyer, 2002; Dolan et al., 2005).

The display of digital content can be manipulated to meet the diverse needs of a variety of learners, including those with physical, sensory, and learning disabilities (Edyburn, 2003; Rose & Meyer, 2002). This, in turn, can enable teachers to differentiate their instructional methods and materials in multiple ways, thus reducing barriers to learning for many students.

These media can also be used to differentiate classroom-based assessment of student learning, supporting timely intervention at the point of instruction (Bennett, 2001; Chudowsky & Pellegrino, 2003). New media also offer the opportunity to assess skill learning in a deeper and more meaningful way (Bennett et al., 1999; Russell, 2002). For example, virtual/digital lab experiments may provide a clearer indication of science students' understanding of processes, methods, and outcomes than do written or verbal tests (Rose & Meyer, 2002). Moreover, by tracking what supports a student uses, the kinds of strategies that he or she follows, the kinds of strategies that seem to be missing, and the aspects of the task environment that bias the student toward successful or unsuccessful approaches, classroom-based assessment can provide information about students as learners. If these data are combined with student responses and scores and teachers are given support in using these data to inform subsequent instruction, it may be possible to develop assessment approaches that can truly transform education. Such techniques allow for the development of large-scale assessments that provide a broader set of constructs than traditional testing techniques allow.

CURRENT EFFORTS IN UNIVERSAL DESIGN AND ASSESSMENT

The 2004 reauthorization of IDEA explicitly called for application of universal design principles to assessment. Nevertheless, efforts to apply universal design to assessment have generally been limited to improving old practices—namely, making print-based assessments more accessible. While providing important guidance for the generation of current, traditional tests, these applications do not realize the full potential of UDL and digital technologies. Advances in technology have made computer-administered testing a possibility. Although the overall focus on computer use for assessment has been on decreasing costs and increasing timeliness associated with large-scale testing, a few states, most notably Kentucky (HumRRO, 2003; Salyers, 2002; Trimble, Lewis, Dolan, & Kearns, 2006), have been exploring the role of technology in improving statewide test accessibility for students with disabilities. In addition, guidelines are emerging for making computerized tests more accessible (Allan, Bulla, & Goodman, 2003; Association of Test Publishers, 2002; Thompson, Thurlow, Quenemoen, & Lehr, 2002).

Clearly, more research and development is also needed in this area. Following are examples of research and practice that suggest future considerations and directions for the field.

Keyboarding Versus Handwriting

As the nature of classroom instruction changes, and in particular the technologies used in the classroom evolve, there is an increasing disconnect between the media with which students learn and the media with which they are assessed. Research by Russell and colleagues (Russell & Haney, 1997; Russell & Plati, 2000) demonstrates quite clearly the broad importance of developing assessment forms that match the needs of students and reflect the technologies that they are using in the classroom.

Recognizing the increasing incongruity between computer use in the classroom and assessment technology, Russell and Haney (1997) conducted a study investigating mode of administration effects on performance on standardized assessment. One hundred twenty-one students in grades 6, 7, and 8 completed each of three assessments: an open-ended assessment with writing, science, math, and reading questions; a test composed of National Assessment of Educational Progress (NAEP) language arts, science, and math items—primarily multiple choice; and a performance writing assessment requiring extended written response. Students randomized to the control group completed all assessments using pencil and paper. Students randomized to the experimental group completed the open-ended assessment on paper, but completed the NAEP and performance writing assessments using a computerized version whose layout was matched to the printed version as closely as possible.

Russell and Haney's findings plainly reveal the impact of test medium on student performance. Comparison of student responses clearly demonstrated a significant mode of administration effect: students completing the short-answer and extended written responses on the computer performed significantly better than students completing these assessments by hand. A secondary analysis of the NAEP multiple choice and open-ended items individually revealed a large and significant mode of administration effect for the science and language arts short-answer questions, favoring the computerized administration. In addition, the average student score on the performance writing assessment was significantly higher on the computerized versus paper-and-pencil administration.

These findings were confirmed and extended in a later study with 525 typically achieving students in grades 4, 8, and 10 who responded to the 1999 MCAS Language Arts Composition Prompt on paper or computer (Russell & Plati, 2000). In all three grades, the mean writing score was significantly higher for students composing on the computer versus with paper and pencil, with a mean difference in scores of 1.6, 1.9, and 1.5 points for grades 4, 8, and 10, respectively.

Russell and Haney proposed that increased student familiarity with writing on the computer was likely responsible for the mode of administration effects; indeed, students in both studies had a high level of access to computers. However, the broader importance of these findings is quite clear given the increasing role computers play in students' lives, both inside and outside of school.

These results have important implications for the future of large-scale assessment, demonstrating that student performance may be strongly sensitive to differences in the mode of administration. As noted by Russell and Haney (1997), assessment validity must take into account not only the content of instruction but also the medium. For assessment results to be valid, to avoid construct-irrelevant variance in test scores, the assessment environment must provide access and supports comparable to those available and familiar to students during instruction. From a UDL perspective this means providing students with multiple options for expression. In view of the increasingly digital classroom, it also means that test designers need to find a valid means to incorporate computers and computer-based supports into large-scale assessment.

Thus not only is mode of administration important to students with disabilities, as Russell and colleagues' work shows, but mode of administration can also greatly impact the scores of students without disabilities. Thus, while the needs of students with disabilities have provided a strong impetus for those interested in applying universal design to assessment, the issue of matching assessments to the needs of the student is in fact far more fundamental. Russell and colleagues' findings provide support for the UDL premise that designing for the needs of students with disabilities can have far-reaching benefits. Their findings also highlight an important shortcoming of accommodations, which are geared solely toward problems affecting students with disabilities and thereby divert attention from the value of reducing construct-irrelevant variance for all students. To avoid construct-irrelevant variance in test scores, it is essential to match the assessment technology to the student—whether the student has a disability or not.

Kentucky Online System Technology Skills Checklist

This need to establish a good match between assessment technology and the student was the primary consideration of the Kentucky State Department of Education when they developed an accessible online format for their statewide assessment, the Commonwealth Accountability Testing System (CATS). Development of CATS Online was part of a comprehensive, statewide UDL initiative (Trimble et al., 2006). The process underlying this development speaks directly to the considerations that must be made when developing universally designed, technology-based tests.

IDEA '97 requires that students be provided with appropriate test accommodations, alterations in test materials, or procedures to minimize the impact of disability on assessment performance. The CATS Online leverages technology to accommodate students with disabilities more elegantly and less intrusively than with traditional accommodations and paper-and-pencil tests. The CATS Online delivers the Kentucky Core Content Test via an interactive Web site hosted by the eCollege of Denver. The test items and scoring rubrics are identical to those on the paper-and-pencil test, but the assessment includes built-in accessibility supports for students with disabilities.

A key feature of the CATS Online is the availability of read-aloud support. The read-aloud is the most common test accommodation addressing test presentation for students with learning disabilities (Sireci et al., 2003; Tindal, Heath, Hollenback, Almond, & Harniss, 1998), and research studies have repeatedly demonstrated its ability to improve the performance of test takers with learning disabilities (Calhoon, Fuchs, & Hamlett, 2000; Fuchs, Fuchs, Eaton, Hamlett, & Karns, 2000; Meloy, Deville, & Frisbie, 2002; Thompson, Blount, & Thurlow, 2002; Tindal & Fuchs, 1999). Most read-aloud accommodations involve a live reading by teacher or aide to a group of students taking individual tests. However, in the CATS Online, students can use a mouse or keyboard to select text to be read aloud by the computer using text-reader or screen-reader software. This removes from the testing equation a number of potential problems with the traditional read-aloud, including potential differences among readers, which can lead to nonequivalent test conditions (Landau et al., 2003) and imposition of a linear navigation path and set pace, which can negatively affect test performance (Hollenbeck, Rozek-Tedesco, Tindal, & Glasgow, 2000). Thus, the digital read-aloud capability of the CATS Online provides greater accessibility, by offering an alternative to the written text, and greater flexibility—particularly, independent, self-paced navigation. In this way, the read-aloud helps to reduce the effect of reading ability as a construct-irrelevant factor affecting students with disabilities. In addition to this read-aloud capability, students are permitted to use any computer-based writing supports they use in the classroom. Thus, students are flexibly supported via multiple means of recognition and expression, which are somewhat customizable to the student.

Development of the CATS Online was a three-part process whereby the Kentucky Department of Education defined the population of students who would take the assessment, provided student supports for using the assessment technology, and engaged in ongoing state and local planning and organization to implement the CATS Online. The digital nature of the CATS Online and the prominent role of text-reader and text-to-speech (TTS) software raised important issues regarding the technology expertise of students and support staff. Thus, a key activity during the development of CATS Online was to address the question, What prerequisite technology skills do students need in order to use accessible computer-based accountability assessments?

Kentucky's approach to this question was to identify, directly observe, and validate a set of technology skills needed by students to access the CATS online, culminating in a technology skills checklist (Fleming, Kearns, Dethloff, Lewis, & Dolan, 2006). The fundamental rationale for the CATS Online checklist is that understanding of students' construct-irrelevant KSAs is important to providing students with the right assessment—minimizing the occurrence of irrelevant constructs and maximizing assessment validity.

Initial development of the technology skills checklist involved a variety of activities, including student and teacher observations, focus groups, and interviews; review of national, state, and school district technology standards and skills; and analysis of the CATS Online Demonstration Area, a Web-based tool designed to offer students and teachers the opportunity to gain experience with the assessment interface. The first draft of the checklist was subsequently validated based on input from teachers.

The resulting checklist includes 121 items distributed across five categories: basic computer skills (e.g., move mouse pointer on screen), keyboarding skills (e.g., use Enter/Return key), word processing skills (e.g., open existing document from a specific location), text-reader/screen-reader skills (e.g., change voice quality of text/screen reader), and skills needed for interaction with CATS Online, specifically (e.g., type in login password). This checklist can be used to prepare students and school staff—in Kentucky and elsewhere—for use and administration of electronic accessible assessments. Although the skills identified are necessarily specific to the CATS Online, they are likely to have overall relevance to other technology-based assessments.

The impact of the CATS Online on students has been assessed in two survey-based studies (Abell & Lewis, 2005. Preliminary evaluation indicates that the assessment had a highly positive impact on students. For example, data show widespread student improvement in the ability to work independently and stay on task. In addition, data show widespread improvement in students' self-concepts. Data from the second study show that the overwhelming majority of students preferred testing on the computer and suggest that greater control and independence were important contributing factors.

The Kentucky experience demonstrates the potential of an approach that integrates UDL with a technology-based assessment to anticipate student needs, including differences in technology experience, and improve the testing experience. The success of the CATS Online likely also reflects important changes in the classroom and in policy. As part of their UDL initiative, Kentucky trained twenty-seven teachers in UDL and text-reader or text-to-speech software, and acquired a site license for text-reader software in 95 percent of schools. This not only provided an important foundation for UDL but also increased students' opportunities to work with technology at the point of instruction. Policy changes were equally significant. Senate Bill 243, 2002-KRS 156.027 stipulated that publishers who provide an accessible digital copy of textbooks for the state adoption would be given "Preferential Procurement" during the next textbook adoption cycle; these publishers were given first preference by local schools. In addition, a Kentucky Accessibility Materials Consortium—a state repository for the distribution of accessible digital curriculum materials for students with disabilities—was established. Publishers have provided over 1,300 individual digital textbooks to the consortium, encompassing social studies, arts and humanities, practical living and vocational studies, and language arts. These policy changes directly support the development of digital curricula, which can itself have a significant impact on the success of technology-based assessment.

Pilot Study of a Computerized Test System with Text-to-Speech Read-Aloud and Universally Designed Supports

The Kentucky experience provides highly valuable practice and policy information regarding computer-based testing with built-in supports. However, for universally designed computer-based testing to gain acceptance within the testing community, research studies are vital. The read-aloud accommodation—a prominent feature of the CATS Online—has been researched fairly extensively and demonstrated to improve the performance of students with learning disabilities (Burk, 1999; Brown & Augustine, 2000; Calhoon, Fuchs, & Hamlett, 2000; Fuchs, Fuchs, Eaton, Hamlett, & Karns, 2000; Hollenbeck, Rozek-Tedesco, Tindal, & Glasgow, 2000; Meloy, Deville, & Frisbie, 2002; Thompson, Blount, & Thurlow, 2002; Tindal & Fuchs, 1999). However, most of these studies have used a human read-aloud, which is now recognized to have several associated problems that pose threats to construct validity (Harker & Feldt, 1993; Hollenbeck, Rozek-Tedesco, Tindal, & Glasgow, 2000; Landau et al., 2003; Lee & Tindal, 2000; Meloy et al., 2002).

Although these concerns might lead some to reject or severely restrict use of the read-aloud, we argue that the issue is one of need for greater diversity and flexibility in the read-aloud accommodation. It has become increasingly clear that not all students with disabilities benefit from the read-aloud accommodation (Helwig Rozek-Tedesco, & Tindal, 2002;

Helwig et al., 1999; Sireci et al., 2003), with responsiveness varying by student (Elliot, Kratochwill, & McKevitt, 2001; Tindal, Glasgow, Helwig, Hollenbeck, & Heath, 1998) as well as by grade, test form, and problem type (Fuchs et al., 2000; Helwig et al., 1999). Indeed, prominent assessment researchers have asserted the need for greater attention to individual effects of accommodations (Elliot et al., 2001; Helwig et al., 1999; Tindal, Heath, et al., 1998), a request that is consonant with UDL. Thus, there are compelling reasons to consider implementation of a more individualized read-aloud accommodation.

In this regard, computer-based read-aloud may hold potential, its digital nature providing much greater flexibility, particularly if coupled to principles of UDL. In a previous pilot study (Dolan et al., 2005) we addressed this possibility by investigating the effectiveness of computer-based testing with TTS and universally designed supports as a means to provide individualized support to students with learning disabilities during multiple-choice testing.

Ten grade 11 and grade 12 students with specific learning disabilities were administered two equivalent forms of a U.S. history and civics test on separate days. One form of the test was administered using traditional paper-and-pencil methods, the other using computer-based testing with TTS. Students were randomly assigned to four groups, controlling for any effects of test order and form. The two test forms were assembled using released items from the NAEP U.S. history and civics tests. Both test forms included two accommodations typically provided for students with learning disabilities: one-at-a-time presentation of test item sets (i.e., a reading passage and associated question or questions) and elimination of a separate answer sheet. The computer-based administration included an additional accommodation, a TTS-based read-aloud feature with which students could select words, sentences, or entire sections in the reading passages, test questions, or student responses to be read aloud on demand, with or without synchronous highlighting. The computerized test was designed to offer students navigation options similar to a paper-and-pencil test (figure 12-1). For example, students could view the reading passage, questions, and responses at the same time, mark questions for review, and proceed through the test in any order and direction using a navigation bar.

FIGURE 12-1 Screenshot of the prototype computer-based testing system with TTS support (CBT-TTS).

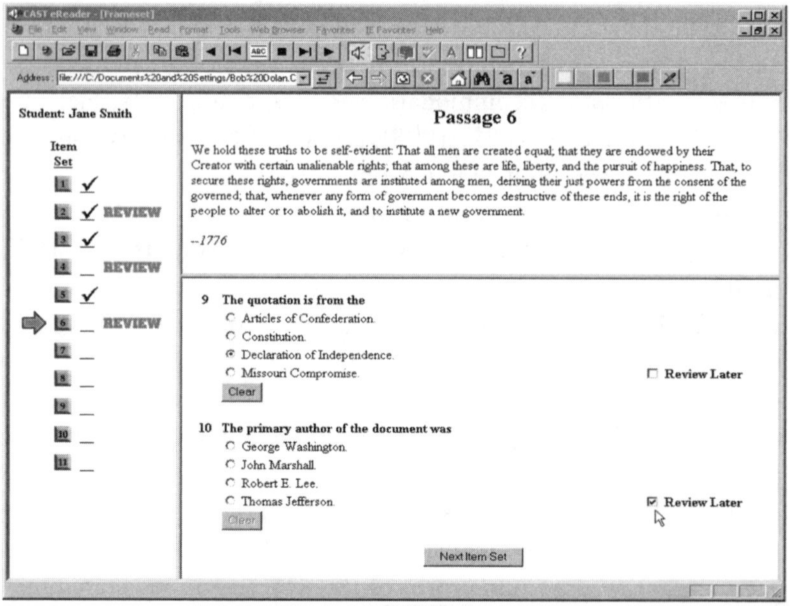

Evaluation of student test scores showed that overall performance was slightly but not significantly better (approximately 7 percentage points higher) on the computerized version of the tests than on the paper-and-pencil versions (figure 12-2). However, reanalysis of the data after grouping items by question type (long or short reading passages) unmasked a marked difference in performance between the two test administrations. When responding to items associated with long reading passages (longer than one hundred words), students scored approximately 22 percentage points higher on the computerized administration than on the paper-and-pencil administration, a statistically significant difference ($t = 2.26$; $p = 0.05$).

An important objective of this study was to look beyond group differences for potential individual differences in accommodation effects. Thus, we conducted further analyses to examine individual student per-

FIGURE 12-2   Mean test scores for the computerized (CBT-TTS) and paper-and-pencil (PPT) administrations for all test questions, test questions with long passages, and test questions with short passages.

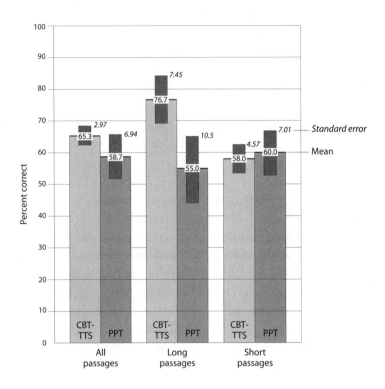

Source: Data collected on composite tests created from NAEP U.S. history and civics test items. See Dolan et al. (2005) for more information on how the study was conducted.

formance across the two conditions. Test performance was reexamined at the individual level after categorizing students according to "low-average" (WIAT-II reading composite scores below 80) or "average" (WIAT-II reading composite score above 80) reading ability. For the short-passage items, type of test administration did not impact the performance of low-average or average readers in any consistent way. However, for the long-passage items, all three low-average readers performed better when using the computerized versus paper-and-pencil test administration, scoring

17, 42, and 75 percentage points higher. In contrast, performance of the seven average readers was variable across the two test administrations. These results suggest that within the overall population of students with learning disabilities, the computer-based accommodation may be more effective for students with low-average reading ability.

Students' overall impressions of the computerized test system were uniformly positive and suggested broad usability. Nearly all students responded with a "definite yes" when asked if they recommended the use of the computerized system to other students. An overwhelming majority of students (90%) reported having very few, if any, technical problems with the system. In fact, students said that the computerized system was "easier to use" and "easier to understand" than the paper-and-pencil system.

Our analyses suggested that the greater appeal of the computerized system derived from its promotion of independence and flexibility, and from the TTS feature. Although 70 percent of students reported having no or limited experience with TTS, all of them used it to read passages during the study, and 70 percent said that TTS definitely helped their passage comprehension. In general, students preferred TTS to a human reader, a preference that seemed to be related to the tool's ease of use and opportunity for control. A typical comment: "TTS is easier to use. You can see and at the same time listen to it. I have more control when I use the computer." However, the inauthentic tone and expression of the TTS was irritating to students. We found that the item display and item navigation features of the computer-based test were appreciated, but there was little indication that they made much difference to students relative to the TTS feature.

The results of this pilot study, while preliminary, underline the potential of technology and universal design for reducing construct-irrelevant variance during testing. Construct-irrelevant variance is a significant problem for students with disabilities, and a key factor in evaluating the effectiveness of any accommodation. The computerized read-aloud may be a potentially valuable tool for addressing the current problems inherent within the human-mediated read-aloud accommodation.

TTS read-aloud supports students' diverse ways of recognizing, strategically interacting, and engaging with an assessment by offering individualized, independent, and self-paced multimodal access to test content—on demand. Individual differences in each of these domains can be sources of construct-irrelevant variance. Unlike a human read-aloud, a TTS read-aloud provides students with consistent readings, free of potentially directive or misleading intonation. In the Dolan et al. study (2005), students appreciated the control available to them with the TTS tool, including the ability to select their own pace and review text on demand. This is consistent with the Kentucky Department of Education's feedback on the CATS Online. Participants in the Dolan et al. study also appreciated the computer-based test's navigation features. Future investigations might directly address the relationship between the various features of the computerized test administration and changes in performance.

Students' usage patterns and responses suggest that they would use the computerized test system in real-world testing situations. Although a relatively small percentage of students in the study reported having experience with TTS, its availability during testing offers the potential for greater continuity between instruction and assessment, as listening is a core literacy activity in the classroom. Indeed, equivalence between the approaches and technologies used during instruction and assessment is essential to providing students with optimal assessment support (U.S. Department of Education, 2001). Ultimately, the link between instruction and assessment may be greatly strengthened through the use of embedded assessment approaches.

The results of this study provide yet further rationale for attention to individual differences when investigating the effects of accommodations. Meeting the challenge of diverse student needs is made easier by flexible, technology-based assessments. However, much more research is needed to establish effective means to realize this potential.

IMPLICATIONS OF UNIVERSAL DESIGN, TECHNOLOGY, AND ASSESSMENT

The research and practice described in this chapter generally support the idea that universally designed assessment can improve student performance, but it is clear that we are only beginning to discover the full extent of variability in student needs and how to support them. It is our hope that future work in research and development, policy making, and school-based practices will address some of the critical questions that follow.

Universal design and technology have the potential to transform the development of assessments so that they are richer and more authentic measures of student learning. It is important to remember, however, that universally designed assessments must *from the outset* be built to serve the needs of diverse learners: universal design is not a system for retrofitting poorly constructed assessment delivery systems. To reduce the effects of construct-irrelevant factors, the universal design approach must begin during test development (Dolan & Hall, 2001; Thompson, Johnstone, & Thurlow, 2002).

A universal design approach to test development also considers the full range of challenges facing diverse learners. Providing access for those with physical or sensory disabilities is essential. However, assessment systems should also support and scaffold the assessment process for individuals with learning disabilities and those with executive function/organizational supports as well as those with cognitive disabilities.

To improve accuracy, attention must be paid to how best to engage students in the assessment process. Engagement is as important in assessment as it is in other areas of instruction, such as content presentation. Providing choice can be a powerful way of increasing the engagement of some (though not all) learners, especially if it develops their metacognitive awareness of how they learn best. Test developers need to explore the effects of providing students greater choice during testing, keeping in mind the results of the aforementioned study by Russell and Plati (2000), in which students did poorly even with the most basic decisions about mode of response. Although this chapter focuses largely on the benefits of text-to-speech supports, there are many other areas of supports that could be investigated and implemented into the assessment environment.

Test developers also need to be aware of the importance of matching instruction and assessment techniques and technologies. For example, assumptions are still often made about students' cultural experiences and reading comprehension abilities (on subject area tests); these assumptions cannot be "accommodated away" through retrofitting. Instead, they must be addressed during item development. Equally important is that the use of technologies such as TTS be matched to students' abilities and challenges as readers, and that such matching start in the classroom. The fact that in the third study summarized here only a few students had prior experience with TTS tools underscores the need for more appropriate use of such accommodations during the instructional process, not only during testing. Only then can we be assured that students are receiving the supports necessary to ensure their ability to learn and to be assessed fairly and accurately. A significant challenge lies in determining just how well matched the instructional and testing technologies must be. For example, in implementing the CATS Online, the Kentucky Department of Education ensured that all students had access to exactly the same TTS software they used in the classrooms. However, for commercial test publishers developing solutions for use in multiple states, this requirement may prove problematic. It is therefore imperative that we better understand just how much difference in implementation is tolerable to students and is still consistent with the accommodations provided during instruction.

Finally, assessment needs to be woven into all levels of the instructional process so that it supports the most efficient and effective achievement of learning goals and standards. What do we want to achieve in the classroom? What do learners need to learn—and how? How can we leverage the power of universal design and new technologies to provide assessments that not only offer summative information about the learning process but, perhaps more important, provide the kinds of formative data that teachers need at the point of instruction to support successful learners in learning even more and to support struggling learners before events of failure turn into patterns of failure? With these questions in mind, test makers, policy makers, and school practitioners need to work together in developing and promoting the use of universal design and new technologies to provide effective formative assessment in the classroom to support all learners as they engage in high-quality content.

CONCLUSION

To the extent that increased accountability can improve education, it must be accurate and inclusive, a goal that universally designed assessments can help us reach. Only by creating fair and accurate tests that consider diverse students from the start and that allow them to demonstrate their learning progress, regardless of how they learn, can we ensure that we are holding educational systems accountable for all students, including those with disabilities.

A small but growing body of evidence suggests that the UDL principles can inform the appropriate use of technology in assessment and that technology can help realize the flexibility necessary to accurately and fairly assess diverse students. Applying the principles of UDL makes it possible to create a new generation of assessments that leverage new media and technologies to more accurately assess the knowledge and abilities of all students by expanding the range of constructs that can be assessed. In the process, we must distinguish measuring individuals' progress toward standardized goals from standardizing the means by which we measure.

REFERENCES

Abedi, J., Leon, S., & Mirocha, J. (2001). *Validity of standardized achievement tests for English language learners.* Paper presented at the Annual Meeting of the American Educational Research Association, Seattle, Washington.

Abell, M., & Lewis, P. (2005). Universal design for learning: A statewide improvement model for success. *Information Technology and Disabilities, 11*(1). Retrieved July 8, 2009 http://people.rit.edu/easi/itd/itdv11n1/abell.htm.

AERA, APA, & NCME. (1999). *Standards for educational and psychological testing.* New York: AERA.

Allan, J. M., Bulla, N., & Goodman, S. A. (2003). *Test access: Guidelines for computer-administered testing.* Louisville, KY: American Printing House for the Blind.

Association of Test Publishers. (2002). *Guidelines for computer-based testing.* Washington, DC: Author.

Bennett, R. E. (2001). How the Internet will help large-scale assessment reinvent itself. *Education Policy Analysis Archives, 9*(5).

Bennett, R. E., Goodman, M., Hessinger, J., Kahn, H., Ligget, J., Marshall, G., & Zack, J. (1999). Using multimedia in large-scale computer-based testing programs. *Computers in Human Behavior, 15*(3-4), 283–294.

Brown, P. B., & Augustine, A. (2000). *Findings of the 1999–2000 screen reading field test.* Dover, DE: Delaware Department of Education.

Burk, M. (1999). *Computerized test accommodations: A new approach for inclusion and success for students with disabilities.* Washington, DC: A.U. Software, Inc.

Calhoon, M. B., Fuchs, L. S., & Hamlett, C. L. (2000). Effects of computer-based test accommodations on mathematics performance assessments for secondary students with learning disabilities. *Learning Disability Quarterly, 23*(4), 271–281.

Chudowsky, N., & Pellegrino, J. W. (2003). Large-scale assessments that support learning: What will it take? *Theory into Practice, 42*(1), 75–83.

Dolan, R. P., & Hall, T. E. (2001). Universal design for learning: Implications for large-scale assessment. *IDA Perspectives, 27*(4), 22–25.

Dolan, R. P., Hall, T. E., Banerjee, M., Chun, E., & Strangman, N. (2005). Applying principles of universal design to test delivery: The effect of computer-based read-aloud on test performance of high school students with learning disabilities. *Journal of Technology, Learning, and Assessment, 3*(7). Retrieved May 13, 2009 from http://escholarship.bc.edu/jtla/vol3/7/.

Dolan, R. P., & Rose, D. H. (2000). Accurate assessment through Universal design for learning. *Journal of Special Education Technology, 15*(4).

Edyburn, D. L. (2003). Measuring assistive technology outcomes: Key concepts. *Journal of Special Education Technology, 18*(2), 53–55.

Ehri, L. C. (1994). Development of the ability to read words: Update. In R. B. Ruddell & M. R. Ruddell (Eds.), *Theoretical models and processes of reading* (4th ed., pp. 323–358). Newark, DE: International Reading Association.

Elliot, S. N., Kratochwill, T. R., & McKevitt, B. (2001). Experimental analysis of the effects of testing accommodations on the scores of students with and without disabilities. *Journal of School Psychology, 39*, 3–24.

Elmore, R. F., & Rothman, R. (Eds.). (1999). *Testing, teaching, and learning: A guide for states and school districts.* Washington, DC: National Academy Press.

Fleming, J., Kearns, J., Dethloff, A., Lewis, P., & Dolan, R. (2006). Technology skills checklist for online assessment. *Special Education Technology Practice, 8*(1), 19–32.

Fuchs, L. S., Fuchs, D., Eaton, S., Hamlett, C. L., & Karns, K. (2000). Supplementing teacher judgments of mathematics test accommodations with objective data sources. *School Psychology Review, 29*(1), 65–85.

Graham, S., & Harris, K. R. (1996). Addressing problems in attention, memory, and executive functioning: An example from self-regulated strategy development. In G. R. Lyon & N. A. Krasnegor (Eds.), *Attention, memory, and executive function* (pp. 349–365). Baltimore, MD: Paul H. Brookes Publishing.

Harker, J. K., & Feldt, L. S. (1993). A comparison of achievement test performance of nondisabled students under silent reading and reading plus listening modes of administration. *Applied Measurement in Education, 6*(4), 307–320.

Helwig, R., Rozek-Tedesco, M. A., & Tindal, G. (2002). An oral versus a standard administration of a large-scale mathematics test. *Journal of Special Education, 36*(1), 39–47.

Helwig, R., Rozek-Tedesco, M. A., Tindal, G., Heath, B., & Almond, P. (1999). Reading as an access to mathematics problem solving on multiple-choice tests for sixth-grade students. *Journal of Educational Research, 93*(2), 113–125.

Hollenbeck, K. (2002). Determining when test alterations are valid accommodations or modifications for large-scale assessment. In G. Tindal & T. M. Haladyna (Eds.), *Large-scale assessment programs for all students: Validity, technical adequacy, and implementation*. Mahwah, NJ: Lawrence Erlbaum Associates.

Hollenbeck, K., Rozek-Tedesco, M. A., Tindal, G., & Glasgow, A. (2000). An exploratory study of student-paced versus teacher-paced accommodations for large-scale math tests. *Journal of Special Education Technology, 15*(2), 27–36.

HumRRO. (2003). *CATS Online: Logistic and construct evaluation of computer administered assessment* (No. FR-03-40). Alexandria, VA: Human Resources Research Organization.

Johnstone, C. J. (2003). *Improving validity of large-scale tests: Universal design and student performance* (Technical Report 37). Minneapolis, MN: University of Minnesota, National Center on Education Outcomes.

Landau, S., Russell, M., Gourgey, K., Erin, J., & Cowan, J. (2003). Use of the Talking Tactile Tablet in mathematics testing. *Journal of Visual Impairment and Blindness, 97*(2), 85–96.

Lee, D., & Tindal, G. (2000). *Differential item functioning (DIF) as a function of test accommodation*. Dover, DE: Delaware Department of Education.

Liberman, I. Y., Shankweiler, D., & Liberman, A. M. (1989). The alphabetic principle and learning to read. In D. Shankweiler & I. Y. Liberman (Eds.), *Phonology and reading disability: Solving the reading puzzle* (Vol. viii, pp. 1–33). Ann Arbor: University of Michigan Press.

Mace, R. (1991). Definitions: Accessible, adaptable, and universal design (fact sheet). Raleigh, NC: Center for Universal Design, NCSU.

Meloy, L. L., Deville, C., & Frisbie, D. A. (2002). The effect of a read-aloud accommodation on test scores of students with and without a learning disability in reading. *Remedial and Special Education, 23*(4), 248–255.

Meyer, A., & Rose, D. H. (2005). The future is in the margins: The role of technology and disability in educational reform (updated). In D. H. Rose, A. Meyer, & C. Hitchcock (Eds.), *The universally designed classroom: Accessible curriculum and digital technologies*. Cambridge, MA: Harvard Education Press.

Nolet, V., & McLaughlin, M. J. (2000). *Accessing the general curriculum: Including students with disabilities in standards-based reform*. Thousand Oaks, CA: Corwin Press.

Olson, J. F., & Goldstein, A. A. (1996). Increasing the inclusion of students with disabilities and limited English proficient students in NAEP (NCES document 96-894) *Focus on NAEP 2*(1): 1–5.

Parkes, J. T., Suen, H. K., Zimmaro, D. M., & Zappe, S. M. (1999). *Structural knowledge as a pre-requisite to valid performance assessment scores*. Paper presented at the Annual Meeting of the National Council on Measurement in Education, Montreal, Quebec, Canada.

Rose, D. (July, 2001). Testimony given by D. Rose on July 25, 2001 before the Committee on Appropriations of the Subcommittee on Labor, Health and Human Services, and Education.

Rose, D., & Meyer, A. (2002) *Teaching every student in the digital age: Universal design for learning.* Alexandria, VA: Association for Supervision and Curriculum Development.

Russell, M. (2002). How computer-based technology can disrupt the technology of testing and assessment. In *Technology and assessment: Thinking ahead—proceedings of a workshop.* Washington, DC: National Academy Press.

Russell, M., & Haney, W. (1997). Testing writing on computers: An experiment comparing student performance on tests conducted via computer and via paper-and-pencil. *Educational Policy Analysis Archives, 5*(1). Retrieved September 28, 2006, from http://epaa.asu.edu/epaa/v5n3.html.

Russell, M., & Plati, T. (2000). *Mode of administration effects on MCAS composition performance for grades four, eight and ten.* Report prepared for the Massachusetts Department of Education.

Salyers, F. (2002, August). Field study of Web-based core content tests goes statewide this fall. *Kentucky Teacher* (newsletter). Lexington, KY: Kentucky Department of Education.

Sireci, S. G., Li, S., & Scarpati, S. (2003). *The effects of test accommodation on test performance: A review of the literature* (Center for Educational Assessment Research Report no. 485). Amherst, MA: School of Education, University of Massachusetts–Amherst.

Stanovich, K. E. (1988). Speculations on the cause and consequences of individual differences in early reading acquisition. In P. Gough (Ed.), *Reading acquisition.* Hillsdale, NJ: Lawrence Erlbaum Associates.

Swanson, L. (1999). Reading research for students with LD: A meta-analysis of intervention outcomes. *Journal of Learning Disabilities, 32*(6), 504–532.

Thompson, S. J., Blount, A., & Thurlow, M. (2002). *A summary of research on the effects of test accommodations: 1999 through 2001* (NCEO Technical Report 34). Minneapolis, MN: University of Minnesota, National Center on Educational Outcomes.

Thompson, S. J., Johnstone, C. J., & Thurlow, M. L. (2002). *Universal design applied to large-scale assessments* (NCEO Synthesis Report 44). Minneapolis, MN: University of Minnesota, National Center on Education Outcomes.

Thompson, S. J., Thurlow, M. L., Quenemoen, R. F., & Lehr, C. A. (2002). *Access to computer-based testing for students with disabilities* (NCEO Synthesis Report 45). Minneapolis, MN: University of Minnesota, National Center on Education Outcomes.

Thurlow, M. L., McGrew, K. S., Tindal, G., Thompson, S. J., Ysseldyke, J. E., & Elliott, J. L. (2000). *Assessment accommodations research: Considerations for design and analysis* (NCEO Technical Report 26). Minneapolis, MN: University of Minnesota, National Center on Educational Outcomes.

Tindal, G., & Fuchs, L. (1999). *A summary of research on test changes: An empirical basis for defining accommodations.* Lexington, KY: Mid-South Regional Resource Center/OSEP.

Tindal, G., Glasgow, A., Helwig, R., Hollenbeck, K., & Heath, B. (1998). *Accommodations in large-scale tests for students with disabilities: An investigation of reading math tests using video technology*. Washington, DC: Unpublished manuscript with Council of Chief State School Officers.

Tindal, G., Heath, B., Hollenback, K., Almond, P., & Harniss, M. (1998). Accommodating students with disabilities on large-scale tests: An experimental study. *Exceptional Children, 64*(4), 439–450.

Torgesen, J. K. (1993). Variations on theory in learning disabilities. In G. R. Lyon, D. B. Gray, J. F. Kavanagh, & N. A. Krasnegor (Eds.), *Better understanding learning disabilities: New views from research and their implications for education and public policies* (pp. 153–170). Baltimore, MD: Paul H. Brookes Publishing.

Trimble, S., Lewis, P., Dolan, R., & Kearns, J. (2006). Universal design for learning: Assessment applications. Project report. Lexington, KY: Human Development Institute, University of Kentucky,

U.S. Department of Education. (2001). *Clarification of the role of the IEP team in selecting individual accommodations, modifications in administration, and alternate assessments for state and district-wide assessments of student achievement.* Washington, DC: Author.

We dedicate this chapter to the memory of our dear colleague Sandy Thompson, who helped pioneer the application of universal design to educational assessment.

This article originally appeared in C. C. Laitusis and L. L. Cook, Eds., (2007). *Large-scale assessment and accommodations: What works?* Arlington, VA: Council for Exceptional Children. Copyright 2007 by Council for Exceptional Children. Used with permission.

CHAPTER THIRTEEN

Accurate for All

Universal Design for Learning and the Assessment of Students with Learning Disabilities

DAVID H. ROSE, TRACEY E. HALL, AND ELIZABETH MURRAY

EDITORS' NOTE

This chapter makes a claim that applying universal design principles to assessments is not sufficient to tell us what diverse learners actually know and can do, since they typically address issues of access, not pedagogy. Rather, we need to apply the principles and practices of universal design for learning and all that they tell us about learning.

The chapter begins with a description of the movement in the field toward making assessments that are universally designed. However, the authors claim that increasing the accessibility of assessments is just the first step in achieving a much more complex goal. They illustrate how applying the three principles of UDL will lead to more accurate measures of students' learning and will ultimately lead to a new way of thinking about assessment.

In recent years, assessment has seemed to play a much more prominent role in American education than ever before. This is true primarily because of the increased priority on accountability, both within the current administration and within the standards-based reform movement. The pressure for greater accountability has intensified demands for the measurement of student outcomes. Statewide and standardized assessments are the most visible signs of this greater accountability and its measurement.

But accountability is only one role for assessment, and large-scale standardized assessment is only one of its forms. Within almost any theory or practice of education, assessment plays a critical role. Other roles for assessment in education may include:

- *Diagnosis:* Identifying patterns of abilities and disabilities in individual learners
- *Measuring progress:* Assessing changes over time as a result of instruction (assessment *of* learning)
- *Informing instruction:* Probing responses to instruction to optimize the course of learning (assessment *for* learning)

It will not be possible to address each of these in full measure. We will focus our remarks primarily on large-scale assessment, because of its prominence and gate-keeping function, but our arguments apply to the other purposes of assessment as well. This is true in large part because one critical aspect of assessment is common across all of its forms: accuracy. We shall argue that most forms of assessment as they are now constituted, and especially standardized large-scale assessments, are systematically inaccurate for students with learning disabilities. That is a serious problem for both the students and the tests.

ASSESSMENT AND LEARNING DISABILITIES: THE PROBLEM OF ACCURACY

The most critical aspect of any assessment is the accuracy and validity of its measurement. No matter what the purpose of an assessment—to measure progress, to predict outcomes, to inform instruction—accurate measurement is its *sine qua non*. As noted earlier, in recent years education has increasingly turned to formal "standardized" testing to improve the accuracy of measurement—replacing or supplementing less formal assessments like teacher observations or subjective evaluations of student behavior. But the accuracy and validity of standardized testing—as now administered—is increasingly under question. Leading professionals and researchers in measurement are beginning to realize that the longstanding focus on standardization of items cannot be sustained in the era of modern cognitive science (Dawson & Fischer, 2006). In the modern era, much more care in the design of measurement will be required in order to standardize not the item or its difficulty, but what is being measured. To understand this issue requires a short digression into the concept of construct relevance.

Let's start with an example. Consider an assessment item that includes a paragraph of text as the stimulus—for example, a paragraph in the U.S. history section of the National Assessment of Educational Progress (NAEP) large-scale assessment. While measuring knowledge of U.S. history would clearly be the focus of this assessment item, successful completion of the item actually requires a much broader set of abilities and skills; only some of those are directly relevant to U.S. history. Students with disabilities often highlight the unintended requirements that are imposed by the measurement instrument. Consider first an extreme case: a blind student. For that student, the item's visual requirements—recognizing the letters of the text by their visual shape—are a demanding (perhaps impossible) requirement introduced by the particular measurement instrument. In that case, accurate measurement of the blind student's knowledge of U.S. history would be jeopardized by the visual acuity demands of the assessment item.

In the jargon of the testing industry, historical knowledge is *construct relevant* for this part of the assessment; it is what we are interested in measuring (Dolan, Rose, Burling, Harms, & Way, 2007). Visual acuity is *construct irrelevant*; it is *not* what we are interested in measuring. But when a blind student takes a text in a print-only format, the medium interferes with the ability to measure knowledge of U.S. history accurately, at least for this student. As a result, our measurement is contaminated (distorted) by construct-irrelevant demands inherent in the measurement instrument. Said another way, our test is inadvertently measuring visual acuity, which is construct irrelevant, and thereby confounds our ability to accurately measure knowledge of U.S. history, which is construct relevant. The problem, of course, is that we will draw erroneous inferences or conclusions from our assessment; it is like a GPS that is inaccurately locating us in space.

As a more germane example, consider a student who has a learning disability. For that student, too, using the medium of print alone may lead to erroneous conclusions about knowledge of U.S. history. That is because the measurement instrument (the passage of text to read) places many construct-irrelevant demands on the student—decoding English text and language, applying effective strategies for comprehending information in text, accessing prior word knowledge, distinguishing key points and details, and so on. For students with learning disabilities, each of these introduces impediments to optimally demonstrating their social studies knowledge.

What is important in this context is to realize that the performance of students with learning disabilities is especially vulnerable to construct-irrelevant demands of the testing instrument. Let us turn to that point.

Standardized Tests for Nonstandardized Students

For many students, especially so-called average students, many forms of standardized assessment are reasonably accurate. This is true for at least two reasons: (1) because the construct-irrelevant demands of the measurement instrument are relatively trivial, and (2) because the effects of those measurement demands are roughly equivalent for the majority of students. For the most part, accurate assessment is not differentially distorted, and construct-irrelevant demands introduce the same type and amount of error.

For students who are not "average," however—students with learning disabilities, English language learners, students from differing cultural backgrounds—the construct-irrelevant demands of the measurement instrument may not be trivial, and the effects of those demands cannot be expected to be the same as for the population as a whole (Dolan et al., 2007). These are students who are by definition "in the margins," and their pattern of abilities and disabilities is demonstrably *not* average.

For students with learning disabilities the issue of construct irrelevance is a pervasive problem. The reading demands of assessment instruments are the most obvious source of difficulty for students with learning disabilities, who may struggle with multiple areas of reading literacy (Liberman, Shankweiler, & Liberman, 1989; Swanson, 1999; Torgesen, 1993).

Reading is an irrelevant construct in many assessments that should have little to do with reading; math is a striking example (Clarkson, 1983; Helwig, Rozek-Tedesco, & Tindal, 2002; Helwig, Rozek-Tedesco, Tindal, & Heath, 1999). It poses a barrier to some students with learning disabilities, undermining their test performance regardless of their proficiency with the subject or skill area being tested. But reading is only one barrier. Students with learning disabilities frequently have difficulties with fundamental testing tasks; selectively attending to a test item and recording responses on a separate answer sheet can potentially undermine some students' performance. Because of primary difficulties like these, assessment instruments often require considerably more effort for students with LD than for other students (e.g., an extended passage may be much more time consuming for a student with LD to read); or the instrument elicits negative expectancies or emotions because students with learning disabilities have a negative association with reading long passages under time constraints.

As a result, for students who are not "average," measurement instruments standardized for "average" students are very likely to introduce "standardized" errors. Blind students will do poorly on a U.S. history exam if the items are presented only visually. Students with LD will do more poorly on items that contain long passages of challenging texts. Compared to typically achieving students, their results are less likely to be either accurate or valid estimates of their construct-relevant abilities (Elliott, 1998).

How can we make assessments that are more accurate? To measure the same construct validly and accurately for all students in a diverse population requires that the construct-irrelevant aspects of the assessment instrument be variable and customizable, not fixed or rigid. For students who are demonstrably *not* standardized—and this certainly includes students with learning disabilities as well as others—it is critical that assessment instruments be flexible enough to measure the same construct accurately and equivalently, even though the students will vary considerably in their facility with the demands of the assessment instrument. Accurate measurement of U.S. history content knowledge requires multiple options in the way that knowledge is assessed—rather like the way that a GPS requires multiple satellites, not one, to accurately assess location.

Current Approach to Improving Accuracy: Accommodations

The most common approach for making assessments more accurate for students with learning disabilities is to offer "accommodations" in the assessment process through alterations in test materials. In fact, procedures to minimize the impact of disability on assessment performance are mandated by special education law (IDEA, 1997), which specifically requires that students be provided with appropriate test accommodations. An example of a test accommodation is reading aloud test directions and items. Reading aloud is the most common test accommodation provided for students with learning disabilities (Sireci, Li, & Scarpati, 2003; Tindal, Heath, Hollenback, Almond, & Harniss, 1998). As with all test accommodations, its intent is to level the playing field without violating the equality of test conditions in other significant ways. While the read-aloud accommodation has repeatedly been shown to improve the performance of test takers with learning disabilities (Calhoon, Fuchs, & Hamlett, 2000; Fuchs, Fuchs, Eaton, Hamlett, & Karns, 2000; Meloy, Deville, & Frisbie, 2002; Thompson, Blount, & Thurlow, 2002), there are some concerns with its use that highlight the challenges of almost any accommodation.

One concern with accommodations is that they may not be properly chosen or implemented for a particular student and thus not actually reduce the measurement error. For example, human read-aloud accommodations may fail to provide adequate supports for students (Landau, Russell, Gourgey, Erin, & Cowan, 2003). The accuracy of a live human reader will naturally vary, and some readers mispronounce or misread words, leading to inaccurate interpretations. Additionally, it is not realistic to assume that students will (or are able to) ask human readers to repeat portions of the text in the way that competent readers typically reread many portions to improve understanding.

Another concern with accommodations is that they may not be well matched to measure the relevant constructs accurately. For example, it has been observed that human readers may actually influence—through intonation, unscripted comments, or even well-intentioned support that is inappropriate—student's responses, attention, or attitude (Dolan , Hall, Banerjee, Chun, & Strangman, 2005). Such alterations in delivery may invalidate the test as they may affect performance independent of any differences in knowledge of the actual relevant construct. An even larger problem is that the same accommodation applied to different students may have very different effects. While the human reader may properly support some students with learning disabilities, there are many for whom that same support would be useless or detrimental.

Another shortcoming of accommodations relates to continuity between instruction and assessment. "Assessment accommodations should be chosen on the basis of the individual student's needs and should generally be consistent with the accommodations provided during instruction" (IDEA, 2004). This is not always the case. For example, computer-based text to speech, which offers the benefit of independent, self-paced access to the text, is a commonly used accommodation during instruction but is rarely available to students during large-scale testing (Dawson, Venn, & Gunter, 2000; Farmer, Klein, & Bryson, 1992; Hebert & Murdock, 1994; Lundberg & Olofsson, 1993; McCullough, 1995; Strangman & Dalton, 2005). Thus, attempts to simplify and standardize the administration of the read-aloud accommodation through human readers are generally at odds with the requirement to maintain continuity between instruction and testing on an individual student basis.

One final problem with accommodations shown in the research is that there are wild differences between teachers, schools, and districts in *what* accommodations are available, *how* they are applied, and *to whom* they are offered. These differences in implementation inevitably render the results less accurate across different students.

A Different Approach: Universal Design and Universal Design for Learning

An alternative approach to providing ad hoc accommodations is to design assessment systems differently from the start, creating them from the outset to be accurate for a wide range of students, including those with disabilities. The general approach is called universal design, and our specific approach is called universal design for learning. For those unfamiliar with these concepts, a short introduction follows.

Universal design (UD), a practice originally formulated by Ron Mace at North Carolina State University, was initially developed in the field of architecture. The goal of the universal design movement is to eliminate barriers through designs that consider the needs of diverse people from the start, rather than overcoming barriers later through individual adaptation. Because the intended users are whole communities, universally designed environments are engineered for flexibility and designed to anticipate the need for alternatives, options, and adaptations to meet the challenge of diversity. In that regard, universal designs are often malleable and variable rather than dedicated. They are not unique or personal but universal and inclusive. The practice of universal design is now commonplace in architecture and has spread to many other fields in the last two decades. In all of these fields, what developers and consumers have learned is that designs that increase accessibility for individuals with disabilities—those who are typically "in the margins"—tend to yield benefits for all users. That is what makes them "universal."

UDL echoes the universal design movement in its emphasis on reaching all individuals, including those in the margins. However, its principles are specific to education since, of course, teaching people is vastly different from designing built environments or products. UDL guides curriculum developers, teachers, and administrators in how to design curricula, including the goals, methods, materials, and assessments that from the outset make effective learning accessible to the widest range of students (Rose & Meyer, 2002). Its purpose is to identify potential barriers to learning in a curriculum or classroom and to reduce those barriers through better initial designs, designs with the inherent flexibility to enable the curriculum to be easily adjusted to individual learners (Rose & Meyer, 2002; Müller & Tschantz, 2003).

The term UDL emphasizes the special purpose of learning environments, which is not merely to transmit information but to support and foster the changes in knowledge and skills that we call learning. UDL requires that we not only make information accessible but also design an accessible pedagogy. In general terms, pedagogy is the science of teaching and learning—the educational methods that skilled educators use to highlight critical features, emphasize big ideas, clarify essential relationships, provide graduated scaffolds for practice, model expert performance, and guide and mentor the student. All of these and more are what teaching is, and the measure of their success is what we call learning. The goal of practicing UDL is to ensure that learning is equally accessible to all students, including those with disabilities.

While the purpose of UDL is essentially the same as the purpose of universal design in any field, its practices reflect the different goals and activities that education requires. The framework for UDL, the foundation of its practices, is therefore not based on architectural principles, but in the sciences of learning. The learning sciences, including cognitive science, cognitive neuroscience, affective science, and neuropsychology, provide a foundation for understanding what learning is, what the range of individual differences in learning is, and what the effective methods of differentiating instruction will require. By taking advantage of research in the learning sciences, and specifically by taking advantage of research on individual differences in learning abilities and disabilities, UDL seeks to build learning environments that are designed from the outset to meet the challenge of individual differences. Meeting that challenge requires not one universal fixed pedagogy but a pedagogy that is varied and flexible enough to provide sufficient options and alternative paths to success for every student.

ASSESSMENT AND UNIVERSAL DESIGN

Within most curriculum frameworks, there is no separation between instruction and assessment. On the contrary, assessment is considered an integral and critical element of instruction. Indeed, instruction without assessment is profoundly disabled. Unfortunately, the present overfocus on assessment for accountability rather than for guiding instruction has limited the application of universal design principles primarily to large-scale assessments. Within the world of large-scale assessment the concepts of universal design have taken strong root of late, motivated by the recognition that standardized large-scale assessments are inaccurate for students with disabilities and that ad hoc accommodations are inherently problematic for the reliability and validity of the ultimate measurement. It is to these efforts that we now turn our attention, but we will return to a more balanced view of assessment at the end of this chapter.

The primary goal of universal design in large-scale assessment is to ensure accurate measurement and educational accountability for all participating students. To accomplish this goal requires careful attention to two things: the constructs that are actually being measured (identifying what is construct relevant) and the students who are being assessed. Successful application of universal design principles requires that the right constructs be assessed accurately across the full spectrum of students for whom the assessment is intended. This means that the full spectrum of abilities and disabilities must be considered from the earliest stages of item development, through test construction, validation, and final test administration. In reality, there are probably no assessments that are fully universally designed in this way. But there has been considerable progress. Early advocates of universal design in large-scale assessment, like the National Center on Educational Outcomes (NCEO) at the University of Minnesota, have made great progress on making tests more accessible. In their approach, similar to the earliest stages in any innovation, the application of universal design principles has been largely applied to improving old practices rather than generating fundamentally new ones.

These early approaches are based primarily on the original seven universal design principles developed by Mace and his architectural colleagues (Johnstone, 2003; Thompson, Johnstone, & Thurlow, 2002). In combination, the seven elements provide a framework for examining tests and their level of accessibility. Many large-scale assessment programs now use these universal design elements to varying degrees, and students with disabilities are more frequently being included in the design and validation of assessment instruments. These are important steps.

ASSESSMENT AND UNIVERSAL DESIGN FOR LEARNING

The next stages require more fundamental changes. For example, the architectural principles, created for designing fixed and permanent physical structures, are an awkward fit for the dynamic and developmental processes that education requires. Among other limitations, these principles concentrate primarily on reducing physical and sensory barriers and very little on the cognitive, linguistic, executive, and affective barriers that are of prime importance to students with learning disabilities. Another, perhaps more important, issue is that the early approaches and principles focus primarily on how to make print-based assessments more accessible. Unfortunately, that approach fails to capture the transformative power of universal design.

The next stage in the application of universal design will not be about how to make print-based items more accessible but about how to use the power of UDL to generate new kinds of assessments that transcend the limitations of print entirely. As the basis for that approach, we will apply principles and foundations not from architectural design but from the design of the learning environment and the curriculum—from universal design for learning. Using the framework of the learning science as a foundation, the UDL approach addresses three critical aspects of any learning activity, including its assessment: the means for representing information to students, the means by which students are expected to express their knowledge, and the means for engaging students in learning. (For further details, see Rose and Meyer [2002] and Rose, Meyer, and Hitchcock [2005].) A short summary of these principles and their applications follows. (For fully articulated guidelines, see www.cast. org.)

Principle One: Multiple Means of Representation

Assessments typically present information in some format. The presented information ranges from merely providing the directions for completing a task, to the stems for multiple-choice items, to extended informational texts and graphics that must be read and comprehended in order to answer related questions that depend on that information.

Students, however, differ in the ways that they access that information. At the extreme are students with sensory disabilities (e.g., those who are blind or deaf), for whom some of these forms of presentation are completely inaccessible. More prevalent are students with cognitive and learning disabilities who, because of their particular profile of perceptual or cognitive strengths and weaknesses, find information in some formats much more accessible than others. Even more common are students who are English language learners, have limited cognitive strategies, or have trouble with the culture of the average classroom, and who therefore face barriers in accessing information when presented in a manner that assumes a common background and ability among all students. There is no common means of representing information that is optimal to address the needs of such a diverse population of learners.

That is why we cannot expect to find a single common means of presenting information that will make an assessment "fair" or accurate for all students. Options and flexibility are essential to ensure that information in the assessment is accessible to all students and that the instrument itself does not introduce unintended, construct-irrelevant barriers by providing information in single formats. Without such options, the assessment will be much more accessible to some students than to others and thus much more accurate for some than for others. That is why, as a first principle, UDL requires multiple representations of all key information in an assessment.

Within a UDL assessment framework, options in representations are carefully constructed at the outset so that what is construct relevant and irrelevant can be carefully considered and addressed. This process reduces the problems of after-the-fact accommodations cited earlier, problems that continually threaten the validity of the assessment. But how will these options be actualized? Here is where the limitations of print become obvious and problematic.

One way modern digital technologies differ from print technologies is their ability to provide a flexible base from which assessment items can be presented and the equivalence of underlying constructs can be maintained (Honey, Pansnik, Fasca, 2007; Rose, Meyer, & Hitchcock, 2005; Meyer & Rose, 2006). With new multimedia technologies as a base, the same underlying construct can have many different "surface" representations. As with print, text can be presented visually, but, unlike print, the size, color, or font can vary. In addition, with digital technologies, text can be presented orally (through prerecorded or automatic speech) or haptically (e.g., in refreshable braille). Similarly, a graphic presentation can be easily enlarged with a flick of a key or described automatically. But of most importance to students with learning disabilities is the fact that many other kinds of presentational options can be available. Examples include options that highlight critical features in a text or graphic, provide definitions for vocabulary, or scaffold reading strategies to support comprehension.

New technologies are flexible enough to provide multiple representations, the choice of which can be determined on an individual basis. Existing print materials lack this flexibility and thus are "one size fits all" in a world where students are not one size at all. To measure accurately, it is critical to identify the construct that is the focus of measurement and must be held constant, and then to recognize those construct-irrelevant aspects of the instrument that can be varied and customized in order to get accurate measurement for every student.

Principle Two: Multiple Means of Action and Expression

Almost any form of assessment, even a single item on a large-scale test, requires the construction of some kind of response—from mere selection in a multiple-choice test, to a simple constructed response in a short-answer item, to sustained composition or problem solving. Each of these modes of response adds specific demands to the assessment, demands that are often not construct relevant. This could be a major problem for measurement, as noted earlier, because the demands of responding to the instrument are confounded with the construct being evaluated. To the extent that these response demands are equivalent for all students, no particular students are especially handicapped.

Of course, students are demonstrably *not* equivalent in their ability to construct responses. Students, especially those with disabilities, often have specific difficulties in generating responses that may have nothing to do with the construct being measured. At one extreme are students who have specific motor disabilities, such as cerebral palsy or dyspraxia, that limit the kinds of physical actions they can take as well as the kinds of tools they can use to respond to or construct knowledge. Other students have adequate motor control but have difficulty integrating action into skills (e.g., students with dysgraphia or the spelling challenges associated with dyslexia). Still others, including those with executive function disorders or ADD/ADHD, may be skillful within a domain but lack the strategic and organizational abilities required to achieve long-term goals. Moreover, many students are able to express themselves much more skillfully in one medium than another (using drawing tools or creating video as opposed to writing, for example).

These inequalities in students' facility to handle the response demands of the assessment instrument interfere with accurate measurement of content knowledge. The primary inequalities and barriers also have secondary effects: a student with a learning disability who labors slowly at construct-irrelevant writing or spelling will inevitably have less time for construct-relevant tasks such as thinking, problem solving, preparation, editing, and reviewing. When low-level skills like writing and spelling take a higher cognitive load, they reduce the cognitive resources available for higher-level thinking. The result can be a negative effect on performance that is quite unrelated to actual content knowledge.

When an assessment limits responding to a single common means of response or expression, the assessment is unlikely to be "fair" or accurate for all students. On the contrary, a single form of expression will guarantee that some students face barriers that can have both primary and secondary effects on their performance. Options and flexibility are essential to ensure that the mode of expression or action in the assessment instrument does not introduce unintended construct-irrelevant barriers. Without such options, the assessment will likely be inaccurate for students with learning disabilities and for many others.

What kinds of options are needed? The UDL guidelines provide a full description of the range of options that are important. The most basic motor options include ensuring access to assistive technologies or providing single-switch accessible formats. Other options, such as providing spell-checking and word prediction for writing or allowing answers to be expressed through writing, illustration, or voice recording, support differences in specific skills with different media. Still others support executive functions in preparing and organizing a response. Examples of this level of options include providing organizational aids and checklists or providing prompts for monitoring time and progress.

Principle 3: Multiple Means of Engagement
Assessments almost always require some kind of engagement in the process. To complete any item or activity, the participant must be motivated

to ignore other options in the environment and commit in at least a minimal way to engaging in the assessment item or activity. Some items require only fleeting attention; others, like composition or problem-solving activities, typically involve long-term concentration and self-regulation skills.

Lack of engagement in an assessment poses a considerable threat to its validity. Serious disengagement generally invalidates the results completely, but even minor variations in motivation, engagement, or concentration are potential threats to the validity of measurement. To the extent that all students are assumed to be equally engaged in an assessment, the effects of engagement would not be expected to cause differential problems in validity. But this, of course, is not the case.

In reality, individual students *do* vary considerably in their levels of engagement on any assessment. There is, moreover, considerable evidence that students with learning disabilities exhibit significant differences in their orientation to, and motivation for, many forms of assessment. Their history of relative failure in many educational and testing situations is sufficient by itself to bias them toward very different expectations than other students have. Personal expectations and beliefs about the likelihood of success have been shown to have a great effect on actual performance (Dweck, 2000).

The fact that students with learning disabilities do not approach assessment with the same expectation and motivation as other students raises a concern about how accurate "standardized" assessments are for them. Assessment developers attempt to address this issue by standardizing the conditions: the same stakes for all students, the same amount of limited time allowed for the test, and the same physical and social environment. While it is possible to standardize external conditions, it is not possible to standardize their effects. Students do not respond to these standard conditions, or any means of engagement, in standard ways. Some students, for example, are highly engaged by spontaneity and novelty, but others are disengaged or even frightened by those aspects in the environment. Similarly, some students are engaged by the risk and challenge in a learning or assessment environment, while others seek safety and support. Some are attracted by social comparisons that often accompany assessment, and others shy away and recede from such social comparisons. Students with high chronic levels of anxiety respond very differently to the pressure of time and results than other students. As a result, every assessment is to some extent measuring the student's individual reactions to the motivating conditions of the assessment method. Virtually every measurement instrument is inevitably measuring, and therefore confounded by, variations in individual engagement.

If maintaining the same external motivating conditions is not adequate for validity and accuracy of measurement, what is? Within the UDL framework, the answer is consistent with the previous principles: it is essential to provide options and alternatives in the conditions of testing and engagement. Rather than "standardizing" the means of engagement with rigid external conditions, it may be important instead to vary the external conditions available.

For a student with learning disabilities, there are typically three areas where systematic differences in engagement may negatively affect the accuracy of measurement. First, because of differential histories with different forms of assessment (most of them arguably negative for students with learning disabilities), the means of recruiting attention and interest in the assessment instrument is likely to have a different impact on these students than on others. Second, there are likely to be significant differences in the ability of students with learning disabilities to sustain effort and engagement in the face of difficulty, boredom, pressure, or failure. Although it is common to vary the time limits, few other variations are available in "standardized conditions" that would address this differential ability to sustain effort and concentration. Third, students differ in "self-regulation," the ability to manage their own engagement and effort irrespective of immediate external conditions. Students may need supportive options to ensure that the assessment is not primarily measuring self-regulation when it is intended to measure social studies knowledge. Those options need to be provided in ways that make them accessible for students with very different emotional and attitudinal histories.

Any of these options may turn out to be construct relevant for a specific assessment. For example, the use of a spell-checker would invalidate an assessment of spelling skills, in which case it could not be offered without destroying the test's validity. But for many other assessments, all of these options are *not* relevant to the construct being measured.

Not using them, in that instance, may well jeopardize the validity of the measurement for some students. Within a UDL assessment framework, those options must be carefully constructed at the outset by the assessment designer so that what is construct relevant and irrelevant can be carefully considered. As noted above, solving these problems with after-market accommodations is likely to introduce new problems to accurate measurement.

SUMMARY

The use of any assessment instrument has the potential to introduce errors of measurement imposed by the instrument itself. For many students, these potential errors are not likely to be consequential because their demands are either trivial or typical. For some students, such as students with learning disabilities, the demands of the assessment instrument are likely to be neither trivial nor typical.

As a result, accurate assessment will require instruments that are not "standardized" in the sense that they are rigid or uniform. Instead it will require instruments that can standardize what is measured by being flexible and variable enough to measure constructs accurately even when used by "atypical" populations, populations with widely varying abilities and disabilities. From a UDL perspective, they will need customizable options and alternatives to provide that flexibility. The flexibility to customize the instruments is critical in much the same way that eyeglasses must be customized, not standardized, in order for two individuals to see the same object with the same acuity. Only through intentional design of flexibility can assessments be accurate for individuals who are not standardized.

Is UDL for assessment really practical? In education, where modern tools often seem in short supply, and where print still dominates assessment, the barriers to practicality are more evident than the opportunities. But this is changing rapidly. It is safe to say that every publisher of large-scale assessments already provides, or is working on, digital versions—even universally designed versions—of their assessment instruments (e.g., Dolan et al., 2007). When the demand is sufficient, they will find these easy to provide.

REFERENCES

Calhoon, M. B., Fuchs, L. S., & Hamlett, C. L. (2000). Effects of computer-based test accommodations on mathematics performance assessments for secondary students with learning disabilities. *Learning Disability Quarterly, 23*(4), 271–281.

Clarkson, P. (1983). Types of errors made by Papua New Guinean students. *Educational Studies in Mathematics, 14*, 355–367.

Dawson, L., Venn, M. L., & Gunter, P. L. (2000). The effects of teacher versus computer reading models. *Behavioral Disorders, 25*(2), 105–113.

Dawson. T., & Fischer, K. (2006). Implications of assessments for learners. *Measurement: Interdisciplinary Research and Perspectives 4*(4), 240–269.

Dolan, R. P., Rose, D. H., Burling, K., Harms, M., & Way, D. (April, 2007). *The universal design for computer-based testing framework: A structure for developing guidelines for constructing innovative computer-administered tests.* Paper presented at the National Council on Measurement in Education Annual Meeting, Chicago, IL.

Dolan, R. P, Hall, T. E., Banerjee, M., Chun, E., & Strangman, N. (2005). Applying principles of universal design to test delivery: The effect of computer-based read-aloud on test performance of high school students with learning disabilities. *Journal of Technology, Learning, and Assessment, 3*(7) Retrieved July 8, 2009 from http://escholarship.bc.edu/jtla/vol3/7/.

Dweck, C. S. (2000). *Self-theories: Their role in motivation, personality, and development. Essays in social psychology.* Philadelphia, PA: Psychology Press.

Elliott, S. N. (1998). Performance assessment of students' achievement: Research and practice. *Learning Disabilities: Research and Practice 13*(4), 233–241.

Farmer, M., Klein, R., & Bryson, S. (1992). Computer-assisted reading: Effects of whole-word feedback on fluency and comprehension in readers with severe disabilities. *Remedial and Special Education, 13*, 50–60.

Fuchs, L. S., Fuchs, D., Eaton, S., Hamlett, C. L., & Karns, K. (2000). Supplementing teacher judgments of mathematics test accommodations with objective data sources. *School Psychology Review, 29*(1), 65–85.

Hebert, B. M., & Murdock, J. Y. (1994). Comparing three computer-aided instruction output modes to teach vocabulary words to students with learning disabilities. *Learning Disabilities Research & Practice, 9*(3), 136–141.

Helwig, R., Rozek-Tedesco, M. A., & Tindal, G. (2002). An oral versus a standard administration of a large-scale mathematics test. *Journal of Special Education, 36*(1), 39–47.

Helwig, R., Rozek-Tedesco, M. A., Tindal, G., & Heath, B. (1999). Reading as an access to mathematics problem solving on multiple-choice tests for sixth-grade students. *Journal of Educational Research, 93*(2), 113-125.

Honey, M., Pansnik, S., & Fasca, C. (2007, July/August). Survival of the skilled. *School Counselor.* Retrieved July 8, 2009, from http://cct.edc.org/report_summary. asp?numPublicationId=243.

Individuals with Disabilities Education Act Amendments of 1997, 20 U.S.C. §§ 1400. (1997).

Individuals with Disabilities Education Improvement Act of 2004, P. L. No. 108-446, 118 Stat. 2647. (2004). (Amending 20 U.S.C. §§ 1400 *et seq.*).

Johnstone, C. J. (2003). *Improving validity of large-scale tests: Universal design and student performance* (Technical Report 37). Minneapolis, MN: University of Minnesota, National Center on Education Outcomes.

Landau, S., Russell, M., Gourgey, K., Erin, J., & Cowan, J. (2003). Use of the Talking Tactile Tablet in mathematics testing. *Journal of Visual Impairment and Blindness,* 97(2), 85–96.

Liberman, I. Y., Shankweiler, D., & Liberman, A. M. (1989). The alphabetic principle and learning to read. In D. Shankweiler & I. Y. Liberman (Eds.), *Phonology and reading disability: Solving the reading puzzle* (Vol. viii, pp. 1–33).

Lundberg I., & Olofsson A. (1993). Can computer speech support reading comprehension? *Computers in Human Behavior* 9(2–3), 283–293.

McCullough, C. S. (1995). Using computer technology to monitor student progress and remediate reading problems. *School Psychology Review,* 24(3), 426–439.

Meloy, L. L., Deville, C., & Frisbie, D. A. (2002). The effect of a read-aloud accommodation on test scores of students with and without a learning disability in reading. *Remedial and Special Education,* 23(4), 248–255.

Meyer, A., & Rose, D. (2006). Preface. In D. Rose & A. Meyer (Eds.), *A practical reader in universal design for learning* (pp. vii–xi). Cambridge, MA: Harvard Education Press.

Müller, E., & Tschantz, J. (2003). Universal design for learning: Four state initiatives. Alexandria, VA: Project Forum/National Association of State Directors of Special Education. http://www.nasdse.org/forum.htm.

Rose D. H., & Meyer, A. (2002). Teaching every student in the digital age: Universal design for learning. Alexandria, VA: Association for Supervision and Curriculum Development.

Rose, D. H., Meyer, A., & Hitchcock, C. (Eds.). (2005). *The universally designed classroom: Accessible curriculum and digital technologies.* Cambridge, MA: Harvard Education Press.

Sireci, S. G., Li, S., & Scarpati, S. (2003). *The effects of test accommodation on test performance: A review of the literature* (Center for Educational Assessment Research Report no. 485). Amherst, MA: School of Education, University of Massachusetts–Amherst.

Strangman, N., & Dalton, B. (2005). Using technology to support struggling readers. In D. Edyburn, K. Higgins, & R. Boone (Eds.), *Handbook of special education technology research and practice.* Whitefish Bay, WI: Knowledge by Design.

Swanson, L. (1999). Reading research for students with LD: A meta-analysis of intervention outcomes. *Journal of Learning Disabilities,* 32(6), 504–532.

Thompson, S. J., Blount, A., & Thurlow, M. (2002). *A summary of research on the effects of test accommodations: 1999 through 2001* (NCEO Technical Report 34). Minneapolis, MN: University of Minnesota, National Center on Educational Outcomes.

Thompson, S. J., Johnstone, C. J., & Thurlow, M. L. (2002). *Universal design applied to large-scale assessments* (NCEO Synthesis Report 44). Minneapolis, MN: University of Minnesota, National Center on Education Outcomes.

Tindal, G., Heath, B., Hollenback, K., Almond, P., & Harniss, M. (1998). Accommodating students with disabilities on large-scale tests: An experimental study. *Exceptional Children, 64*(4), 439–450.

Torgesen, J. K. (1993). Variations on theory in learning disabilities. In G. R. Lyon, D. B. Gray, J. F. Kavanagh, & N. A. Krasnegor (Eds.), *Better understanding learning disabilities: New views from research and their implications for education and public policies* (pp. 153–170). Baltimore, MD: Paul H. Brookes Publishing.

CHAPTER FOURTEEN

Perspectives on UDL and Assessment

An Interview with Robert J. Mislevy

CONDUCTED BY THE EDITORS

EDITORS' NOTE

Dr. Robert Mislevy is a leading expert in educational assessment, technology, and cognitive science. He was a distinguished research scientist at Educational Testing Service (ETS), where he worked for nearly two decades. ETS develops, administers, and scores some 50 million standardized tests per year, including the SAT, AP, GRE, and TOEFL. Dr. Mislevy is currently Professor of Measurement, Statistics, and Evaluation at the University of Maryland. He also collaborates with Cisco Learning Institute on advances in assessment. Dr. Mislevy holds a PhD in the methodology of behavioral research from the University of Chicago. He was elected to the National Academy of Education in 2007.

As co-principal investigator of Principled Assessment Designs for Inquiry (PADI), Dr. Mislevy is well positioned to comment on UDL and assessment (visit http://padi.sri.com/). A joint project of the University of Maryland, CAST, and SRI International with funding from the National Science Foundation, PADI aims to develop a framework for high-quality assessments for science inquiry projects. In 2007, the team began working with CAST to infuse UDL principles into the assessment framework.

In this 2009 interview, Dr. Mislevy shares his insights on the histori-cal background of assessment, the current state of assessment for students with disabilities, the integration of UDL and assessment, and the implica-tions for policy makers. He emphasizes the value of large-scale assessment but also notes that the field has not kept up with advances in the learn-ing sciences. UDL is a way of applying those advances, and Dr. Mislevy points out that a principled application of UDL can in fact increase the value and even the validity of large-scale assessment for a greater number of students.

How has the landscape of assessment changed over your career?

Over the past thirty years, advances in the field of psychology have given us a better understanding of how people learn and of the nature of knowledge. In the 1980s, we started to see the impact of information processing and cognitive science in assessment. In the 1990s, sociocog-nitive perspectives began to shape our understanding. Yet the funny thing is that the practice of large-scale testing really has not changed that much! Informal and local assessments have been changing over the years, but there have been few adjustments to the way in which we mea-sure student learning on a large scale. The eighty-year-old perspective that a couple of questions answered over a couple of hours can give you an adequate understanding of what people know and what people can do persists in large-scale assessment. There are still reasons for doing some large-scale assessment. However, you no longer can assume that the little snippets from large-scale assessment tell you everything that is important to know. You get some information, but now it needs to be contextualized. And, you also need to understand what the information *does not tell you* as well as what it does.

What *has* changed with regard to large-scale assessment is the public's growing dissatisfaction with what we are learning from standard meth-odology. No Child Left Behind (NCLB) has spurred frustration with large-scale assessment because its accountability measures hang on these tests results. A good outcome of NCLB has been to direct more attention to the need for assessment and for knowing what kids are learning. But as [Harvard researcher] Dan Koretz's research suggests, the steps that you take to maximally improve NCLB scores are not necessarily the best steps that you would take to improve student learning, and reliance on test-score information alone can lead to bad policy.

What is the value of large-scale assessment for accountability?
One of the values is what you might call "chain of custody." Chain of custody is a term from the law that describes the chronological documentation of a piece of evidence. For example, after a piece of evidence is discovered at a crime scene, the names of all of the different people who examine the evidence and all of the protocols that are followed are recorded. This documentation enables you to make inferences from that evidence a year or maybe three years later. The evidence is "protected" so it can be used at times and places quite distant from its initial discovery.

Think, for example, about the SAT. The SAT still has value not simply because it is measuring people's innate capabilities as a be all and end all, but because it serves as a little chunk of evidence. For a finite, reasonable amount of money, you know something about how evidence was collected, and you roughly know something about the chain of custody of that evidence. It is evidence that is gathered at locations throughout the country, summarized, and used by people at distant times and places. Despite its limits as evidence about what the students know and can do, it brings some credibility in terms of the chain of custody.

You sometimes hear the argument that we should not have large-scale, common assessments because teachers are better able to assess their students. It is claimed that teachers know their students better and that we should trust our teachers more in terms of their ability to conduct relevant, meaningful assessments that guide their instruction from day to day. Part of that argument holds water. In the local context, you can get more targeted and more useful information from students. However, such assessments—for different students, in different classrooms, and in different courses of study—while useful in local contexts, do not communicate value to people in distant times and places (policy makers, for example) who are removed several steps from the instructional episode. Ideally, you would really like to see large-scale assessments as working *with* rather than working *against* the local assessments that are used to determine how students learn, to obtain feedback, and to guide teachers' instruction for the next day.

So perhaps large-scale assessment does not offer much in terms of improving classroom instruction and learning except as it can help lead to systemic changes or investments that in turn could be used for local improvement.

I would agree. However, this does not mean large-scale assessment could not be more informative for instruction. As an example, I would mention a project funded by the National Science Foundation that we are working on with our colleagues at CAST, SRI, and Pearson that focuses on the Minnesota Comprehensive Assessment Program. We're working with large-scale science assessment at the middle school level. Minnesota's assessment is computer administered, which allows them some flexibility in making the assessment more interactive. However, despite being computer administered, it is still traditional in that every kid in the eighth grade in Minnesota looks at and interacts with the same test items. Our project is building design patterns around the science standards and benchmarks in Minnesota that can be used for both assessment and instruction. These design patterns help you build learning tasks, group work, and extended investigations in the classroom that are compatible with the same state standards and benchmarks. And, because the same design patterns are also used in assessment, the content included on the large-scale test, the Minnesota Comprehensive Assessment II (MCA-II), is made up of little snippets from the design patterns that teachers are using in their classrooms. By using the same design patterns for both instruction and assessment, teachers and curriculum developers begin to understand what the standards and benchmarks are really about and the various ways to teach them and assess them in the classroom. When the MCA-II test comes at the end of the year, teachers can be assured that there will most likely be some tasks included in the assessment that are similar to the activities that have been taking place in the classroom all year long. Students are going to do better on the items, not because they studied and focused just on the MCA-II kinds of tasks, but because they learned the ways of thinking that are compatible with what you do on those MCA-II tasks in the simpler forms that can be presented there. This is just one example of how the large-scale testing can be compatible with learning goals without subverting teaching.

In an ideal world, how would large-scale assessment and other measures, such as curriculum-based measurement or progress monitoring, integrate to give us reliable measures for accountability purposes?

To answer this question, I will give you another example from industry: the Cisco Networking Academy, a global e-learning initiative that focuses on developing introductory skills in network engineering. Cisco has designed simulation-based tasks for courses that deal with troubleshooting, network design, and setting up networks. The simulation tasks range in their level of complexity. Some may require students to work collaboratively for a number of hours, while less complex tasks may require only ten minutes of individual work. The final exams are based on smaller segments of the same kinds of simulation tasks. At the end of the course, students are well prepared for the exam because the assessment is compatible with the ways in which they have been learning—and the skills that they need in the real world. In fact, their focus of study and their final exam will also be compatible with some of the tasks on their certification test should students decide to pursue the area further. The final exams are not developed simply from a measurement point of view; they are derived from the same learning goals and the same psychology of learning used to create the courses.

The Cisco case also shows how technology can help to make congruency between instruction and assessment even stronger. Technology is loosening the constraints we have experienced over the eighty years of large-scale testing, and these constraints are being loosened in ways that make it easier to connect what happens in learning to what happens in assessment. For example, if you were conducting large-scale testing on the computer, students could build interactive models to solve problems, they could design their own graphics, or they could map information from one form of representation to another. Technology removes the layer of artificiality that develops from the tight constraints of traditional large-scale assessments.

*What is the current state of assessment for students with disabilities,
English language learners, and others marginalized by traditional
curricula? Do you believe we are currently able to accurately measure
the learning of all students?*

I am not an expert in everything that is being done in the field regarding assessing students with disabilities, but I have done a lot of thinking around the challenges of traditional assessment. The traditional way of building assessment arguments has always been to present everyone with the same stimulus material and have them interact and respond in the same ways. It was believed that this traditional method allowed you to obtain comparable evidence that could be in interpreted in the same way for everyone who is tested. However, there is a big problem with this approach; it forces you to make assumptions about students' ability to see, to hear, to physically interact with their surroundings, to concentrate, and so on. Although many people realized that including students with these types of varying abilities would lead to invalid inferences, the students were often tested nonetheless because the alternative was to exclude them from the assessment altogether. The real challenge is finding ways to make assessment arguments when different students might be interacting with different stimuli and responding in different ways. The traditional educational measurement and assessment machinery, conceptual as well as statistical, does not help us to address this issue. However, I hope that the work that is being done in the field will lead us to some answers.

The PADI project seeks to lay out a rigorous conceptual basis for assessment using principles for universal design for learning (UDL). We are working to develop more tailored assessment situations for different individuals that still make sense using the same frame of interpretation across individuals. That frame of interpretation is driven by clearly defining the specific knowledge, skills, or abilities that we want our students to develop. Oftentimes, a "one size fits all" assessment is developed, and adaptations and accommodations are made only after the fact. This is the hard way to build accessible assessments; the adaptations are constrained by the "one size fits all" conception of how you develop and interpret tests. This method does not tell you how to think in a principled way about the students for whom the "one size fits all" test does not work. After-the-fact adaptations might make some improvements to accessibility, but they are not a part of the framework for drawing the inferences that you want to make. In the PADI project, we are thinking about the range of students' abilities and disabilities from the very beginning. It is a different way of thinking about what assessment is.

What kind of a role do you see UDL playing in assessment?
UDL prompts you to target learning goals; you identify what we call the "focal knowledge, skills, and abilities," or "focal KSAs," that you want your students to develop. When applying UDL to assessment, you are evaluating these focal KSAs in order to determine if students are making progress in those capabilities.

UDL also encourages us to carefully consider *all* of the knowledge, skills, or abilities that might tangentially be involved in assessing the focal ones. These "non-focal KSAs" might prevent students from accurately being able to demonstrate what they know and what they can do. For example, students with a visual impairment might do poorly on a science assessment not because they do not know the content but because they are unable to see the material. Other students may do poorly on a specific item simply because they were not given some construct-irrelevant information that they would need to know in order to interact with the task. In both of these examples, non-focal KSAs interfere with students' learning and performance on tests, and lead to invalid assessment. UDL pushes us to think about the ways in which we can support students' non-focal KSAs so that we can target and address the actual learning goals.

Questions have arisen about the impact of UDL upon the validity of assessment. From your perspective, what impact does the application of UDL to large-scale assessment have on construct validity?
The historical conception of construct validity was built for the situation in which "everybody gets the same test and does the same thing so that we have the same data." The conceptual and statistical machinery for thinking about validity was built upon this framework as well. However, if you apply UDL to assessment and assess different kids in different ways, the procedures and the methods that went along with

ensuring validity based upon that framework no longer apply. Integrating UDL into assessment takes away all of the tools for thinking about validity that we have relied upon in the past. It requires a different way of thinking.

The application of UDL to assessment has the potential to either increase or decrease construct validity. A straight ad hoc application of UDL without identifying the focal knowledge and skills that are being assessed will most likely lead to a decrease in construct validity. However, if UDL is applied in a *principled manner*, it will actually increase construct validity for a larger population of students. Our PADI project focuses upon ways of growing the population of students for whom we can obtain valid measures. We are working to develop tools and procedures that make the application of UDL explicit and that help us make a rigorous assessment argument for when different students might be presented tasks in different ways, or interact with them or respond to them in different ways, to be able to get at the focal knowledge and skill. We want to help the field to understand that a principled application of UDL can increase construct validity for a bigger population of kids. But simply applying the UDL principles in and of itself is no guarantee.

What are some ways in which policy can support this more thoughtful, more "principled" application of UDL to large-scale assessment?
There is a big challenge in implementing policy around assessment. Many people believe that they know everything there is to know about teaching and about testing because they have been taught and because they have taken tests. That sort of "everyday thinking" about testing will not bring to bear what we are learning from cognitive science nor will it support the integration of UDL and assessment. Policies that are made using eighty-year-old ways of thinking about learning and assessment can sometimes make the job of improving assessment more difficult.

Policy can play a role in instituting the UDL framework as an ingrained part of the assessment design process. Creating tasks that have this principled reasoning throughout them needs to be a part of development from the very beginning. At first, this new approach to design will require more thought and more money for test development, administration, and review. For eighty years, tests have been thought of as "one size fits all," and it has been acceptable to make that "one size" as fast and as cheap as possible. This way of thinking has left a bad legacy. The notion that what you can do fast, cheap, and large scale is in fact sufficient for everybody still persists, often at the policy-maker level. Recognizing that test development requires thoughtful consideration and significant funding would be a very big step forward. It is true that this new thinking around assessment design takes a little more money, and the procedures for creating and administering tests are a little more involved. However, there are ways to make this assessment design process more economically feasible. The use of technology and the sharing of design patterns and assessment delivery mechanisms across states and across testing companies will save on time and resources. In summary, policy makers can do two things to promote assessment for a wider range of students: (1) they can make it a priority to understand the current barriers that are preventing us from obtaining accurate measures of learning for a broad range of students, and (2) they can support the development of new technologies, design patterns, and assessment delivery mechanisms that can be shared by all.

Furthermore, it is important to promote examples of successful initiatives in order to generate support for this new way of thinking around assessment. Many other sectors are using more innovative assessment and progressing at a much faster rate than our public schools. In the medical profession, for example, the use of simulations has made a positive impact upon both assessment and learning. The National Board of Medical Examiners has now included computer case management problems as part of the licensure sequence. In medical schools, students continue to memorize the names of the bones, muscles, et cetera, but the use of simulations encourages them to spend more time thinking through how that knowledge applies to interactions with patients, to diagnosis, and to treatment. The military provides another example. The military places a real value in having people learn to do things better. They have the motivation to improve instruction and assessment as best they can because the consequences are so real. The defense community is a bureaucracy as much as any school district, but the military has the impetus to be creative in their approach to learning and assessment. Finally, community colleges seem to be a bit more flexible, innovative, faster to change. The lay of the land seems a little more favorable in community colleges than it does in K–12 or in university systems. Publicizing examples of success such as the Cisco Networking Academy, the use of simulations in medical schools, and the innovation within the military and many community colleges will help the public to understand that this new way of thinking about assessment is actually possible. Once parents, teachers, and citizens see the effectiveness of these examples, they will become a little less tolerant of the policy makers who are not working to move these developments forward.

Universal Design for Learning and Universal Design Provisions in the Higher Education Opportunity Act (P.L. 110-315)

(A SUMMARY OF SELECTED PROVISIONS)

EDITORS' NOTE

The Higher Education Opportunity Act (HEOA) of 2008, passed with strong bipartisan support, established the statutory definition for Universal Design for Learning. This definition incorporates the three principles of UDL—representation, expression, and engagement—and emphasizes reducing barriers with appropriate supports and challenges built into instruction.

In addition to defining UDL, HEOA emphasizes that pre-service training through teacher education programs should incorporate instruction on strategies consistent with UDL. If future teachers are taught the principles of UDL, they will be able to better meet the diverse needs of their future students.

The National UDL Task Force—representing more than two dozen general education, special education, and civil rights organizations—led the effort to include an additional definition of UDL and specific provisions for its implementation in the statute. In doing so, the task force made the convincing case that UDL was more than just UD applied to educational materials—that the emphasis on learning required considerations encompassing instructional goals, assessments, and methods as well as materials. Furthermore, the task force emphasized that more than just physical access to educational environments and materials was at stake—that fair and equal opportunities for learning are owed to those with learning disabilities or other cognitive and intellectual challenges, English language learners, learners from disadvantaged backgrounds, and others who might otherwise be marginalized in the one-size-fits-all classroom.

The inclusion of UDL in HEOA indicates a federal recognition of the potential for UDL to improve practice in classrooms and provide opportunities for students to succeed. With NCLB and IDEA up for reauthorization, the inclusion of UDL in HEOA establishes a strong foundation for UDL to be incorporated in these K–12 policies.

SEC. 103. ADDITIONAL DEFINITIONS.
(a) Additional Definitions.—

(23) UNIVERSAL DESIGN.
The term "universal design" has the meaning given the term in section 3 of the Assistive Technology Act of 1998 (29 U.S.C. 3002). [This meaning is: "The term 'universal design' means a concept or philosophy for designing and delivering products and services that are usable by people with the widest possible range of functional capabilities, which include products and services that are directly accessible (without requiring assistive technologies) and products and services that are interoperable with assistive technologies."]

(24) UNIVERSAL DESIGN FOR LEARNING.
The term "universal design for learning" means a scientifically valid framework for guiding educational practice that—

(A) provides flexibility in the ways information is presented, in the ways students respond or demonstrate knowledge and skills, and in the ways students are engaged; and

(B) reduces barriers in instruction, provides appropriate accommodations, supports, and challenges, and maintains high achievement expectations for all students, including students with disabilities and students who are limited English proficient.

PART A—TEACHER QUALITY PARTNERSHIP GRANTS

SEC. 202. PARTNERSHIP GRANTS.

d) Partnership Grants for Pre-Baccalaureate Preparation of Teachers.—An eligible partnership that receives a grant to carry out an effective program for the pre-baccalaureate preparation of teachers shall carry out a program that includes all of the following.

(1) REFORMS.—

(A) IN GENERAL.—Implementing reforms, described in subparagraph (B), within each teacher preparation program and, as applicable, each preparation program for early childhood education programs, of the eligible partnership that is assisted under this section, to hold each program accountable for—

(i) preparing—

(I) new or prospective teachers to be highly qualified (including teachers in rural school districts who may teach multiple subjects, special educators, and teachers of students who are limited English proficient who may teach multiple subjects);

(II) *such teachers and, as applicable, early childhood educators, to understand empirically-based practice and scientifically valid research related to teaching and learning and the applicability of such practice and research, including through the effective use of technology, instructional techniques, and strategies consistent with the principles of universal design for learning*, and through positive behavioral interventions and support strategies to improve student achievement;

SEC. 204. ACCOUNTABILITY AND EVALUATION.

(a) Eligible Partnership Evaluation.—Each eligible partnership submitting an application for a grant under this part shall establish, and include in such application, an evaluation plan that includes strong and measurable performance objectives. The plan shall include objectives and measures for increasing—

(G) as applicable, *the percentage of teachers trained—*

(i) *to integrate technology effectively into curricula and instruction, including technology consistent with the principles of universal design for learning*; and

(ii) to use technology effectively to collect, manage, and analyze data to improve teaching and learning for the purpose of improving student academic achievement.

SEC. 205. ACCOUNTABILITY FOR PROGRAMS THAT PREPARE TEACHERS.

(a) Institutional and Program Report Cards on the Quality of Teacher Preparation.—

(1) REPORT CARD.—Each institution of higher education that conducts a traditional teacher preparation program or alternative routes to State certification or licensure program and that enrolls students receiving Federal assistance under this Act shall report annually to the State and the general public, in a uniform and comprehensible manner that conforms with the definitions and methods established by the Secretary, the following:

(F) USE OF TECHNOLOGY.—*A description of the activities, including activities consistent with the principles of universal design for learning*, that prepare teachers to integrate technology effectively into curricula and instruction, and to use technology effectively to collect, manage, and analyze data in order to improve teaching and learning for the purpose of increasing student academic achievement.

(b) State Report Card on the Quality of Teacher Preparation.—

(1) IN GENERAL.—Each State that receives funds under this Act shall provide to the Secretary, and make widely available to the general public, in a uniform and comprehensible manner that conforms with the definitions and methods established by the Secretary, an annual State report card on the quality of teacher preparation in the State, both for traditional teacher preparation programs and for alternative routes to State certification or licensure programs, which shall include not less than the following:

(K) A description of the activities that prepare teachers to—

(i) integrate technology effectively into curricula and instruction, including *activities consistent with the principles of universal design for learning*; and

(ii) use technology effectively to collect, manage, and analyze data to improve teaching and learning for the purpose of increasing student academic achievement.

PART B—ENHANCING TEACHER EDUCATION

SEC. 231. PROGRAM AUTHORIZED.

(a) Program Authority.—The Secretary is authorized to award grants to, or enter into contracts or cooperative agreements with, eligible consortia to pay the Federal share of the costs of projects to—

(3) *assess the effectiveness of departments, schools, and colleges of education at institutions of higher education in preparing teacher candidates for successful implementation of technology-rich teaching and learning environments, including environments consistent with the principles of universal design for learning,* that enable kindergarten through grade 12 students to develop learning skills to succeed in higher education and to enter the workforce.

SEC. 232. USES OF FUNDS.

(a) In General.—An eligible consortium that receives a grant or enters into a contract or cooperative agreement under this subpart shall use funds made available under this subpart to carry out a project that—

(2) transforms the way departments, schools, and colleges of education teach classroom technology integration, including the principles of universal design, to teacher candidates.

(b) Uses of Funds for Partnership Grants.—In carrying out a project under subsection (a)(1), an eligible consortium shall—

(2) build the skills of teacher candidates to support technology-rich instruction, assessment and learning management in content areas, technology literacy, an understanding of the principles of universal design, and the development of other skills for entering the workforce;

SEC. 233. APPLICATION REQUIREMENTS.

To be eligible to receive a grant or enter into a contract or cooperative agreement under this subpart, an eligible consortium shall submit an application to the Secretary at such time, in such manner, and containing such information as the Secretary may require. Such application shall include the following:

(1) A description of the project to be carried out with the grant, including how the project will—

(B) transform the way departments, schools, and colleges of education teach classroom technology integration, including the principles of universal design, to teacher candidates.

Subpart 3—Preparing General Education Teachers to More Effectively Educate Students With Disabilities

SEC. 251. TEACH TO REACH GRANTS.

(c) Activities.—An eligible partnership that receives a grant under this section—

(1) shall use the grant funds to—

(A) develop or strengthen an undergraduate, postbaccalaureate, or master's teacher preparation program by integrating special education strategies into the general education curriculum and academic content;

(B) *provide teacher candidates participating in the program under subparagraph (A) with skills related to*—

(i) response to intervention, positive behavioral interventions and supports, differentiated instruction, and data driven instruction;

(ii) *universal design for learning;*

(iii) determining and utilizing accommodations for instruction and assessments;

(iv) collaborating with special educators, related services providers, and parents, including participation in individualized education program development and implementation; and

(v) appropriately utilizing technology and assistive technology for students with disabilities; and

(C) provide extensive clinical experience for participants described in subparagraph (B) with mentoring and induction support throughout the program that continues during the first two years of full-time teaching; and

. . . .

Subpart 1—Demonstration Projects to Support Postsecondary Faculty, Staff, and Administrators in Educating Students With Disabilities

SEC. 762. GRANTS, CONTRACTS, AND COOPERATIVE AGREEMENTS AUTHORIZED.

(b) Duration; Activities.—

(2) AUTHORIZED ACTIVITIES.—A grant, contract, or cooperative agreement awarded under this subpart shall be used to carry out one or more of the following activities:

(A) TEACHING METHODS AND STRATEGIES.—*The development of innovative, effective, and efficient teaching methods and strategies, consistent with the principles of universal design for learning,* to provide post-secondary faculty, staff, and administrators with the skills and supports necessary to teach and meet the academic and programmatic needs of students with disabilities, in order to improve the retention of such students in, and the completion by such students of, postsecondary education. Such methods and strategies may include in-service training, professional development, customized and general technical assistance, workshops, summer institutes, distance learning, and training in the use of assistive and educational technology.

(G) ACCESSIBILITY OF EDUCATION.—*Making postsecondary education more accessible to students with disabilities through curriculum development, consistent with the principles of universal design for learning.*

Subpart 3—Commission on Accessible Materials; Programs to Support Improved Access to Materials

SEC. 772. ESTABLISHMENT OF ADVISORY COMMISSION ON ACCESSIBLE INSTRUCTIONAL MATERIALS IN POSTSECONDARY EDUCATION FOR STUDENTS WITH DISABILITIES.

(b) Duties of the Commission.—

(C) RECOMMENDATIONS.—

(ii) CONSIDERATIONS.—In developing the recommendations under subparagraph (C), the Commission shall consider—

(V) solutions utilizing universal design;

SEC. 773. MODEL DEMONSTRATION PROGRAMS TO SUPPORT IMPROVED ACCESS TO POSTSECONDARY INSTRUCTIONAL MATERIALS FOR STUDENTS WITH PRINT DISABILITIES.

(f) Required Activities.—An eligible partnership that receives a grant or contract under this section shall use the grant or contract funds to carry out the following:

(1) Supporting the development and implementation of the following:

(G) Awareness, outreach, and training activities for faculty, staff, and students related to the acquisition and dissemination of instructional materials in specialized formats and instructional materials utilizing universal design.

Subpart 4—National Technical Assistance Center; Coordinating Center

SEC. 777. NATIONAL TECHNICAL ASSISTANCE CENTER; COORDINATING CENTER.

(4) DUTIES.—The duties of the National Center shall include the following:

(B) ASSISTANCE TO INSTITUTIONS OF HIGHER EDUCATION

(ii) *development and provision of training modules for higher education faculty on exemplary practices for accommodating and supporting postsecondary students with disabilities across a range of academic fields, which may include universal design for learning* and practices supported by the grants, contracts, or cooperative agreements authorized under subparts 1, 2, and 3 . . . .

About the Editors

David T. Gordon is director of communications at CAST (Center for Applied Special Technology), where he is helping to launch a National Center on Universal Design for Learning. At Harvard University (1999–2004), he edited the award-winning *Harvard Education Letter*, winning a National Press Club Award for distinguished reporting and analysis of the national board certification program for teachers. He has been a college writing instructor at Emerson College (1998–1999) and a staff editor, writer, and researcher for *Newsweek* (1989–1997). Gordon is the editor of three previous books for Harvard Education Press, including *A Nation Reformed? American Education 20 Years after A Nation at Risk.*

Jenna W. Gravel is a research associate and instructional designer at CAST, where she has played a central role in the development of CAST's UDL Guidelines. Her expertise in education policy and her experience in special education serve as a foundation for her work. Before joining CAST, Jenna was a middle school inclusion specialist in Malden, Massachusetts and a staff assistant for the Federation for Children with Special Needs in Boston, an advocacy group for parents of children with disabilities. She is certified in special education from preK–12. She earned an MEd in education policy and management from Harvard Graduate School of Education and a BA in government and Spanish from Colby College.

Laura A. Schifter is a doctoral candidate in the Education Policy, Leadership, and Instructional Practice program at Harvard Graduate School of Education where she is studying the experiences of and policies related to students with disabilities. Prior to attending Harvard, Laura served as an education fellow for Senator Chris Dodd (D-CT) on the Senate Health, Education, Labor and Pensions Committee in Washington, DC and taught elementary school in San Francisco. Laura earned an MEd in mind, brain, and education from Harvard Graduate School of Education and a BA in American studies from Amherst College.

About the Contributors

Peggy Coyne is a research scientist and senior professional development associate at CAST, where she concentrates on bringing research-based instructional practices to educators. Coyne works with educators to change instructional practices by integrating UDL and technology into classroom instruction to improve student learning outcomes. She has been project director of federally funded studies on digital literacy environments that support with disabilities.

Robert P. Dolan is a senior research scientist in assessment and information at Pearson Education. Prior to joining Pearson in 2007, he was a senior research scientist at CAST, where he was principal investor on projects around the universal design of instructional environments and the design of large-scale assessments for students with disabilities.

Tracey E. Hall is a senior research scientist at CAST, where her work focuses on assessment and instructional design grounded in effective teaching strategies. Hall directs a number of federally funded initiatives to create and evaluate digital supported environments based on UDL principles. She served as director of curriculum for the National Center on Accessing the General Curriculum (1999–2004).

Ted S. Hasselbring is a research professor of special education at Peabody College of Vanderbilt University. Over the past thirty years, Hasselbring has conducted research on the use of technology for enhancing learning in students with mild disabilities and those who are at-risk of school failure. His research has resulted in several widely used computer-intervention programs for struggling learners, including READ 180 and FASTT Math. He is the author of numerous publications, including *Assistive Technology Planner: From IEP Consideration to Classroom Implementation (2006)*.

Thomas Hehir is a professor of practice at Harvard Graduate School of Education. He served as director of the U.S. Department of Education's Office of Special Education Programs under President Clinton from 1993 to 1999. He is the author of *New Directions in Special Education: Eliminating Ableism in Policy in Practice* (Harvard Education Press, 2005).

Chuck Hitchcock is the chief officer of policy and technology at CAST. As director of the federally funded, NIMAS Technical Assistance Center, Hitchcock works with states, school boards, and publishers to raise awareness of and implement the National Instructional Materials Accessibility Standard. He is also codirector of the AIM Consortium, a fifteen-state initiative to improve the procurement and delivery of accessible instructional materials for students with disabilities.

Joanne Karger is a staff attorney for the Center for Law and Education, an organization that focuses on the right of all students to a high-quality education. Before joining CLE, she worked as an educational consultant, evaluating the special education programs in New York City, Washington, DC, and several districts in Massachusetts. She is a graduate of Boston College Law School and holds a doctorate from the Harvard Graduate School of Education.

Grace Meo is director of professional development and outreach services at CAST, where she leads initiatives across the United States to train teachers and administrators in universal design for learning at the preK–12 and postsecondary levels. Meo also oversees a national consortium of school practitioners who collaborate with CAST on researching and implementing universally designed materials and practices.

Martha L. Minow is the dean of the faculty and the Jeremiah Smith, Jr. Professor of Law at Harvard Law School. An expert in human rights and advocacy for members of racial and religious minorities and for women, children, and persons with disabilities, she also writes and teaches about privatization, military justice, and ethnic and religious conflict. She is the author or editor of numerous articles and books, including *Just Schools: Pursuing Equality in Societies of Difference (2008)* and *Making All the Difference: Inclusion, Exclusion, and American Law (1990).*

Robert J. Mislevy is a professor of measurement, statistics, and evaluation at the University of Maryland. He was previously a distinguished research scientist at ETS and a research associate at National Opinion Research Center. Mislevy is a widely recognized expert in educational assessment, technology, and cognitive science.

Elizabeth Murray is a senior research scientist at CAST, where she is a principal investigator of "Science Writer: A Universally Designed Thinking Writer," a project funded by the U.S. Department of Education's Steppingstones of Technology Innovation program. Murray brings to her work experience in mathematics instruction, special education, and clinical work with individuals with disabilities.

David H. Rose is the founding director and CEO of CAST, where with his colleagues he has defined the theoretical and practical framework of universal design for learning. Since the early 1980s, he has taught neuropsychology, technology, and universal design for learning at the Harvard Graduate School of Education. He is the author or editor of four books, including *Teaching Every Student in the Digital Age: Universal Design for Learning* (ASCD, 2002) and *A Practical Reader in Universal Design for Learning* (Harvard Education Press, 2006).

Christina A. Samuels is a staff writer and reporter for *Education Week* where she covers issues including special education, gifted education, and health and nutrition.

Kim Moherek Sopko is the executive director of the MOKO Education Services, a consultancy. Sopko holds an EdD in special education, an MA in early childhood special education, and a BA in psychology, all from George Washington University. She has taught at the Darden College of Education at Old Dominion University.

Skip Stahl, director of technical assistance at CAST, is a nationally recognized expert in accessible digital materials and universal design for learning. As project director for the NIMAS Development Center, he leads a national initiative implementing the transformation of K–12 textbooks into specialized accessible formats for students with print disabilities. He is also codirector of the AIM Consortium, a fifteen-state initiative to improve the procurement and delivery of accessible instructional materials for students with disabilities.

Nicole Strangman is the founder and director of SciMedCom, a communications company specializing in scientific, medical, and educational writing. She holds a PhD in neuroscience from Brown University, and is the coauthor of numerous articles on education and universal design for learning. She is also a contributing author of *Teaching Every Student in the Digital Age: Universal Design for Learning* (ASCD, 2002).

Joy Zabala, a pioneer in special education and assistive technology, works at CAST, where she is project manager of the AIM Consortium, a federally funded fifteen-state initiative to improve the procurement and delivery of accessible instructional materials for students with disabilities. Zabala is the developer of the SETT (Student, Environment, Task, Tools) Framework for gathering data to make effective assistive technology decisions, and is a founding member of the QIAT (Quality Indicators for Assistive Technology) List.

Index